THE ART OF THE COPTS

BY

PIERRE M. DU BOURGUET, S.J.

Translated by Caryll Hay-Shaw

GREYSTONE PRESS/NEW YORK · TORONTO · LONDON

Title-page:

Fish and Cross. Stone. Erment. Fourth century. Height 26 cm., width 34 cm.
Paris, Louvre, Christian Antiquities. Photo: Bulloz.

FIRST PUBLISHED IN 1967
GERMAN EDITION © 1967 BY HOLLE VERLAG G.M.B.H., BADEN-BADEN, GERMANY
ENGLISH TRANSLATION © 1971 BY METHUEN & CO. LTD.
LIBRARY OF CONGRESS CATALOG CARD NUMBER: 78-147350
PRINTED IN HOLLAND

LIST OF PLATES

LIST OF FIGURES

ACKNOWLEDGMENTS

The following museums and institutions kindly allowed reproduction of the plates on the pages listed below:

Baltimore, Walters Art Gallery 44
Berlin, Staatliche Museen 153
Berne, Abegg-Stiftung 55
Boston, Museum of Fine Arts 135, 136
Cleveland, Museum of Art 134
Detroit, Institute of Art 159
Khartoum, National Museum 189
Leningrad, Hermitage Museum 78
London, British Museum 87

Moscow, Pushkin Museum 77
Old Cairo, Coptic Museum 24, 53
Paris, Institut Catholique 177
Paris, Louvre 3, 23, 41, 42, 43, 54, 56, 65, 66, 75, 76, 89, 100, 101, 102, 107, 108, 109 (below), 110, 115, 116, 133, 152, 154, 160, 178
Trieste, Civico Museo di Storia ed Arte 88
Zurich, Collection Ch. Grand 145

The following photographs were taken *in situ*:

Egypt 11, 12, 13, 14, 90, 109 (above), 146, 151, 187, 188

Ethiopia 190

The coloured plates on the following pages were kindly supplied by:

P. Brice 14
Messrs. J. E. Bulloz, Paris 3, 56, 133, 152, 160, 178
M. Chuzeville, Vanves 41, 108, 110, 115
P. du Bourguet, Paris 11, 12, 13, 90, 99, 109 (above), 146, 151, 187, 190
Ch. Grand, Zurich 145

A. Held, Lausanne 24, 53, 177, 188
A. Javor, Berne 55
'La Photothèque', Paris 76
Max Seidel, Mittenwald 23, 42, 43, 54, 65, 66, 75, 77, 78, 89, 100, 101, 102, 107, 108, 110, 133, 154

The figures were drawn by Thérèse Moreau, Paris from information provided by the author.

CONTENTS

I. HISTORY AND DISCOVERY

The notion of 'Coptic art' barely emerges from the depths of time. Yet its belated discovery and appreciation make it seem a kind of revelation. Is it a genuine one?

The people from which this art springs is not an unknown one. But history has been unsparing in its depredations, and this without, in return, conferring that fame which is often the concomitant of such misfortunes.

For all that, it can point to an illustrious ancestry, and count to its credit qualities and achievements of the first order.

The Copts are, in fact, the direct descendants of the Egyptians of pharaonic times. 'Copt' is merely an abbreviation, by suppression of the initial diphthong, of 'Aigyptios' – itself doubtless modelled by the Greeks on the pharaonic word 'Het-Ka-Ptah', 'the house of the Ka (soul) of Ptah',[1] the name of the ancient shrine at Memphis. The word was further transformed by the Arabs, whose written language admits of neither vowels nor initial diphthongs. Conquerors of Egypt in the seventh century, they used it to designate the inhabitants of the Nile valley, at that time practically all of them Christians. In its new form the word reached Europe through the intermediary of travellers, notably in the seventeenth and eighteenth centuries, who doubtless brought it back with them from Moslem Egypt. From that time on, the term has been taken to mean those Egyptian Christians who were of Egyptian stock, a community which has survived, in imposing numbers (more than three million today), up to the present time. It is also customary to apply it, in a more restricted sense, to a period of Egyptian history extending, effectively, from the fourth to the middle of the seventh century A.D., the time of the Arab conquest. But in this so-called Coptic period all the inhabitants of that time who came of Egyptian stock, whether Christian or pagan, are necessarily included. Finally, when used to define the rite of the Christian Church in Egypt, it also covers the rite borrowed from Egypt by the Ethiopians, who observe it to this day.

The term has thus passed from a purely *ethnic* sense to a sense that is either *ethnico-religious*, when it refers to Christians of Egyptian stock, or purely *religious*, when applied to the Coptic liturgy, whether practised by Egyptians or Ethiopians.

In this work, the word 'Copt' will be used in the first place to designate the entire population of the country during the so-called Coptic period, including the indigenous people, whether middle-class or peasant, and the Egypto-Greeks assimilated to them, and consequently, with reference to this period, the pagans equally with the Christians. In addition, it will be used to designate the Christian community of Egyptian race which, after the Arab conquest, diminished in number, though surviving in the Nile valley. It will exclude, by definition, the Ethiopians and the Nubians.

The Copts have no mean claims on our attention.

The most striking one is of great value to the historian: it was among the Copts that Christian monasticism originated and developed – this immense movement, of which the widely varying forms, in the domains of contemplation, of thought and of action, whether evangelistic or charitable, have never ceased to grow and multiply over the surface of the globe.

The Coptic language is of interest to a more restricted circle. It was written and spoken by the Egyptians up to the thirteenth century,[2] at which time it finally had to give way to Arabic, though it remained until very recently the liturgical language of the Christians of Egyptian stock. It represents the last phase of the language of the pharaohs, with the addition of a vocabulary corresponding to new realities in the religious and administrative fields. Using the Greek alphabet, instead of hieroglyphics, with the addition of seven characters of its own, it was of no little service to Champollion in deciphering hieroglyphic writing, and remains indispensable to the Egyptologist with a philological bent.

In this language were written a number of texts, some on papyrus, others on flat stones or fragments of pottery, but mainly on parchment. These consist of translations – sometimes from very early sources – of the Old and New Testaments, as well as the works of the Greek Fathers, whether in the form of narratives or of original monastic treatises. To this literature are linked the books of the 'Gnostic library' of Nag Hammadi, of which the comparatively recent discovery is – for the early history of the Christian era – comparable in importance to that of the Dead Sea Scrolls for students of the Bible or of the Jewish social structure of that time. It was in the thirteenth century that, in Egypt, among the Copts themselves, the Coptic language gave place to Arabic as the language of everyday affairs. Retained to the present day in the recital of the monastic Office and, doubtless, in the vocabulary of colloquial Arabic in Egypt, it remains of interest mainly to scholars. Two seventeenth-century humanists compete for the honour of having made it known in Europe: the German Jesuit, Athanasius Kircher (who spent most of his life in France) and Nicolas de Peiresc, of Aix.[3]

Religious and literary history; linguistic studies – these are the fields in which the legacy of the Copts has made itself felt for more than three centuries.[4]

COPTIC
ART

The contribution of the Copts to the human heritage was indeed appreciable. Can they also be considered as creators of an art of their own?

In earlier centuries the idea was undreamed of.

At first the Copts were an indigenous people totally without political power and then a Christian minority merely tolerated by the Moslem overlord. Mainly composed of very poor peasants, small landowners, and civil servants generally of subordinate rank, they have from the first been denied that degree of respect which might have led to a closer examination of the facts.

Certainly they were credited with some works of reasonable quality, though of a minor order, which appeared at the time most favourable for them – the so-called Coptic period. The most important of these are tapestries and sculptures. To these were added small objects: bronzes, articles in bone, sometimes in ivory, most

Monastery of St. Anthony the Great. Red Sea desert. Photo: P. du Bourguet.

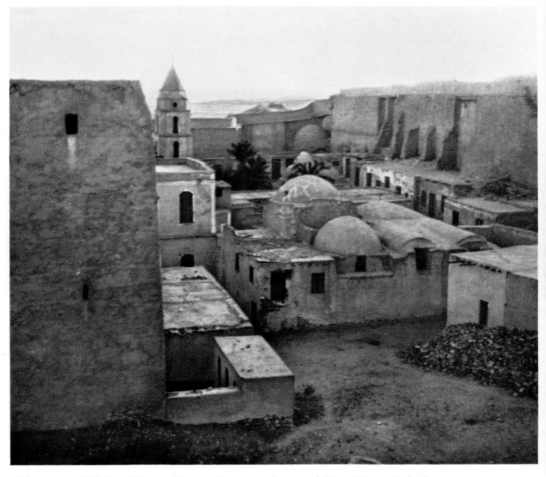

Monastery of Wadi en-Natrun. Western desert, north-west of Cairo. Photo: P. du Bourguet.

Page 13 (above): Monastery of St. Paul the Theban. Red Sea desert. Photo: P. du Bourguet.
Page 13 (below): Monastery of St. Paul the Theban: the Office for the Night. Photo: P. du Bourguet.

13

Church of Dendera, near the *mammisi* of the temple of Hathor. Fifth century. Photo: P. Brice.

of them intended for liturgical use. As for architecture, the field seemed to offer nothing which could conceivably be credited to the account of an original art. The surviving examples were solely of a religious character, and since churches in this area were usually constructed on a basilican – and thus 'imported' – plan, the question seemed not to arise. One author, and one moreover who should be well informed, has recently gone so far as to deny the name of art to the whole body of Coptic work, on the ground that there can have been no great Coptic monuments.[5] An extremely arbitrary conclusion, to say the least, if one thinks of, say, 'the art of Luristan', accepted as such without objection being raised on the grounds that it includes no architecture whatever. But in any case such an assertion is a denial of the facts, as we shall see. Leaving aside such extreme views, however, it remains true that Coptic work has never been valued at higher than craft level; quality crafts if you like, but no more.

Looked at more closely, this attitude towards Coptic work is, quite simply, the result of a conjunction of prejudices, the unfavourable nature of which, though readily understandable, constitutes no less gross an injustice.

Sandwiched in time like a thin slice – for its duration was short – between the two giant strata of the pharaonic and the Moslem periods, the so-called Coptic period has long seemed crushed to extinction between them. The more restricted number of Coptic monuments and objects could not stand comparison with the large body of masterpieces produced by these two civilizations. Inevitably, under a ruling power identified with a different religion whose tolerance, always relative, was subject to periodic eclipse, the monuments came, little by little, to be destroyed. Placed as they often were on top of, or inside, pharaonic temples, they were frequently sacrificed by Egyptologists in pursuit of more spectacular prizes. Finally, having only recently come under the protection of the Egyptian Antiquities Service, they have seldom ceased to be at the mercy of tomb-robbers and of treasure-seekers hoping – on the advice of the 'Book of Hidden Pearls' – to find precious stones behind the old paintings, which they had no compunction in destroying in pursuit of this ever illusory aim. Thus to Time, which spares nothing, was added Man, to reduce even further the volume of Coptic work. The chances of its being recognized as having the merits of original art were thus severely compromised.

History, in another way, seemed bent on destroying the last scruple. In general, art is the expression, on the aesthetic level, of a civilization whose destinies are presided over by a régime, whether monarchic, aristocratic or democratic.

After the Roman conquest, Egypt found herself in the unenviable position of being no more than a possession, first of the Roman and then of the Byzantine empires, before falling under the Moslem yoke. She was to be, for nearly two thousand years, a mere occupied territory. As such, she could not maintain an autonomous civilization, and an essential condition seemed lacking from her productions in the field of art: that direction of effort which assures its unity and its grandeur of expression.

Alexandria might conceivably have filled this role. In fact, cut off as it was officially from the rest of the country, and psychologically from a peasant mass wedded to the soil, it could hardly have been less concerned. The mass of the people was therefore left to its own devices, and at first sight it would seem totally unreasonable to expect from them artefacts rising much above the level of mediocre craftmanship.

Neither could one, from the start, expect to find any homogeneity in what was produced. As it was, the slight importance accorded to Coptic monuments and art objects, the rarity of scientifically conducted excavations and the risk inherent in purchases from antique dealers, could only operate in its disfavour. Also, among the experts there has been a constant tendency to attribute to the Coptic period everything of the Christian era in Egypt which did not quite clearly belong to pharaonic, Alexandrian, Byzantine or Moslem art.

But in this case all previous assumptions now appear outmoded. When one considers all the art objects upon which the label 'Coptic' has been bestowed, the mind may well boggle. The most heterogeneous themes and styles appear: subjects from Greek or Hellenistic mythology – and from the moral point of view the most daring subjects – rub shoulders not only with secular representations but with Christian iconography as well, even where this bears the sign of the Cross;[6] Sassanid influences can be detected, as well as Roman, Palmyrene, Byzantine or Moslem, and even Indian, contributions. Graceful figures elbow disproportionate manikins with crude features and odd shapes; elegant decorative motifs are associated with others of primitive execution, sometimes barely recognizable. A certain vigour, a certain imaginative power – these have been freely granted to the workmanship.[7] But this is far short of the conception that a Coptic art, in the full sense of the term, existed. At the best, one could look on the Egypt of that time as a meeting-place of forces, both autochthonous and foreign. It was seen as a field of study, and a difficult one, for specialists, usually drawn from other spheres; at best a period of transition, but in no sense a period of art.

Efforts have, however, continually been made to bring a modicum of order into this chaos.

Interpretations The most seductive hypothesis saw in this period a continuation of the pharaonic period. But this theory had a predictably short life. Pharaonic subjects are extremely rare, and how could one see in Coptic forms, crude as they often were, any trace of the formalized perfection of the earlier art? Moreover, between the pharaonic and Coptic periods there stretched the period of Hellenistic influence which had sounded the knell of the former.

Weightier reasons led, and still lead some, to look to the East for hardier roots, and to see in Coptic works of art either a local offshoot of Byzantine or, more often, a transposition of Christian Syrian art.[8] In some Coptic centres one does in fact find, about the ninth and tenth centuries and later, a direct Byzantine influence. Elsewhere, in the sixth and seventh centuries, basket capitals seem to indicate a Byzantine influx, while at the same time numerous decorative motifs seem to be copied from those favoured in Syria. Finally, in the pre-Byzantine period, Coptic work appears to have been carried along in the general reaction against Hellenism.

16

However, to postulate from this an 'imported' art, whether of Byzantine or Syrian origin, is premature, and in the last resort erroneous. From the fact of influences, localized in space and time, one is not entitled to jump to the hypothesis of a single source – whether such source be put in Byzantium or in Syria – and to make it responsible for all the rest of the art produced. A community of subject-matter, and to some extent of style with other pre-Byzantine arts, clearly link it to the Graeco-Roman art of Alexandria, but not as yet with Constantinople. Furthermore, borrowings from Palestine, from Palmyra, and from as far as Persia, are also detectable in Coptic work. Finally, it is clear that, while restricting its decoration to the interior, and thereby departing radically from the practice of the Syrian Church in the general orientation of its architectural ornament, the Coptic Church did not, for all that, model itself on the Byzantine Church, either in its programme, which remained, as we shall see, consistent, or in its forms, which are massive and geometric. If, then, Coptic Egypt turned periodically towards Byzantium and Syria, she looked as often elsewhere, preserving in this, if in no other way, her independence.

The great archaeologist Strzygowski, basing his hypotheses more upon a close study of the monuments – in other words, on the facts – sees Coptic art as a local continuation of Hellenistic art; an art which certainly contributed much more to this than it did to other pre-Byzantine arts.[10] In his own day, however, insufficient was known to facilitate the development of his hypothesis, which could thus lead only to datings of an almost completely subjective nature. It also excluded the supposition that Coptic artistic activity continued beyond the Moslem conquest, thus leaving an area of confusion in which, until very recently, all Coptic art studies were bogged down. As it was, his concern to trace the sources and describe the monuments led him to see Coptic art as a homogeneous entity, and to present it as such.

The possibility of a continuance of Coptic art into Moslem Egypt, which had been divined by a few scholars, when faced with certain precisely dated monuments, was given substance by E. Drioton, who gave the name 'art of the Copts' to these survivals.[11] The formula remains, however, a restrictive one, and while retaining it for the sake of clarity, its scope must now be extended up to about the twelfth century, as against Drioton's limit of the eighth, it having become possible since his time, to trace the artistic activity of the Copts up to this later date. It is, however, thanks to him that Coptic art was liberated from one of its shackles. Quite recently, one author of a book on Coptic art,[12] unhappily guided by preconceived ideas, has tried to circumscribe too rigidly what he himself regards as specifically Coptic. He rightly excludes all that is properly Roman, notably the famous Egypto-Roman painted portraits, and masks carved in the round, which some would still insist on adding to the ensemble of Coptic work. Ignoring, however, in quite arbitrary fashion, the architecture of a civilization which has left us so many churches and monasteries, he extends the Copts' understandable hatred for the Byzantine occupiers of Egypt to include everything of Greek origin; he goes on to distinguish two streams, one pagan – that of the Greeks established in Egypt during the so-called Coptic period, who inherited the Hellenistic myths and gradually transformed them in accordance with the abstractionist tendencies of the times – and the other a Christian art as practised by the Copts. These latter are represented as uncultivated peasants, fanaticized by the monks – monks sprung from among their number – and applying a purely barbaric technique to Christian themes, of which the sole merit, prior to the Arab conquest (which is supposed to have made a clean sweep of it all) would be to have proclaimed, through its very primitivism, the early Middle Ages.

The very simplicity of such a hypothesis renders it seductive. But the denial of any artistic value to a work because it is Coptic, and a theory according to which a given work is the more certainly Coptic the greater its barbarity[13] is wholly gratuitous and based on aprioristic reasoning which is inadmissible.

In fact, the hypothesis rests upon over-simplified postulates and on selective historical data. The equation of pagan Greek with Byzantine is, to say the least, surprising. The supposed hatred of the Copts for everything Byzantine calls for reservations, and cannot be presented, as it is in this case, without substantial qualification. To do so is to forget the patronage of St. Helen, revered as she was throughout the whole of Coptic Egypt; the cult of Constantine – considered as a saint by the Copts even before his canonization in Byzantium;[14] the relations which existed between well-known Copts and particular Byzantine functionaries, and even certain emperors;[15] above all, it is to forget the Byzantine influence, duly recorded as it is, in several Coptic centres before as well as after the Arab conquest.[16] The assertion that the Copts must have helped the Arabs to conquer Egypt rests on no firm foundation. At every step the basic hypothesis meets its refutation, since the author is obliged to admit the frequent use and transformation of Hellenistic, Christian and Byzantine themes by the Copts.[17] Furthermore, to deny to the Coptic craftsmen – frequently heirs to the skills possessed by artists of the Ptolemaic period – to deny them the possibility of having imitated, even to their elegance, the techniques of their co-workers of Graeco-Roman origin, is a pure intellectualization. Finally, to consider this whole people as lacking an élite capable of directing their efforts is, as we shall see, to ignore history. It is, in fact, too facile a hypothesis, which overlooks too many shades of difference; ignores or misreads too many facts, and thus ends by destroying without constructing anything in its place.

This exaggerated systematization takes to an extreme an all too common view – for the formulation of which Strzygowski must accept some blame, though he did not accept it at all points – which at first sight does appear to accord with the general aspect of objects described as Coptic. This view regards the whole mass of Coptic productions as a tardy, local prolongation of Graeco-Roman art. Such a reaction is quite understandable; everything seems to combine to lend credence to it. The basic themes are Graeco-Roman ones. In Egypt – as elsewhere – they are charged with a symbolism which, in keeping with the mysteries held in esteem, gives a new and more universal meaning to the old legends of mythology. In all late antique art contemporaneous with the first productions regarded as Coptic, the tendency to abstraction, and consequently towards a decorative style, is noticeable; we find it in the mosaics of Piazza Armerina in Sicily and especially in North Africa – for example at Tabarka, as also in the paintings in Roman catacombs, in imperial sculpture or in reliefs on sarcophagi.[19] In Alexandria, too, the departure from natural proportions is obvious in certain objects, which show a deformation of the antique style; for example, in the ivories – and how fine they are – mounted on the pulpit of Henry II at Aix-la-Chapelle.[20] Despite the interdicts, relations between Alexandria and the outlying countryside, or at least between it and the towns, were by no means negligible. At first sight, therefore, nothing seems to preclude the belief that Coptic work is no more than a late Egyptian deformation of Graeco-Roman art, parallel to that which took place in the provinces of the empire, caused partly by the absence of an aristocratic or aulic direction and partly by the decline of craftsmanship.

In fact, the problem seems to have been wrongly stated, or, rather, the question has not been taken far enough. To regard the work of the Copts as one of the waves set in motion on the surface of the Mediterranean by the impact of Graeco-Roman art is to admit that a certain number of elements of undeniable originality have been overlooked: in particular the style itself, sustained by an appropriate technique, which sacrifices harmony of the subject to the great masses of the composition. This is not deformation but transformation. To the casual observer, or on mere cursory examination, the Coptic oeuvre is naturally confusing, the more so in that the themes are Graeco-Roman. To anyone fully conversant with 'Coptic art' – for the style is consistent throughout the more important works – no such error is possible. This consistency permits us to group together those Coptic works which at first sight may appear as deformations, and then proceed to separate them from late Graeco-Roman art in general.

By broadening the question in this way, our approach will be adequate to Coptic art as a whole. Deformation may be found in works of aristocratic or official inspiration from Alexandria or from some of the more important centres of Egypt, more directly dependent upon Rome or Byzantium. This is not so in what one may call Coptic Egypt, which both socially and psychologically was separated from the main centres by a veritable hiatus.[21] In the religious, social, linguistic, literary and technical spheres, Coptic Egypt alone, apart from Italy and Byzantium, was able to pursue its own course of development and bring it to a level of which no one contests the validity or the originality—even to the point of 'absorbing Alexandria itself', as it were. A dynamic entirely its own appears to have operated in the profoundest depths of Coptic Egypt. It is hardly conceivable that this force should not have made itself felt in the domain of art, as in other spheres, differentiating it both from the last manifestations of official Graeco-Roman art and from the impulses radiating from Byzantium, even though it remained unafraid to borrow from one or the other. We are not trying to raise Coptic art to that eminence from which Byzantium reigns and must always reign. To anyone who considers it without preconceived ideas, however, this art does constitute a coherent entity. On its own level it outshines all others. This can only be explained as a result of certain positive drives having taken on new life from the final convulsions of antique art.

From this point onwards, instead of making extravagant efforts to find an exotic source for the best products of Coptic Egypt, we can more profitably, and more naturally, adopt a positive attitude from the outset. Let us take the work generally accepted as Coptic in its entirety, without preconceived ideas, and refusing it that designation only in the rare cases where a foreign influence is manifest in the style, rather than in the themes; in this way we may hope to introduce some order into the oeuvre, and at the same time to establish firm criteria for its assessment. The equation of 'Copt' with 'Christian' is only valid in Egypt after the Arab conquest. Up to that time many monuments were of Christian inspiration, but on one hand numerous Coptic fellaheen and other Egyptians were still pagans, and on the other many Greek residents, for example, perhaps pagans themselves, had become assimilated to the autochthonous population, especially in Middle and Upper Egypt. The work of these latter, therefore, should be credited to the account of Coptic art. Doubtless foreign influences can be detected in such work, but these remain of only relative importance, and for the most part, as happens in all art, they are carried along by a current of which, under a cloak of diversity, the unity of inspiration and of development is clearly apparent to anyone who looks closely.

Diversity of themes and styles

Diversity unquestionably appears in the themes, as is natural. The Coptic current, as first undoubtedly pagan, and later Christian, flowing on Egyptian soil – soil occupied successively by the Greeks, the Romans, the Byzantines, the Persians and the Arabs (whose civilizations were themselves nourished on borrowings) – carried, in its journeyings over the centuries, themes utterly foreign to each other. Nevertheless the Copts, faced with this heterogeneous legacy, did excercise a certain selectivity. It is remarkable that, among the various forms of Christian architecture employed in the Graeco-Roman world, upon which they were so dependent, the Copts retained only the basilica. This exclusive choice cannot have been the result of chance; it proclaims a unity of concept in that branch of art which is the foundation of all the others. We shall endeavour at a later stage to elucidate the reasons for this choice. It is equally noticeable that, with certain exceptions, the themes employed during the Coptic period group themselves for the most part into Egypto-Alexandrian syncretist cycles, to the exclusion of all others. It is into this already well-constituted ensemble that the Christian figures of Christ himself, the Virgin and the saints came to be assimilated. If, therefore, on cursory inspection, the ensemble appears heterogeneous, one is forced to recognize in it firstly the element of choice and finally – after a study of the evolution through which the elements replace one another – a unity which it would be difficult to deny.

There is also an apparent diversity of style. Three elements seem to war with each other: harmony (in certain works of a style in which we again find a trace of Hellenistic elegance); disproportion, at times to the extent of barbarity, where one perceives however something of the former; and finally, strange representations in which nothing remains of either of these.

The diversity is, in fact, purely the result of random juxtaposition of one with the other. When one takes the trouble to group them by affinities, and then to compare specific details in them with the same subjects treated in other works of the period, and finally to follow their transformation from one point of reference to another, it can be seen that this diversity of style derives naturally from the evolution of the style itself.[22] Beneath this diversity we can now detect the unity inherent in the age. It is characterized mainly by the translation, either of an idea or of an effect to be rendered; by insistence – at the expense of the natural proportions of the subject – on the contrast or harmony of surface areas. This applies equally to the plastic and the colouristic arts. This conception places Coptic art among what are described as the symbolist arts, as opposed to the naturalistic, and is it through the failure to recognize this, by a too exclusive attachment to classical norms, that one can easily misjudge it altogether.

This same conception is responsible for a technical characteristic in the treatment of relief which, though by no means exclusive to Coptic art, was used by them to the exclusion of any other: that of contrasting forcibly, and at right angles, the two levels, the upper of which is flattened. The same effect, of a light surface area standing out against a dark one, is also found in the colouristic arts. Admittedly Coptic art appears to have moved progressively towards this stage, but it was quickly reached and never afterwards abandoned; they made it completely their own.

In sum, it is through a failure to take into account the choices exercised and the evolution, whether in the programmes or the subjects, whether in the style or even in the technique, that one may be misled, and allow oneself to become blind to the homogeneity of Coptic art. An art can only be said to exist if, in a number of sufficiently important works arising within the relevant limits of place and time, there appear distinct individual characteristics. The Copts manifested their consistent selectivity in choosing a single architectural programme for their church building, with details entirely their own; in the use of a coherent ensemble of subjects, within the cycles of themes treated; in their symbolist conception, pushed to a degree which clearly distinguishes it from the arts of their contemporaries; in a style, and even a technique which answers fully to this conceptual approach. Is it possible to account for such a constellation of exclusive traits other than by the existence of true individuality?

The reality of Coptic art, local, popular and devoid of pretensions to great art as it is, cannot be denied.

The history of Coptic art must, for a start, be reinstated in contemporary Egyptian history as such, in which political, social and religious factors are intimately involved.

THE COPTS IN HISTORY

There are three principal periods to be considered. They are marked by three dates: in 30 B.C. Egypt was incorporated into the Roman Empire; in A.D. 313 a new era was inaugurated in Egypt, as it was in the rest of the Mediterranean world, by the official recognition of the Christian religion, and by the transfer of the imperial capital from the West to Byzantium; and in A.D. 641 Egypt was conquered by the Moslems. One must therefore distinguish a Roman Egypt, a Christian and Byzantine Egypt, and a Moslem Egypt.

After the battle of Actium,[23] which left Egypt in the hands of Octavian, the latter attached it directly to his person and, from the moment when he became Augustus, as Tacitus puts it, 'in his own house',[24] depriving it of the privileges of a Roman province. This was because Octavian saw in Egypt, essentially, the granary of Rome and a source of wealth for his own treasury. The role thus envisaged for Egypt weighed more heavily upon it than had the impositions of the pharaohs and the Ptolemies – of which the product, at least, remained in the country, and endured until the time of the Tulunids, and more particularly the Fatimids. It was to weigh so heavily upon the Egyptians, whether indigenous or assimilated, as to reduce them for centuries to an exploited and subjected mass.

At the head of the country we find a prefect, representing the emperor and combining both civil and military functions. He resided in Alexandria, which was administered by *archontes* and always enjoyed a dispensation special to itself. From the time of Vespasian, three *epistrategies* were installed, under the authority of the prefect, in Lower, Middle and Upper Egypt. Under their orders functioned various officials at the level of the *nome* (province), the town and the village, chosen from among Greeks or hellenized Egyptians. Diocletian, however, separated the civil and military powers, on the model of provinces of the empire. He gave to the army a commander-in-chief, called the *dux* (duke) and retained the division of Egypt into three parts, under other names, placing at the head of each a prefect responsible directly to the emperor. In the south, in order to stem the continual nomadic raids with the minimum expense, he withdrew the frontier to Syene (Aswan) and provided it with a garrison drawn partly from the Nuba. From that time onwards Nubia ceased to form part of Egypt.

The population, consisting of more than eight million souls, included the very few Roman citizens, the privileged Greeks and, above all, the mass of the Egyptians. In principle, mixed marriages were forbidden, but the enforcement of the law was riddled with exceptions, such as the concession granted to the inhabitants of Antinoë by Hadrian in the second century, and for much of the time remained a dead letter, so much so that the Egypto-Greeks, while sometimes managing to live among the Greeks, most often went to swell the indigenous population.

Land and, to a lesser extent, skilled labour, constituted the wealth of the country. To a great extent this accrued to the emperor and to his favourites, but also to certain 'veterans' and – it is important to note – to a certain number of free landowners. These were Egyptians who lived on their own lands, or in the towns, when they did not themselves become high officials or even governors.[25] The land, cultivated by fellaheen – day-labourers or tenant-farmers – who were additionally subject to forced labour, had to provide, first and foremost, a tribute, the *annona*, in the form of a quantity of corn fixed annually according to the harvest and to requirements, which was destined for the provisioning of Rome. In addition to this tax in kind both direct and indirect taxes were levied. The former was in the first place the land tax, levied on both the agricultural and the industrial product,

Basket capital. Limestone. Bawit. Eighth century. Height 53 cm. Paris, Louvre, Christian Antiquities. Photo: Max Seidel.

Birth of Aphrodite. Stone. Ahnas. Fourth century. Length 78 cm. Cairo, Coptic Museum.
Photo: A. Held.

on built-upon land, on workshops and on domestic animals, which fell on all landed proprietors, apart from the rare holders of Roman citizenship. To this must be added the head-tax, which fell on all subjects, i.e. – with the exception of Roman citizens – on Egyptians and assimilated foreigners, whether proprietors or fellaheen and, though generally reduced by half, on Greeks and other foreigners. The *curiales* or tax-collectors, usually of native origin, to whom the taxes were sometimes 'farmed', also took advantage of every opportunity to enrich themselves at the expense of the Egyptians, in particular the fellaheen.

The troubles which accompanied each succession to the imperial throne had few repercussions in Egypt. They did, however, make possible, during the third century and for a limited time afterwards, control of the country by the rulers of Palmyra: first Odenathus and then, after the ephemeral reign of his son Vaballathus, Queen Zenobia.

The most striking development, in the absence of great political events, was the establishment of Christianity.

Whatever may have been its beginnings, traditionally attributed to the preaching of St. Mark the Evangelist, the establishment of the new religion appears as a firm fact by the end of the second century.[26]

Thus, about the year 190, we find in Alexandria the 'Great Church' in epistolary relations with the Churches of Palestine and Syria regarding the date of Easter, and also the mention of some forty episcopal sees under the jurisdiction of the bishop of Alexandria; these were as yet confined to the north of the country.

It was, in fact, in Alexandria that Christianity was organized. The efforts of Bishop Julian (178–88) were responsible for the founding of the famous Didascalium (School of Catechists) which established the Canon of the Scriptures and, while opposing all deviations of thought, dispensed instruction of a quality comparable to the highly honoured teaching of the Museum. According to Eusebius, Origen, who directed it throughout the early part of the third century, 'employed more than seven tachygraphers who worked in relays at fixed hours, [and] as many copyists and young girls skilled in calligraphy'. The aim in view was, clearly, a conquest of the intellectual élite. To judge from the position which Athanasius and Cyril were to occupy in the city during the following centuries, this aim was soon largely achieved.

The common people were not overlooked and, in the Delta and in Faiyum, were already deeply affected, as we may judge from the use of marginal glosses and translations of the Holy Scriptures.

The young Christian Church, however, suffered from waves of persecution. These emanated from Septimius Severus (202), Decius (250), Valerian (258), Diocletian (303), Galerius (304), and Maximinus Daia (311–13). That of Diocletian was sufficiently bloody to serve Coptic writers as a point of departure for their history.

In the intervals, stimulated by the siege of Alexandria with consequent troop movements involving the importation of soldiers, themselves often Christian, and by the fervour generated by the witness of the martyrs, Christianity made headway. It first infiltrated simultaneously into the Faiyum,[27] which was visited by Bishop Dionysius about the year 257, and for about a hundred kilometres to the south, but does not seem to have penetrated beyond this limit in the time of Decius. The edict of tolerance promulgated by Gallienus (260) was followed by a substantial leap forward as far as the Thebaid, as we know by implication from the accounts of the great persecutions of Diocletian. Nevertheless it was not, even in the north, the religion of the majority of the Egyptians. Along the route of its penetration churches were built which, to judge from the terms of the edict of Gallienus, which restored them to the Christians, must already have been official buildings for the practice of the cult, and not what we might call 'parish halls'. By the end of the third century some one hundred bishoprics could be counted in Egypt.

The Christian life, wherever it appeared, displayed its fervour, even among the humblest, by the search for an environment more conducive to asceticism and contemplation than were the surroundings of ordinary life. This search coincided with the necessity of finding a refuge from the persecution of Decius and incited them to flee to the desert. Among them must be counted Cheremon, PLATES PP. 11, 13 the old bishop of Nilopolis – a town later to be rendered illustrious by Anthony – and also a Theban living in Alexandria, Paul of Thebes.

Eremitism was born. Gallienus' tolerance allowed this form of life to develop for itself an embryonic organization by grouping the hermits' cells about one of their number, notably around that of Anthony, the most famous among them, about the year 270. The first outlines of monastic life had been drawn.

Christian and Byzantine Egypt

The administrative reforms made by Diocletian appear to have endured up to Justinian, at the beginning of the sixth century.[28] The latter reunited the civil and military powers, putting them in the same hands. He broke the power of the prefect, who continued to represent him, by dividing Egypt into four duchies, directly answerable to the prefect of the East at Byzantium. Each duchy was divided into two eparchies, themselves divided into smaller areas, the *pagarchies*. The dukes, the prefect himself and many of the officials were at this time frequently chosen from among Egyptians, a custom legalized by Justinian in 569. This system, which brought Egypt into line with the other imperial possessions, soon caused all the institutions of specifically Egyptian character, and among them the privileges enjoyed by the Greeks and the hellenized towns, to fall into decay.

The taxes and, from this time onward, the full head-tax, fell on all alike, with the exception of the rare Roman citizens and, soon afterwards, the clergy.[29] Confirming a state of affairs in existence since Augustus, Justinian laid down in his decree of 538 that the transport of wheat to Constantinople, with the carriage[30] tax (*naulage*), destined to cover the cost even of the transport, should be the first care of the Egyptian dukes, from whom no mercy could be expected thereafter by those liable for the contributions, i.e., the Copts. The *curiales*, on whom devolved the levying of the taxes, themselves managed to evade these ruinous obligations. The general impoverishment resulting from the fiscal charges brought the Greeks nearer and nearer to the level of the popular masses and had, additionally, the effect of diminishing the middle classes of Greek origin. The indigenous mass, the Copts, whose cohesion was thereby more firmly consolidated, gained in importance and strength.

Three developments in the religious field were to give full force to their improved position. These were the edict of 313, the foundation of monastic institutions and the Council of Chalcedon.

The edict of Licinius and Constantine which, in 313, liberated the Church, now brought about an overt flowering of Christianity in Egypt. Documents, notably episcopal lists and monastic writings reveal a sudden and mass conversion of the Egyptian peasantry.[31] But after this date it is no longer Alexandria which is responsible for the propagation of Christianity. Local groups had been constituted: priests and deacons, whose role in the community as intermediaries between the civil authorities and the population had no little influence on the conversion of the latter. Very soon, however, their role became fused with that of the monks.

About 323, with Pakhom (St. Pachomius), the founder of cenobitism (KOINOS BIOS – communal life),[32] monasticism attained institutional form. The monasteries, from the middle of the fourth century onwards, formed an almost unbroken chain along the edge of the desert which bounded the Egyptian countryside on either side of the Nile. Being in permanent contact with this area, they found therein a constant field of recruitment, while simultaneously exerting a profound influence upon it. It is certainly due to their activities that, apart from a few centres of paganism, Egyptian as well as Greek, situated mainly in Alexandria and the towns, the whole of Egypt had been Christianized by the fifth century. The closure of the temple of Philae in the sixth century, by order of Justinian, put the seal on the disappearance of these forces of the past.

The third factor was the condemnation, by the Council of Chalcedon in 451, of the Monophysite heresy, which was supported by Dioscorus, Patriarch of Alexandria. Following Dioscorus to a man, Christian Egypt broke with the rest of the Christian world.

Provoked by differences of a political rather than a religious nature, the separation represented something of a crisis of national conscience. It affirmed a veritable spiritual independence from Constantinople, the political capital of the Christian world and, while uniting the Copts, in other words the mass of the Egyptian people, against the imperial power and its representatives, both secular and religious, prepared the way for a political separation, which was accomplished at the first opportunity.

Already a Persian occupation, from 619 to 629, made easier in Egypt by the division of power instituted by Justinian, had operated to the advantage of the Monophysites, who were officially supported by the occupying power. Forming as they did a majority of the Egyptian people, they could not but aspire to a similar state of affairs after the return of the Byzantines.

The conquest of Egypt by the Arabs took place in 641.[33] It remains unproven, whatever may be said to the contrary, that the Egyptians in a sense betrayed Constantinople by favouring the Moslem conquest. There were, for instance,

Moslem Egypt

27

Monophysites as well as Melkites (Christians under Byzantine rule) among those who fled before the advance of Islam as far as Nubia.[34] It remains true, however, that the Coptic Church was overjoyed at being finally liberated from 'Roman tyranny'. It is certain, furthermore, that, well treated at the beginning by their conquerors, the Copts hoped for a more liberal dispensation under them. In the event they found themselves under an even heavier yoke, by reason of their being Christians, which rendered them suspect to the Moslem power. This new servitude, which weighed ever more heavily upon them, caused defections among the Copts to Islam, and by the tenth century the Christian Copts had even ceased to be in a majority.

The Moslems in general preserved the Byzantine machinery of administration. The division of the country was simplified by reducing the four Byzantine duchies to two, Upper and Lower Egypt, which were then subdivided into districts called *kura*, corresponding to the old pagarchies. At the head was the prefect, whose duties included presiding over the Friday prayers, direction of finance and the police. At first nominated by the caliph and answerable to him, then, under the Abbasids, by the heir to the caliph or by a high-ranking military official of the household, he was in principle a simple governor. In fact, the first in date, Amr, the conqueror of Egypt, and those who succeeded him, frequently dreamed of making themselves independent of the caliph. Under the Omayyad caliphs, and under the first of the Abbasids, these were no more than idle dreams. Under the Abbasids, as they became more and more dominated by military leaders of Central Asian origin, Ibn Tulun, himself a Turk, did achieve it, and this state of affairs persisted under his successors for a quarter of a century. A few decades later Egypt was conquered by the Fatimid caliphs from North Africa, who this time installed themselves for several centuries.

Before the Fatimids, the fiscal system had functioned on the sames lines as it had under the Byzantines. The contribution in corn now found its way to the holy cities of Arabia. The monetary tax, on the other hand, which was much heavier, was assessed in proportion to the means of the individual taxpayer. It was collected by the district headmen, who corresponded to the old *curiales*, responsible to the prefect. These tax-collectors were almost always chosen from among the Copts, rightly considered by the Arabs to be thoroughly competent. They also constituted what Gaston Wiet has described as 'a sort of buffer-caste between them and the mass of the taxpayers'.[35] For the taxpayers were Copts. No Moslem was subject to the head-tax, which was a sort of tribute from the vanquished, i.e., the non-Moslems. The Moslem, being considered the only suitable fighting-man, was forbidden to engage in commerce, and thus escaped paying indirect taxes.

Moreover, the Moslem community, sole proprietors of all the lands of Islam, let out the Egyptian land on lease, but only to non-Moslems who, by the same token, fell under the land-tax. The entire tax burden therefore fell on the Copts. It is noticeable, however, that the total of the monetary taxes varied annually during the seventh and eighth centuries from ten to fifteen million dinars, while, from the second half of the eighth century to the time of the Fatimid conquest in the tenth century, it fell to little more than three million dinars.

This considerable difference was due to the corresponding fall in the number of Christians. Although they enjoyed a more liberal dispensation than under the Byzantines, it remains true that the tax burden now fell exclusively on them, and therefore increased accordingly for each individual.

Entering a monastery, which until then had brought exemption, no longer sufficed, since at the beginning of the eighth century a census was undertaken of all the monks, who then became liable for a payment of one dinar a head. Flight into the desert, or wandering from village to village, was punished with the utmost severity. Without any deliberate pressure being applied in that direction by the rulers, the result was mass apostasy.

This did nothing to solve the fiscal problem, since conversion to Islam meant, in principle, deliverance from taxation. It is a fact that that section of the revenue provided from the capitation tax suffered accordingly. The new Moslem, however, continued to be liable for the land-tax, whether his property was considered as personal and by that very fact as belonging to the Moslem community, or as part of the wealth of a Christian village to whose total tax burden he still had to contribute, despite his change of religion.

As a result, while the general tribute must necessarily have diminished, the burden carried by an ever decreasing Coptic community grew heavier at almost the same rate. This taxation, and not resistance to persecution, was thus at the root of the numerous revolts among the Copts during the course of the eighth century and part of the ninth. These took place under the Omayyad and Abbasid caliphs, in other words, at the time when the greater part of the tax burden fell on the Copts.[36] These had, in fact, been able to bear it as long as the burden was distributed without too great a change from the preceding period, and as long as the conqueror treated them in other respects with some liberality.

Freedom of worship, guaranteed by charter, seems always to have been assured to them. The destruction of images on the exterior of churches, decreed in 689 and repeated in 722, was in no way peculiar to Egypt. No doubt the move was directed against Christianity, but it was modelled on the iconoclastic measures adopted by the Byzantines in their empire, and seems to have taken advantage of these to make them coincide with Moslem imperatives. In any case, it is only when we come to Harun al-Rashid, at the end of the eighth century, that the Christians were forced to wear distinctive head-dress and clothing, and were forbidden to build new churches or to rebuild those that had fallen into ruin.

We have noted that those converted to Islam had, in practice, to continue payment of the land-tax. They were in effect, and for a long time continued to be, second-class Moslems. It was only in the middle of the eleventh century that the Arabs, properly so called, no longer formed part of the army and were assimilated to an autochthonous mass which had absorbed nothing from them except their religion. This explains – and it is essential to bear this in mind – the continuity, in social behaviour and consequently in the technical field, between Coptic Egypt (if one may risk a pleonasm) and Moslem Egypt. It would have required several centuries to effect a complete change on the religious plane. Although the Coptic community was now a minority group alongside them, the Moslem Egyptians with their vast majority were not distinguished from them in any way, either in their mode of life or in their occupations. Moslem Egypt – and this has never been said forcibly enough – remained firmly Coptic in character on both the social and the technical plane.

Under the Fatimids, whose own interests ran closely parallel with the prosperity and unity of the country, relations between them and the Copts were on the whole good, and even marked by a certain benevolence. One must regard as exceptional – in its extreme savagery and emanating from a caliph regarded as unbalanced by the Moslems themselves – the bloody persecution and destruction of churches visited upon the Copts at the beginning of the eleventh century by Caliph al-Hakim. Individual Copts were even chosen as counsellors by certain rulers, which suggests that there were more of them in the administration than ever before. Suspect as these men became to the populace, less on account of their religion than of the functions they assumed, they must however have remained in close contact with the mass of the people in order to have produced the state of rich prosperity which existed under the Armenian vizier Badr al-Jamali.

After the Fatimids, the Coptic community dwindled progressively, and no longer enjoyed such favourable conditions. It is not until the nineteenth and twentieth centuries, and particularly the support given by the Copts to the independence movement launched by Zaghlul, that their history again acquires any great significance. In that long period of obscurity which runs from the fourteenth to the twentieth century, if they retained their originality, circumstances did not allow them to exercise it in the arts, so that there is no point in taking account of this period here.

COPTIC
CHRISTIA-
NITY

In the light of the foregoing, we may now take a closer look at Coptic Christianity.[37] The birth and growth, the full flowering, and then the decline of Christianity in Egypt, constitute three distinct periods, in each of which it is possible to distinguish its characteristics and also the degrees and particular manifestations of its fervour.

1st period:
birth and
growth

Tradition attributes the beginnings of the conversion of Egypt to St. Mark. The oldest document in which this is mentioned is Eusebius' *Ecclesiastical History*, from the fourth century, in which however he is careful not to give this opinion as a fact. However problematical it may remain in the event, the Coptic tradition does throw some light on the matter. It draws attention to the relations existing between Alexandria and Rome and to the effects due to these relations. Certainly Alexandria was the first point in Egypt to be touched by the Gospel. Its position on the Mediterranean coast, close to centres already Christianized, rendered this natural. But in any case its direct relations with Rome for the conveyance of the product of the *annona* would normally have resulted in the importation of Christianity as it was constituted in the capital of the Empire by the preaching of St. Peter, codified, as we know, in the Gospel of St. Mark.

Alexandria, the centre of Neoplatonism, was also a melting-pot into which poured all the doctrines of the age. The Gnostics, or adherents of Gnosis – a world system, the elements of which were drawn from all the known religions – found a place there, as did the devotees of the cult of Mithras. Apart from the uncultivated mass, such as abounds in every seaport, all levels were represented in the remainder, from the most exalted, through the less distinguished and down to the distinctly inferior; but all, in varying degrees, were affected by the culture, or at least by the ideas and the doctrines, which this intellectual capital attracted. In this population the Jews occupied a special position. Many highly cultivated ones, such as Philo in earlier times, were certainly in touch with Greek or Egyptian thinkers of their own calibre, while remaining in close contact, within their own markedly distinct group, with the humblest of their co-religionists.

One may suppose that the route by which Christianity reached the level of the cultivated Egypto-Greeks passed through these evolved Jews and would, here as elsewhere, have touched the humbler elements of the population in its passage through the Jewish community. The fact is that Christianity very soon counted some rare spirits among its adherents. The foundation of the Didascalium by Bishop Julian, about the year 180, is evidence of this.

It is probable that this élite consisted of Egypto-Greeks, perhaps even of Egyptians with a Graeco-Roman culture. The interest shown by Clement of Alexandria in hieroglyphic writing may be taken as an indication of this.[38] When conflicts of belief arose it was the Egyptians who were most affected. This 'most religious of all peoples', as Herodotus considered them[39] – certainly the people whose hearts were most deeply penetrated by religion – had lost, in the pharaoh,[40] their natural mediator between man and the divine. They found themselves faced by a deeper abyss than did other peoples and it was natural that the most educated among them, those who felt the void more acutely than the others, should turn – in preference to those 'systems' then in favour in Alexandria itself – towards the religion which most nearly satisfied their needs.

This is not to say that the Christian religion was less suited to the mass of Egyptian fellaheen. On the contrary, as elsewhere, indeed more than elsewhere because of the parallelism between Isis and Horus on the one hand and Mary and Jesus on the other, Christianity had every chance of infiltrating the most popular levels of the community.

It is, however, a fact that we find it gaining a foothold in Alexandria. It was sufficiently well established there to be taken into account by Celsus at the end of the second century, and had an intellectual base – the Didascalium – fully in character in this city of the future Neoplatonism. During this period it fanned out towards Faiyum and the Delta, that is to say, in those circles most affected by the ideas current at the time, and where, moreover, doctrinal differences were soon to become exacerbated. We know this well enough in respect of Arianism in Alexandria, and indeed earlier from the controversies regarding Origen and again, even earlier still, from the existence, in the second century, of a Christian Gnosticism centred on Valentinus and Basilides. We also know of it in Faiyum, where, in 257, Bishop Dionysius of Alexandria went in person to inquire into the effects of a book tainted with Sabellianism.[41]

2nd period: flowering
The pagan masses of Middle and Upper Egypt were only to be won over in the course of the fourth century, and then only in stages. In the year 300, in fact, in Oxyrhynchus for example, there were still twelve temples and only two churches whereas in the fifth century this was on the way of being reversed, with a count of twelve churches, and was to be completely so in the sixth century, when the number of churches there had risen to thirty.

What brought about such a change? It is clearly attributable to the freedom with which the edict of A.D. 313 had endowed Christianity, and to the activities in which the latter could engage from then onward.

Inevitably, this liberty acquired through the conversion of Constantine and the prestige derived from it for Christianity, brought in the mass of the peasants. It had doubtless largely rallied the intellectual élite of Alexandria and touched the common people of the Delta and of Faiyum. But it is by comparison with Persia, which after a promising start remained un-Christianized because no Sassanid ruler was converted, that we can measure the repercussion of Constantine's conversion on the masses.

One must be careful not to overestimate the effect of the exemption from taxes which, after this date, favoured the clergy, the monasteries and their inhabitants. While it facilitated recruitment to the monasteries, this measure does not suffice to explain their activity. For this there are two complementary reasons: on the one hand the link between the monks and the fellaheen from whom they were recruited and, on the other, as a glance at monastic literature reveals, an intense mystical fervour.

But, as a result of the activities of the monks, who had taken over from the great Alexandrian catechists, Christianity in Middle and Upper Egypt changed its character. From being doctrinal, as it remained in Alexandria, it became elsewhere more ascetic and mystical.

PLATE P. 11
PLATE P. 12
Egyptian monasticism,[42] as Anthony had founded it, and as it was conceived by those who emulated him – Pakhom, Macarius, Shenute – in fact disclaimed any intellectual preoccupation. The monks devoted themselves to prayer and to manual work, carrying their mistrust of all studies to the point of abhorrence. In contrast to what took place in Asia Minor or in Europe, Coptic monasticism, while it could claim great theorists of asceticism, did not produce a single theologian. Thanks to monasticism, the dissemination of the Gospel was extended and accelerated. It is no less true that this difference between Alexandrian Christianity and the Christianity of the rest of Egypt, i.e. the Copts, came to widen further the gap which had been deliberately created by the Roman governors between the capital and the country.

This difference did not deter the monks, and through them all Copts, from submission to the Patriarch of Alexandria. Quite the contrary, for, while they rejected intellectualism as incompatible with the monastic life, they valued the glory reflected by Athanasius and Cyril upon the Alexandrian episcopal see. Their activities in the service of the Alexandrian bishops was to be outstanding in defence of Cyril, whether in Alexandria against the pagans or at the Council of Ephesus in supporting his views. When the dogmatic formula on the nature of Christ proposed by Dioscorus was condemned by the Council of Chalcedon in 451, they likewise sided whole-heartedly with the dogma and against the Council. National pride played as large a part as did ignorance in their blind submission to Alexandria. But it happened that in breaking with the rest of the Christian world, the head of the Coptic Church was thrown back among his own followers and had to flee from Alexandria, where his place was taken by a patriarch of the Greek rite. From this time on, and over a long period, Egyptian Christianity would be Coptic Monophysite from the patriarch down to the last fellah.

This, then, was the situation at the death of Shenute in 452: Egypt had become a Christian country, but professed a Coptic Christianity, ostensibly Monophysite but in fact without any clearly defined doctrine, yet ferociously attached to its own traditions and customs.

No doubt there were still isolated pockets of paganism. These consisted mainly of a few conservative intellectuals in Alexandria and in some of the towns, perhaps in touch with pagan circles in Constantinople. But, in effect, no trace of paganism remained in Egypt after the Arab conquest.

Coptic Christianity, however, permitted the emergence of many elements which owing to its lack of doctrine it was unable to exorcize. This may account for the continuance of Gnosticism which, in the fourth century, was still militant.[43] We can be more certain of the continuing practice of magic and of certain magical heresies which grew out of Christianity, which are documented in Coptic papyri of the time and even, in fact, up to comparatively recent times.

All this was favoured by the continuing struggle between the Coptic patriarchs in exile, supported by their churches, and the patriarchs of the Greek rite, with their suffragan bishops, installed by Constantinople in Alexandria and in the dependent sees.

Thus we must bow before the weight of evidence: evidence of a Christianity which, although fully identified with the Coptic masses, had not penetrated them very deeply.

Following the Arab conquest all Egypt, apart from a few groups of Byzantine *3rd period:* officials, was Coptic, and the term, from that time onwards, signifies precisely *regression* 'Egyptian Christian'. But, apart from a nucleus of truly devout Christians, what lies concealed behind this façade?

Under the caliphs and the first Omayyads, the stream of conversions to Islam began and continued without let or hindrance. The intensification of the head-tax, over and above all the other taxes which afflicted them, affected a relatively large number of Copts. This tax, however, must have been supportable, since many still remained true to their faith. It would seem that the new Moslems were drawn from the mass of those who willingly followed the faith of the majority, but whose convictions were too weak, and sometimes too recent, to withstand the first pressure brought to bear upon them.

The reduction in the number of taxable individuals, following the conversions to Islam, drove the authorities, in the eighth century, to subject the monks, hitherto immune, to the head-tax. The abandonment of monasteries reached substantial proportions. The small *peculium* which the religious authorities had previously allowed the monks to accumulate out of savings had now to go almost entirely to meet this tax. But this implies that, in the case of many Copts who had entered monasteries, the possibility of a legal escape from the head-tax had played an important part in their choice of the monastic life.[44]

In both cases, pressure of a financial kind operated. The effect was to remove from the Coptic community those elements which were ready to follow the law of the strong, but the cause should properly be attributed to a lack of fervour and, ultimately, to a lack of temper in the religious mentality.

The movement, in any case, continued and evidently began to include those who until then had shown themselves better able to withstand privations. A further cause must therefore have come into play. Can this have been anything else than a lack of reflection on the Christian verities – among the monks and the faithful alike?[45]

We must conclude that, with certain particularly brilliant but rather scattered exceptions, the attitude of suspicion towards matters of doctrine which characterized Egyptian monasticism was the weak point in Coptic Christianity, and was perhaps the main factor responsible for its failure under Moslem pressure. Only a ferocious attachment to its own traditions was to preserve a nucleus of Copts. These men were to become more and more aware of the need for a study of Christian doctrine and would, in fact, form the basis of a new development in our own time.

II. AN IMAGINARY EXHIBITION

It may seem arbitrary, at first sight, to extract from a total oeuvre those examples one may consider the best of their kind, in order to arrange them in a sort of permanent exhibition.

The notion is justified, however, when the works in question are the pride of the museums to which they belong, and when most of them have, at one time or another, been chosen to figure in exhibitions.[1] Moreover, there can be nothing arbitrary in such an approach if it be admitted that the value of any art must be judged firstly by its masterpieces.

On these lines a very strict selection has been made. We have excluded those pieces which, because they help in identifying the sources of Coptic art, are often considered worthy to be shown in conjunction with it; since they belong to the arts of other peoples, they have no place here.

We shall, on the contrary, admit only works of the period under review and possessing the characteristics special to Egypt – in other words, Coptic works – to figure in this collection of prime examples.

Some of these may, even so, be related to earlier arts, or to other contemporary arts, but they are first and foremost Coptic, by virtue, in the former case, of new features which alter their essential aims, or, in the latter, by the persistence of features proper to Egypt.

In order that, despite variations, the judgement reached should be wholly valid, all the works included should be 'located' on the same wave-length, that of the Copts.

Here a word of warning is needed. All too often the distinction between themes and styles is forgotten. Borrowed themes abound in every art. It is not a question of whether or not certain themes are borrowed, nor, indeed, if all are borrowed, but of whether or not they have been assimilated, i.e. transformed, wholly or in part, by the art which adopts them. This transformation will show itself in new characteristics, of which the most important is style – style as the very embodiment of the inspiration. A work may be typical of a given art whatever the origin of the subject represented. An elementary truth, no doubt, but experience proves that it is indispensable to restate it here.

It is clearly impossible to present a monument of vast dimensions in an exhibition; we must be content with small-scale models. But here we have greater freedom. Our freedom will extend even to supplying imaginatively what has been destroyed, and there is nothing to prevent our applying this to the Coptic churches which, in almost every case, lack their entire superstructure.

ARCHI-
TECTURE

This is so in the case of the church of Dendera[2] in Upper Egypt, within the walls of the great Ptolemaic temple of Hathor near the *mammisi*. The roof has disappeared but the walls, enclosing an area 40 metres long by 25 metres wide, are

PLATE P. 14

still quite high. The church appears as a closed rectangle running east and west, with an entrance in the south wall at the extreme south-west end. This entrance does not lead directly into the nave but into a transverse narthex, of which the east wall is pierced by three doorways opening on to the nave while, in the western part, three doors provide entrance to two closed rooms. This arrangement results in a sort of indirect, or baffled, means of entry into the church. The columns are no longer there; only their bases remain, the two rows of which indicate that this was a basilica of three naves, the walls of which, from the narthex to the sanctuary, have hollowed-out niches at intervals along the interior face. These are segmental in plan and surmounted by a shell-form motif. The sanctuary at the east end is trifoliate, and comprises a central apse with five semi-circular niches and two lateral apses. These latter are without niches, and communicate directly with the central apse and indirectly with its corresponding nave. Our choice of a basilica – an architectural programme clearly imported from elsewhere – as the first example of a typically Coptic building, will doubtless give rise to objections. This exemplifies the importance of our preliminary remark on the distinction between theme and style. Here the theme, the programme, is certainly on a basilican plan. But first – and we shall have occasion to emphasize this elsewhere – the Copts, in contrast to all other regions in which this plan was equally used, adopted it exclusively, i.e., as the result of a deliberate choice. Furthermore, if the essential lines could not be changed, certain features – whether borrowed, because particularly dear to the Copts, or whether original – were impressed upon it. These additions, while accommodating themselves to the general scheme, gave it a new character and ended by transforming the ensemble into a Coptic programme. The chief of these are the form of the sanctuary and the hollowed-out niches at intervals along the walls; of the others the indirect or baffled entry is of no little significance.

The monument is still very impressive. Nicely calculated proportions, simplicity of plan, equilibrium of the parts composing the sanctuary, the balance between these and the narthex at opposite ends of the main body, the lines austere, but articulated by the wall-niches, where the eye lingers on the perfection of the carving in the shell forms: all this is satisfying to the mind. It only remains for us to imagine, in an atmosphere of isolation from the world, accentuated by the grey tones of the sandstone and by the gloom once cast by the roof, the ranged colums in their solemn march towards the sanctuary, as towards the supreme mysteries. Is this to say too much? A rigid rectangle, baffled entry, returning galleries; all this is reminiscent of the secrecy in which the Ptolemaic temples enveloped themselves, while the rows of columns up the nave are evocative of their hypostyle halls and the tripartite division of the sanctuary of its counterpart in the pharaonic temples. Be the likeness as it may – a likeness rendered the more natural by the placing of the church within the precincts of one of the most imposing temples of ancient Egypt – the insistence on mystery is inescapable, although it has been modified, in accordance with the Christian viewpoint, to allow the participation of the faithful in the cult rites performed in the sanctuary.

Some surprise may be felt that we have chosen to draw attention in the first place to a work of architecture. But if one agrees that architecture is the foundation of all the arts – since all of them in the last resort exist solely for its enhancement, either by prolonging its lines or by contributing to activities which take place within it – there is nothing really surprising in this choice. It is to architecture that one must look for the prime motivations of a style, the secrets of its inspiration. Sculptural ornamentation serves to prolong the lines of the architecture. Here, as has been said, we shall be content to isolate those Coptic examples which are of outstanding aesthetic quality.

There would be numerous basket capitals to choose from. Most of these come from the monastery church at Saqqara and can be seen in the Cairo Museum; two others, originally from Bawit, are on display in the Louvre.[3] In our imaginary exhibition they might be fittingly placed on top of the engaged columns a little way inside the entrance. The prototype, of course, is Byzantine and even pre-Byzantine in origin.[4] The shape, which broadens out toward the top, allows of a continuous decoration, impossible on the Corinthian capital. The Byzantines certainly did not overlook this possibility, but the Copts seem to have surpassed them in the almost magical charm of their decoration. This is apparent, still in a naturalistic vein – still close, too, to Byzantine models, of which several preserved in the Graeco-Roman Museum were probably imported to Alexandria from Constantinople[5] – in the interlacement of vine-leaves which clothes the Saqqara capitals.[6] The effect is even more striking at Bawit, this time showing a new use of the basic model. Over the entire surface of one of these capitals the closely-packed stems of acanthus leaves seem to jostle one another in a concerted upward movement; in the second, long acanthus leaves, their stems formed of interlacings, each harbouring a fruit or a cross, rise to the upper limit, each attaching itself to its neighbours by the tip of an extended leaf. The technique of relief on two levels produces a veritable lace-like effect.

PLATE P. 23

Another species of decorative element is that of a broken pediment enclosing a scallop-shell, an example of which, originating from Bawit, can be seen in the Louvre.[7] We cannot go far wrong here in giving it a prominent place, say on the end wall of one of our exhibition rooms. The prototype is again an imported one, of Graeco-Roman origin.[8] But the Copts have transformed it to their own taste. The broken ends are directed sharply upwards and what is, in the original model, a horizontal line between the two has in its turn taken the form of an acute angle, the peak of which rises to the level of the other two, thus forming a perfect protection for the shell form. The outer spaces are filled – at the top, between the angles – with a cross contained in a circle and – to right and left of the chief members – by three supple volutes springing from a spray of acanthus which turns inwards, towards the border. The inner spaces carry long, twin-leaved stems of acanthus, following the borders; finally, surmounting the shell form, are three acanthus stems, springing from a central point and directed respectively towards the summit and the two sides. Beneath all this organic exuberance, itself accentuated by the sharply contrasted levels of surface and background, yet

APPX. PL. 3

disciplined in movement and controlled by the lines of the pediment, the scallop-shell radiates long petal-like cells of great sobriety. Here we have an example of elaboration, through the contrast between simple and multiple, which attains the level of great decoration.

APPX. PL. 1   Fairly high on the wall of our exhibition-room we shall now place an archivolt known to have been found in Egypt, though the exact place of origin is not known.[9] This presents a sort of poised equilibrium between the background of organic decoration, with its two – only modestly contrasted – levels of flat carving, and the high reliefs, of a fruit in the centre of the semicircle and an angel-musician on either side. These are, in many ways, related to the best Romanesque reliefs, but the interest and originality of this piece is due to their bold projection against the relative flatness of the plant decoration behind them.

Running along the walls of our imaginary exhibition, again fairly high, we shall
APPX. PL. 4   mount some friezes, originally from Bawit and now on show in the Louvre.[10] Great scrolls of foliated vine-stems, which end in a cross, succeed one another with marked nobility of line, each defining a true circle. Within each scroll an escaping stem springing from above is interlaced with another, this time springing from below, while the terminal leaves bend back and are aligned with the outer circle. The knot uniting each successive scroll with its neighbour is invariably placed on the median line, and each rounded cavity formed by the interlacing of two stems corresponds with another, from scroll to scroll. The space formed by the parting of two scrolls is filled, both above and below, by a long leaf and a bunch of grapes. The surroundings of the right-hand cross are given a special treatment: the separation between two scrolls is slightly accentuated to leave the space necessary for the upright of the cross, the arms of which pass over the top of both. Within these two scrolls a single stem, that which springs from above, breaks away and interlaces, this time with another stem which at the top passes underneath that of the neighbouring scroll, and, at the bottom, underneath that of the other, thus tracing a new circle about the cross. The drawing of the curves is fine and supple, but it is through the contrast of the two levels of flat carving that the stems, the bunches of grapes and the crosses are made to stand out boldly against the background, in that clear contrast of light and shade which is so characteristic of Coptic work.

The pieces which follow one may envisage as being distributed either on plinths or in show-cases. Some will have formed part of the decoration of sanctuaries; others again were in more common, even profane use. Two series may be distinguished, to each of which we may allocate a room. One of these will contain human or animal figures; the other decorative objects of small size, among them certain pieces which will be found markedly original, and even rather odd in some ways, but with which contemporary taste will find itself strangely at ease.

SCULP-   From the start, who could fail to discover some element of charm in a Birth of
TURE   Aphrodite, a limestone relief originally from Ahnas el-Medineh and now to be
PLATE P. 24   seen in the Coptic Museum in Cairo?[11] The head and shoulders of the goddess are presented full-face, while the lower part of the body is turned gradually to a

three-quarter view, with the legs, slightly bent under her, shown in profile. The upper part of the goddess is carved in such high relief against her scallop-shell that it amounts almost to a free-standing figure. The trace of a smile is sketched on the triangular mask of the face, which rises clear of shoulders, slightly elevated by the upward movement of the arms. The left arm is missing while the right is raised above the crown of curly hair to feel for the veil, which passes below the elbow and fans out behind the body, its folds breaking loose as it falls. Against this harmonious background the bust, with barely swelling adolescent breasts, and the elongated waist describe a most graceful curve, setting off to advantage the faintly smiling face poised above the shoulders, the pillar of the neck defined by a collar bearing a massive medallion. Here is the true undine, seeming at a gesture to raise the lid of the shell, whose innocent awakening is already suffused with a sense of her power.

Say what one will, an object so delightful cannot be stripped of its charm. The very bulk of the collar and medallion which, on reflection, one might be tempted to criticize, serves by contrast to emphasize the elegance of the forms and of the pose; the conventionalized head seems made for the smile; the almost excessive elongation of the waist suggests a young, scarcely formed body. All these details, in departing from classical realism, serve further to underline the meaning inherent in the subject.

One really had to take this little masterpiece first. Another example, however, PLATE P. 41 while perhaps less supremely elegant, has still the power to charm. This, now in the Louvre, is a fragment from the central part of a broken pediment, presenting a concave surface from which projects, carved almost in the full round, a Dionysiac subject.[12] In this, prominent against the smoothly carved-out background, but still attached to it by a stony mass, stands a nude figure, entangled in vines. On examination we find a disproportion between the short legs, the again elongated waist – though here with a substantially developed torso – and the exaggeratedly broad neck and shoulders and over-large head. This imbalance between the three parts of the body together with their extreme smoothness and the stylization of the face, with its fixed, staring eyes, the hair treated like a coronet of beads – all this underlines the movement with which the personage thrusts aside the vines which encircle him and advances into the full light.

The merit of a third piece lies in the complexity of the ensemble. This is a group of Pan with a bacchante framed in a broken pediment.[13] Originally from Ahnas el-Medineh, it is now shown at the Coptic Museum in Cairo. Here, at the apex of the angles formed by the broken members of the pediment, sea-lions in high relief spring outwards on either side, their foreparts supported on small shrubs, while the inner faces of the broken members are enriched with bold reliefs of acanthus. Filling the centre space and connecting the broken elements is a round-headed niche, which harbours the group. This latter, carved in high relief, is further enhanced in its effect by the dual contrast, firstly with the almost flat carving of the conventionalized plant forms and secondly with the rounded forms of the sea-lions. The subject is the pursuit of a bacchante by the god Pan. The faces are poorly rendered, but the features which mar them accord well enough with the contrary movement of the rather stylized bodies and, despite the two heads being turned in the same direction, serve to indicate the motives which animate the personages: desire on one hand and escape on the other.

PLATE P. 42 An Annunciation in sculptured and painted wood, now in the Louvre,[14] exemplifies a style highly characterized in its every part. The subject is incomplete, but we recognize Mary, seated, with a basket of wool on her lap. She extends a hand towards the angel, only a leg and a foot of which has survived. The Virgin's head is shown full-face, while the body is turned towards the angel. This disposition of the two parts of the body, at right angles to each other, indicates a manner which makes full use of only two dimensions. In effect, it reduces the third to a barely perceptible recession, and flattens the upper level, without, however, eliminating the features of the subject or the folds of the draperies, which are either rendered by the technique of incision or are picked out with simple colours. The pose, odd enough from the spectator's point of view, accentuated by the rather over-conventionalized drapery and the almost totally unrealistic contours of the face, result in all our attention being drawn to the eyes. Their exaggerated size suggests a slight degree of apprehension which is heightened, even if unintentionally on the artist's part, by the head being turned away from that of the angel. It is perhaps an effort to render that part of St. Luke's Gospel which describes her as being 'troubled'.[15]

PAINTING In painting, our attention is first drawn to an icon executed in tempera on wood, by the highly stylized lines which define the subject. Originally from Bawit, and now in the Berlin Museum,[16] it represents the head and shoulders, with the head curiously stylized, of Bishop Abraham. Fullest use is made of the framed space, and its proportions are used to the greatest advantage. The shoulders fill the available width completely, the halo less so, with the result that the elongated lines describing a figure-of-eight about the bearded head of Abraham, within and in contrast to the perfect circle of the halo, are given full prominence. These curves are reinforced by the elliptical form of the eyes; by the vertical lines of the nose; by the downward curve of the mouth, echoing that of the cranium and accentuated by the deep lines descending from the nostrils. The right hand inclines towards the book carried upright against the left shoulder, and fills the interval between the beard and the lower edge of the frame. The colours used are simple and tender. Pink and yellow predominate, with a deep grey-violet used very sparingly for a few lines defining the drapery and the covers of the book, while this is further enriched with simulated brilliant black stones. The colour areas are outlined with broad black borders. Every element – the austere lines, the supple curves, and even the direction of the hand – combines to focus attention on the brilliance and fixity of the eyes. Inflexibility prevails, and appears, in the stylization of the lines, as the principal characteristic of the subject, as indeed it was of some of the intransigent monks or bishops described in the texts.

In the same technique, another 'icon', also originating from Bawit, and now to be seen in the Louvre,[17] is more reticent in its appeal to the spectator, but proves

Dionysian figure. Limestone. Sheikh Abada (?). Fourth century. Height 61 cm, width 60 cm, depth of niche 7 cm, height of relief 14 cm. Paris, Louvre, Christian Antiquities. Photo: M. Chuzeville.

41

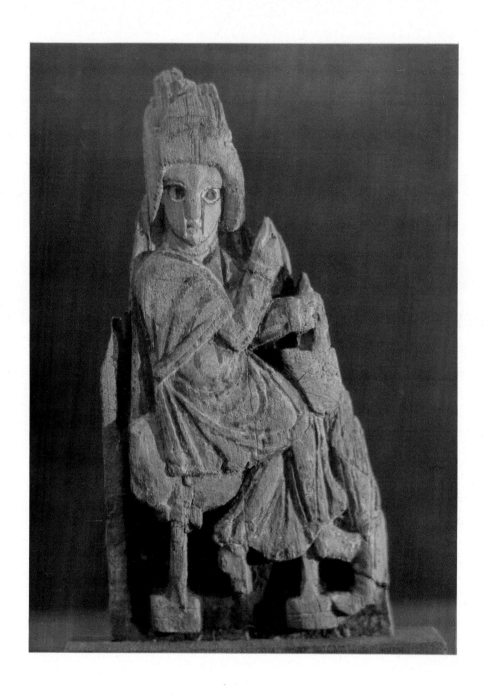

Annunciation (fragment). Wood. Fifth century. Height 28.5 cm, width 14.5 cm, thickness 2 cm. Paris, Louvre, Christian Antiquities. Photo: Max Seidel.

Christ protecting the monk Menas. Tempera painting on wood. Bawit. Sixth-seventh century. Height 57 cm, width 57 cm, thickness 2 cm. Paris, Louvre, Christian Antiquities. Photo: Max Seidel.

to be much richer in evocative power. This is the one representing Christ pro-
tecting the monk Menas. The two personages stand side by side, facing the spectator, each with a nimbus about his head, that of Christ having a cross superimposed upon it. But the 'Saviour', as He is described in the descending inscription on the right, extends His right arm protectively round the shoulders of Menas, a *proeistos*, that is to say, prior of a monastery. The two figures stand out against a background of desert foothills, their haloed heads rising above the line of the horizon.

Certain details here are of Byzantine origin: the nimbus perhaps; the book Christ holds, with its embellishment of simulated precious stones, certainly. Others may appear to be so: the hieratic pose of the two personages standing side by side and full-face; the set facial expressions; the nature of the costumes and the handling of the draperies. Nevertheless, it is a Coptic artist who has, so to speak, put his signature to the work. The first letter of the Greek word *sôtêr* has been contracted with a *p* to form the Greek letter *psi*. But the *p* is the Coptic article.

Above all, even if the pose owes something to Byzantium, it has passed through the Coptic crucible, since the attitude, by virtue of Christ's gesture, is entirely original and in its familiarity both breaks with the general hieraticism of the art of the imperial court and exemplifies the marked humane tradition constant in Egypt throughout the ages.

Christ's Majesty suffers no loss as a result of the gesture, and is underlined by His slightly greater stature and by the head, which is slightly taller and wider. Christ's arm, encircling the shoulders of St. Menas, seems to draw the saint beyond the earthly horizon, where their two haloed heads stand out against a flaming sunset sky. All this evokes, and even goes beyond, the great pharaonic tradition in which the divine sun reigns in splendour, and also the characteristic horizons of Egypt itself.

The style of the work contributes to its symbolic significance. In contrast to the Byzantine manner, the bodies are dwarfed, divided into simple zones of almost equal dimensions, the folds of the pallium effectively concealing the bodily forms. These folds in the pallium, worn over a dalmatic, are arranged in concentric curves which converge on one or other of the two haloed heads, in accordance with the relative importance attributed to each, and on the eyes, where again the curves are strongly emphasized.

The intense 'presence' generated here transcends that generally evoked by the Graeco-Roman portraits, or by their later icons, and renders this painting at the
very least a key work in world art, and certainly the masterpiece of Coptic art.

From these two panels we must pass now to a niche, originally from Saqqara
and now displayed in the Coptic Museum in Cairo, the interior of which bears
a painted representation of extreme naivety.[18]

Virgin enthroned between two angels. Ivory. Ninth century. Height 26 cm, width 11.6 cm, thickness
5 cm. Baltimore, Walters Art Gallery.

45

The Virgin, seated, offers her right breast to the Infant Jesus while, on the same side, above a standing angel, is depicted the bust of a saint. On the other side appears a second angel, symmetrical to the first. The main subject, at the rear, is of Byzantine origin and was doubtless inspired by representations of Isis nursing Horus. However, the piece bears the typical abbreviated sign for the name of Mary, placed between the Virgin's halo and the bust of the saint, and the workmanship is Coptic. The pose of the angel with its fixed gaze; the facial contours of the Virgin, the Child and the saint, their stylized eyes gazing in somewhat unexpected directions, having regard to the personages involved; the disproportion of both hands and faces; the disproportion, too, of the personages in relation to one another; the abnormal position of the Virgin's breast in the gesture with which she offers it to her Son – all this, which at first rouses astonishment, is related to characteristics noted in other Coptic works. Awkward traits, perhaps, which nevertheless take on a certain significance. The standing position of the angel and the fixed stare stress its role as impassive servitor. The saint is reduced to head and shoulders, but the inclination of the head and the general direction of the gaze are both directed towards the Virgin. The disproportion of these two figures with the group of the Virgin and her Son minister to the same effect. In this group it is the gesture, rather than the strange position of the limbs, which attracts attention; the very inaccuracy tends to mobilize it even more forcibly towards that gesture. This gesture, coupled with the Virgin's gaze, directed above and beyond her Son's head, is by these means assured of its prime importance in the scene. The mother feeds her baby, but to prepare Him for certain tasks, of which the distant one, as painful as it is glorious, seems to be before her eyes at this moment. Whether intended or not, the effect, in spite of all the awkwardnesses – indeed, through them – registers fully on the spectator.

IVORY WORK

PLATE P. 44

In a style so far removed from naturalism as to be disconcerting, a Virgin and Child between two angels, in low relief on ivory and belonging to the Walters Art Gallery, Baltimore, is no less compelling in effect.[19] The subject in itself is touching, but our first warm response to this is chilled by the contrastingly harsh treatment in detail: the distended and staring eyes, the elongated rectangular heads and the folds of the draperies ranged in series like organ pipes. Once our eye becomes accustomed, however, we notice that these folds are grouped and make a concerted movement towards the faces. The whole effect of these depends upon the position of the Infant's head, pressed against His mother's cheek, as in the groups known as 'Virgins of tenderness'. In this evocation the harshness of the detail takes on a new meaning which dissipates our first feelings of repugnance. Whether intended or not, this harshness has the effect of bringing out the suffering of the prematurely aged mother and of the divine Child, at the prospect, distant yet tragically close, of the anguish demanded by the Redemption.

Bawit

In many of the apses found at Bawit, one of which has been preserved in the Coptic Museum in Cairo,[20] the hemisphere of the vault is taken up with a scene, painted on two levels. On the lower level the Virgin, shown either standing in prayer or seated, either carrying the Infant Jesus on her lap or suckling Him,

is placed in the centre, flanked on either side by Apostles, each bearing a book. PLATE P. 53
In the upper register Christ is depicted, enthroned within a circular mandorla,
which is supported by the allegorical symbols of the four Evangelists. On either
side, inclined towards the centre, is an angel. This is a Coptic interpretation of the
Ascension. The figures are stiff, their features simplified and practically uniform,
the pleats of their garments fall mechanically from folded arms. The total effect is
rather awkward, but the colours are bright and varied. To a superficial observer
the two registers might seem to be independent of one another, their apparent
independence being accentuated by the frontal stare of the Apostles. In fact, the
dimensions and placing of the mandorla indicate clearly that the subject is entirely
oriented towards Christ triumphant. Even the grouping of the Apostles on either
side of Mary has the effect of bringing her into closer relationship with the upper
register. As for the orientation of the Apostles' faces, placed as they are strictly
in line, this the artist has left us to supply. Like the artist of today, he disdains
perspective or anything resembling it. He is content to juxtapose the elements,
counting on the spectators and their mystical understanding of the subject to
reconstruct, imaginatively, their actual orientation.

That this is intentional is confirmed in a fragment of loop (bouclé) weaving in TAPES-
TRIES
APPX. PL. 9
the Chafik Chammas collection,[21] the subject of which is a seated Virgin carrying
the Infant Jesus. The head of the Child, whose arms are raised in prayer, is formed in
the direct prolongation of the mother's neck, treated as a column, while His right
leg is disposed diagonally. Mary's feet and the hem of her robe can be distinguished.
By this treatment the union of the two heads and the pre-eminent role of Christ
are underlined at the same time.

An interesting point, which the reader will doubtless have noticed, but without
attributing any precise symbolic significance to it, is that, as a result of the stylization which forms an essential part of most, if not all, of these pieces, they present
a markedly decorative appearance. The lines of the composition prompt us to
seek a meaning which transcends the subject depicted. At the same time they
define the unusual proportions, which serve to create a new balance and rhythm.
A total effect is achieved which, as we shall observe, is sought after more and more
for its own sake as time goes on.

Secular decoration was by no means alien to the Copts. Examples can be seen in PLATE P. 54
the Berlin Museum[22] and in the Louvre,[23] on shawls which are crossed by wide
bands of decoration incorporating foliated scrolls and vine branches, with bunches
of purple grapes glittering in the sun among the green tints of the leaves. It can
also be seen in a large wall-hanging in the Louvre – commonly known as 'Sabina's
Shawl'[24] – though here one of the figures displays a cross. Although only a
fragment, it is nevertheless worthy of consideration. Marrying the three sides at
one end are two bands at right angles, which shelter a panel in each of their interior
angles, while further away an *orbiculum* is placed near the centre, among flowers
and amorini. In the bands themselves we find amorini, birds and crocodiles
among water-lilies. In one of the panels is depicted Artemis the huntress, and in
the other the myth of Daphne and Apollo; in the *orbiculum*, Bellerophon and the APPX. PL. 7

Chimera. The subjects are readily identifiable and retain something of classic realism, but are so treated that natural proportions are never completely adhered to. The subjects have abdicated here in favour of the total effect, and this, through the interplay between the varied colours, the lines and the movement of the bodies, is fully attained.

Basically, the aim has already become that of delighting the eye with a shimmering interplay of colour. This can be seen quite clearly in the ornamentation on cushions or on ceramics, where the figures of dancers, of hunters or of animals filter through a tangle of branches, or a mythological scene may be enacted.

As in the paintings just mentioned, but carried one degree further, the subjects participate in this general decorative effect. This can be measured in a small limestone panel to be seen in the Louvre, in a wall-hanging belonging to the Abegg-Stiftung in Berne, and in a carved stone panel acquired by the Brooklyn Museum in New York.

TITLE-PAGE   The first of these[25] bears, in relief, a fish disposed diagonally, head downwards, the body filling the frame on the right-hand side, while the space left free above the head, which bends up towards it, is occupied by a cross. Even if the fact that this was discovered at Erment, in Upper Egypt, did not sufficiently establish its nationality, the piece proclaims its Coptic origin both in the sharp cutting at right angles which separates the parts in relief from the background and in the flattened carving of the two levels. This simplicity in the technique lends even greater effect to the movement of the fish, a movement marked both by the curvature of the body and the downward thrust of the head. This symbolizes also a homage to the cross carried by the fish, which in turn gives to the ensemble its meaning, that of salvation through the Christ-*ichthus*.

PLATE P. 55   The wall-hanging in the Abegg-Stiftung at Berne[26] presents a far more complex subject. In a framework broadly resembling pilasters surmounted by an architrave, two arcatures in the upper part harbour stylized birds; one an eagle with outspread wings and the other a peacock. In the lower part are represented four personages, facing the spectator, their arms raised in the orans attitude and wearing dalmatics; respectively, a man, a child and two women. Here the stylistic effect is achieved through the immediate juxtaposition of contrasting areas of colour and is effected without loss of richness in the colours. This is accomplished independently of the technique, though the latter enhances the effect. A cross at the intersection of the arcades, and another in the eagle's beak, indicate the Christian character of the work.

APPX. PL. 12   This striving after decorative effect makes itself felt in a stone panel belonging to the Brooklyn Museum, which treats the martyrdom of St. Thecla in relief.[27] The saint is standing, stripped to the waist, menaced on both sides by wild beasts and flames, beneath the cross which she raises with both arms above her head. It is curious to note that the lines here are so constrained, and the surface level where they are rendered in relief so flat, that in another material this might be taken for a woodcut, which would only require inking in order to produce, under pressure, a perfect print in a simple contrast of black and white.

48

We may see this tendency pushed even further, to the extreme limit at which the subject becomes no more than a blank canvas, alterable at will and with the colours disposed in areas dictated by fantasy. Although they can by no means be considered masterpieces, two tapestries may serve as examples. Both belong to the Louvre.

One of these is a small square panel, the design of which consists of a very broad PLATE P. 65 outer band, ornamented with closely juxtaposed lozenge shapes, each of a different colour from those of its immediate neighbours. This band encloses a smaller square, occupied by a portrait.[28] Only on careful examination does this reveal itself as a woman's face. With its long nose and shrunken mouth, under a heavy mass of curly black hair, the effect is no longer even human. The thick outlines, however, in conjunction with the elongation of the nose, recall Rouault's use of the same procedure for his portrait in stained glass of St. Veronica.

The other example consists of one end of a band, or runner.[29] The ground colour PLATE P. 66 is blue and upon this, executed in loop-weaving, appears a design of eight-lobed flowers. Below this, i.e., at the extremity of the band, four figures stand out boldly against a bright yellow ground. Experience alone enables us to recognize these as female dancers, for the bodies form a rectangle, composed of the head, the very short torso and the very long legs – all of uniform width.

This utilization of the subject for purely decorative ends appears as the climax of those general tendencies shown in the work we have examined so far. Thus Coptic art may claim successes in several different directions – following, however, a consistent line of development – each of which, while not perhaps attaining to great art, belongs in the category of pure art.

What sort of impression, then, shall we carry away from this exhibition? Or, to put it differently, what tendencies exclusive to Coptic art will stand out in the memory? In contrast with many national arts which have been qualified as great, Coptic art appears to have cherished a horror of academicism. It stylizes to the ultimate degree by altering proportions, at times to the extent of oddity. From thence it proceeds either to express a harmony which no longer resides in the forms, but which is that of a profound symbolism, or to obtain a purely decorative effect, in which only the interplay of lines, of levels, of surfaces or of areas of colour have any part to play. External appearance is sacrificed, whether it be for the realization, through these relationships, of a reality which goes beyond it, though without ceasing to express it, or from a paroxysm of the imagination in the very play of these relationships. At all events, Coptic art transcends the here and now to reach the invisible. If, from the objects which manifest this dual tendency, we turn back to the architecture, we realize the profound unity of this art, which tends essentially to orientate itself towards the unknown, or else to evoke it.

If our imaginary exhibition has succeeded in interpreting these characteristics, it will not have been wasted, as we stand on the threshold of the history of Coptic art.

III. ON THE THRESHOLD: PRE-COPTIC ART

At the moment when the first indications of Coptic art began to show themselves, another art was in occupation of the field.

Could this art still be described as pharaonic?

Certain aspects, and these not inconsiderable, suggest that it can.[1] In architecture, taking their cue from the Ptolemies and from their religious policies, the Roman emperors favoured the construction of new temples dedicated to the gods of pharaonic mythology, and the continuance of the decoration of temples already extant. The architectural programmes were derived, in their essentials, from ancient pharaonic art. They responded, even more than the latter, however, to the desire for separation and for secrecy: the columns of the façade and those which commanded the hypostyle hall were linked by intercolumnar walls, which effectively prevented the gaze from straying beyond them; the rectangle of the temple itself was enclosed in the wall of the precinct, in close proximity, which was apparently intended to offer a further barrier to the indiscreet eye. In the decoration, and notably in the bas-reliefs, human figuration may assume the weightiest forms, taken over from the style introduced by the xxvth (Nubian) dynasty, transforming them after the Greek fashion to give a curious three-quarter view. The subjects hardly differ, as to scenes and personages, from those we find ornamenting the temples of the New Kingdom and beyond. They retain and even accentuate, in this new manner, the pharaonic canon, which aimed at achieving an equilibrium of masses, rather than a harmonious sequence of forms. The statues even affect the same conventional pose as that adopted in Egypt from time immemorial. We find the same thing as regards the personages represented in paintings, as may be confirmed at Tunah el-Gebel, particularly in that which shows a woman dressed as a Roman matron, although represented, almost full-face, between the gods Horus and Anubis.[2] Certain details in the form of the sarcophagi were modified: the lid was no longer carved in the likeness of the supposed attitude of Osiris but is now flat, with the recumbent form of the deceased painted on the upper face.

In fact, however, pharaonic art – even if its official death certificate was not forthcoming until the sixth century – was, on the threshold of the Christian era, irretrievably doomed.

It stood condemned in the first place, despite appearances to the contrary, in its architectural programmes. The monuments surviving from Roman times in Egyptian history are by no means negligible, particularly the temple of Kalabsha in Nubia, and above all that of Philae, the pearl of pharaonic Egypt. But this, truly, was the swan-song. The mass of the temple of Kalabsha is more a reflection of Roman solidity than of religious inspiration. As for the temple of Philae, its artistic merit resides mainly in the Hellenistic grace with which it reclines, like a

DOOM OF
PHARAO-
NIC ART

FIG. I

51

bathing beauty, on the languid curve of the island's surface. Neither one nor the other could really claim to have contributed anything new to religious architecture.

But the doom of pharaonic art was evident also in its themes. These either display Hellenistic or Roman detail superimposed on broadly Egyptian poses, or else have become frankly integrated into Alexandrian art. A statue of Isis in the Louvre[3] is a flagrant example of these borrowings, which finally destroyed the profound symbolism of pharaonic art. True, the arms are hieratically attached to the sides, and the right leg advanced from the body, in conformity with Egyptian tradition. But the lines and volumes of the head, the modelling of the whole body and the folds of the drapery all combine to strip this statue of the last trace of Egyptian personality; without the help of the name which appears at the base we should be hard put to recognize here the most popular goddess of the Nile valley. In her hybrid representation, like so many others, she breathes the last sign of pharaonic art. It is at the source – of the programmes, architectural and decorative, as of the themes and of the style proper to the time of the pharaohs – that the mortal blow has been struck. This source, this well-spring, was the religion, embodied in the ruler himself.[4] He was its high priest, because, as god on earth, he presented himself as mediator between the deities and men. He presided over every manifestation of the cult – and consequently over everything which ministered to the cult – from the monuments within which the ceremonies were performed, to the form of their decoration and the most diverse liturgical equipment, just as he was supposed to have command over the principal events in daily life, and particularly over the cosmic phenomena which engendered and renewed that life. The blood of Horus, which vanished with the last pharaoh of the xxth dynasty, had been the source which nourished pharaonic art, and this source now dried up over the land of Egypt.

For, while assuming the title of pharaoh, the Ptolemies were in no position to take over his religious and cosmic functions. It was obviously impossible for them to claim kinship with the blood of Horus, the essence of pharaonic power. At the most, they passed themselves off as representatives of the god. But this did not suffice to breathe life into the religion, nor, consequently, into the art which had been the expression of it. The monuments which they themselves, and after them the Roman emperors, multiplied on the face of Egypt were no more than a translation into stone of the outward gestures of the religion; along their corridors the breath of the spirit was no longer felt.

ROLE OF HELLE-NISTIC ART This void could never be filled through the activities of the new centre of learning which the Ptolemies had established in Alexandria, and which soon showed itself to be very much alive. This latter was to nourish a flame which, compounded of Neoplatonism on the one hand and Gnosticism on the other, would have an affect on philosophy, and on its advancement throughout the world, and was also to have a profound influence on the development of the Christian religion, at least in its early stages. But, shine as it might throughout the whole of the civilized world, it had not the power needed to take the place of a failing inspiration in

Ascension. Painting. Bawit. Seventh century. Height 100 cm, width 100 cm. Cairo, Coptic Museum.
Photo: A. Held.

Band with pastoral subjects (fragment). Tapestry. End of fifth century. Height 147 cm, width 26 cm. Paris, Louvre, Christian Antiquities. Photo: Bulloz.

Egypt. It could to some extent fill the needs of cultivated circles in Alexandria, and spread from there around the entire periphery of the Mediterranean, and even beyond it; it was too complex, too ethereal, too intellectual and, in a word, too rationalistic to establish a firm hold over the masses. It appealed to the intellect, not to the heart. It could only have succeeded if it had been sustained by a religion capable of comprehending the whole of life, and of making itself equally accessible both to the people and to the élite.

The Greek religion was no longer in a position to assume such a role. The object of sarcastic comments since the fourth century B.C. on the part of Greek philosophers, on account of the far from moral activities attributed to the gods, it offered nothing comparable to the ancient Egyptian religion wherewith to enlist the consciences of the humblest, as of the most cultivated.[5]

Should one read more into the assimilation of the Egyptian gods to those of ancient Greece than a simple superimposition, aimed at bringing the two mythologies closer together? Above all, was the syncretism between the two, which resulted in the appearance of new gods such as Serapis, a positive attempt to inaugurate a new Egyptian religion? This hardly seems likely, however great may have been the infatuation of the Greeks and the Egypto-Greeks with this latter god – an infatuation which persisted until the destruction of the god's shrine by the Christians in the fifth century. In any case, such an attempt would have had no hope of success, since it seems to have lacked any corresponding dogmatic or moral theology, and would, moreover, have required adequate

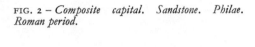
FIG. 2 – *Composite capital. Sandstone. Philae. Roman period.*

foundations in order to take the place of those positive elements which the pharaonic religion had contained in time past. The new symbolisms with which these gods and their life-cycles were decked out by the religious sects of the moment could claim no such thing.

It remains true that, at the same time as these last respects were being paid to pharaonic religion and to the art which reflected it, another art was establishing itself in Alexandria and, through the intermediary of certain large centres – Antinoë, Heracleopolis Magna and Oxyrhynchus – in the Egyptian countryside, just as it spread through the rest of the Mediterranean world. Just as there was a linguistic *koine*, a common language, in use throughout the empire, formed partly from the Greek, but carrying along with it, in simple forms, differing vocabularies, so also was there an artistic *koine*, compounded of various themes and characteristics, but in which Greek themes predominated and in which were presented graceful forms derived from Greek art. This art, composite but with Hellenistic leanings, provided a common fund, to which the local arts, and in particular Coptic art,

FIG. 3 – *Acanthus leaf, inner treatment. After E. Drioton, 'De Philae à Baouît', Coptic Studies in Honour of W. E. Crum', Paris, Institut Byzantin, 1950, p. 445.*

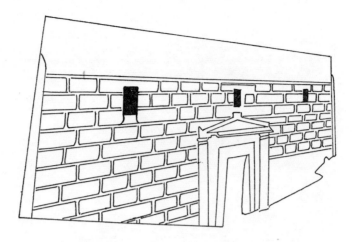

FIG. 4 – *Pediment on colonnettes. Painting. Tunah el-Gebel. Roman period. After S. Gabra and E. Drioton, op. cit., p. 15.*

quite naturally turned for new material. At the base of this art of Hellenistic inclinations lay Greek mythology and philosophy – transformed, however, by Pythagorism – stoicism and the mystery religions, which portended to find the 'world-soul' and a promise of salvation hereafter in the ancient myths.[6] All this ensured a readier welcome for the advent of oriental religions and ideas. For this Alexander's campaigns were partly responsible, but the extension of the empire and the mixing of peoples that resulted from conquests or from recruitment to the legions, all accentuated the movement. The oriental cult of the sun, the dualist religion of Mithras, the Orphic or Dionysiac cults originating from Greece, that of Isis, and also a mentality dominated by superstition or addicted to magic – the magic so prevalent in late pharaonic Egypt – all these met, mingled and overlapped throughout the Mediterranean world. The doctrines of which they were the vehicles interpenetrated one another, keeping speculative thought on Greek philosophy in a constant state of flux. Neoplatonic ideas, developed in Rome by Plotinus, (who was said to have followed the armies of Gordian III into India) predominated in Alexandria. These tended to lay stress on the invisible, and to regard the visible as its expression and outward harmony. Gnostic books proliferated. These were cosmogonic systems seeking to explain the creation of the world on the basis of texts drawn from all religions, and to extract a moral philosophy therefrom. Though sometimes written in Greek, from the end of the second century onwards, they have reached us mainly in the form of Coptic texts of the fourth century – texts discovered about twenty-five years ago at Chenoboskion, near Nag Hammadi, in Upper Egypt.[7] If this stream of ideas, borrowed from all sides, achieved no profound penetration of the Egyptian people, it did however contribute towards a change of viewpoint in their perspective on reality – a perspective they owed to their pharaonic origins.

FIG. 5 – *Triumph of Amphitrite. Mosaic. Constantine. Third century. Height 380 cm, width 200 cm. Paris, Louvre, Greek and Roman Antiquities.*

The result, in effect, was to attach greater value to the meaning of things than to the things themselves. The symbol or the magical power became more important than the object embodying it.

This tendency was widespread. But Alexandria was one of its principal centres, upon which depended the hellenized towns of Egypt, which is to say the metropolises, as minor centres. Hellenized art – this art with Hellenistic leanings – which sought its inspiration not only in such very diverse elements, but also in such composite philosophizing, was nevertheless responsible for some architectural programmes, architectural ornamentation and decorative themes that were unified by their style.

FIG. 6 – *Mask from a female mummy. Painted plaster. Antinoë. Third-fourth century. 34 × 26 × 62 cm. Paris, Louvre, Egyptian Antiquities.*

FIG. 7 – *Portrait of a man. Tempera painting on wood. Thebes (?). First century* A.D. *18.5 × 30 cm. Paris, Louvre, Greek and Roman Antiquities.*

FIG. 8 – *Lady wearing crux ansata. Encaustic painting on linen. Antinoë. Third-fourth century. 216 × 91 cm. Paris, Louvre, Egyptian Antiquities.* ➤

Architecture

The architectural schemes were developed in Alexandria and also in several of the largest centres in Egypt. It is not, however, to Alexandria that we must look for any considerable remains – apart from a few necropolises – of monuments, either religious or secular. A few, such as the Serapeum, were destroyed from the fifth century onwards. The others lie buried under the modern city. Only here and there, thanks to excavations, has one or another become available for examination.

The situation was but little better in the rest of Egypt. The important centres are known: Oxyrhynchus, Antinoë, Heracleopolis Magna, Panopolis... But nothing

FIG. 9 – *The Tetrarchs. Porphyry. About 300* A.D. *Near St. Mark's, Venice.*

remains of them save ruins, and these in a condition which, to the present day, has rendered the study of them disappointing.

A hall forming the core of a Roman fortress at Qasr Qarun in the Faiyum[8] has been put forward as constituting the link with the basilican church plan. The demonstration is not absolutely convincing.[9] Nevertheless, the exclusive preference shown later by Egyptian Christians for the basilican form leads us to suppose that it was extensively adopted in this earlier period and, having regard to the enforced relationship with the capital of the empire, it could well have come from Rome.

Ornament   In the ornamentation of buildings we find a predominance of motifs widespread in the Hellenistic Orient, though originating from ancient Greece. These either conform to a rather mechanical stylization or else are adaptations – to an art already inclined towards ornamentation – of elements utilized up to that time on a large scale and destined solely for architectonic purposes.

To the first group belong the capitals. These may be, as at Hermopolis Magna, of the canonical or Vitruvian type adopted in Rome, in which the three zones: lower acanthus, higher acanthus and leafed calices, are of equal heights. They may equally well be – as in Alexandria, in ruined monuments of the first century B.C. and now stored in the Graeco-Roman Museum – of the type found in the tholos of Epidaurus, which was common in the Near East at that time, in which the zone taken up by the scrolls supporting the abacus is given greater importance at the expense of that occupied by the lower range of acanthus.[10]

At Philae, in the portico flanking the west side of the dromos of the temple, we find capitals bearing cartouches deriving from the second canon, but here the
FIG. 2   scrolls which should support the abacus have been replaced by umbels of papyrus. In these same capitals, however, we must draw attention to the treatment of the acanthus leaf – the work of an Egyptian artist. What little remains of the original form of the leaf and of its indentations is rendered in a few lines, and these moreover stylized. Lines of almost geometric regularity are inscribed within the upper lobe and in the extremities of the second and third lobes, but these latter join together to form concentric circles, unrelated to the nervures of any known leaf, in pursuance of a purely decorative interpretation: the translation of an element
FIG. 3   of Greek origin into the pharaonic style. What we have here, however, is not the short-lived invention of one artist. It must be recognized as the tradition of a school, since it is perpetuated in Corinthian capitals attributed to the third century, which are now stored at Edfu.[11]

In this context we must not omit the friezes, which derive from an ornament much used in the temples of ancient Greece, but which are here on the one hand made narrower, and on the other may run the length of the walls at the most
FIG. 4   diverse levels. Those ornamenting the tombs or Roman houses at Tunah el-Gebel[12] are obviously reproductions of others in relief, but of these latter, however, we have no examples from the Egypt of that time, unless we include a number of friezes from Oxyrhynchus now stored in the Graeco-Roman Museum in Alexandria.[13]

The second type of transformation of elements originating in ancient Greece, and redeveloped in the Hellenistic Orient, is particularly manifested in the use of niches surmounting two engaged colonettes. This may take the form of a pediment as in house No. 21 at Tunah el-Gebel in Egypt,[14] or of a broken pediment, as at Petra,[15] or it may have alternating rectangular and curvilinear aspects, as in the Nympheum of Jerash in Syria.

FIG. 4
FIG. 45

This type of ornament was used either on a flat wall or in a scenic arrangement of pyramidal form, in which a triumphal arch on two columns is featured between two similar arches of smaller dimensions or again in a piling up of niches on columns, in which case the superstructures might be of uniform design or of two alternating designs. The simple type of ornament found on the basilica of Constantine in Rome is found again in Egypt on Alexandrian imperial coinage and in the tomb houses of Tunah el-Gebel, notably in house No. 21 and in the Dionysiac house with the rectangular pediment. The rectilinear arrangement existed in the temple of Baalbek, but there is no surviving example in Hellenistic Egypt. The first harmonic order, in tripartite form, which was common in Graeco-Roman art, for example in the basilica of Trajan in Rome and in the palace of Diocletian at Split, appears in Egypt in a tomb of Mustapha Pasha in Alexandria. The superimposed order, with alternating forms of niched pediments, predominates, for example in the Mausoleum of Diocletian at Split or in the Nympheum of Jerash, and consequently may well have been used to ornament some of the important buildings in Hellenistic Egypt: a supposition which gains support from the fact of its use in churches of the Coptic period.[16]

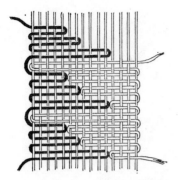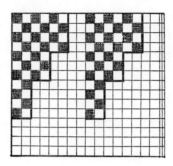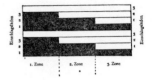

FIG. II – *Hatching. Method of weaving. After unpublished drawings by M. Cauchy (Paris, Mobilier national).*

Themes As in architecture and in architectural ornament, the themes most favoured in Graeco-Roman art are themselves transformations of themes already extant in earlier times.

Most of these originated in ancient Greece. If we find relatively few of them in Graeco-Roman Egypt, there is still every reason to suppose that they flourished there, if one is to judge from the number and variety of those in use during the Coptic period. Although most of the Aphrodisian and Dionysian themes have probably disappeared, it is impossible to doubt – when one remembers the interest shown in Alexandria, as elsewhere, in the religions of mysteries – that such themes were frequently treated. Foliated vine-scrolls, in any case, appear as painted decoration in several Roman houses in Tunah el-Gebel, notably in an arcature.[17] To judge from their presentation, these reflect a Greek rather than a pharaonic origin. On the same site and in the same technique, a series of scenes from the cycle of Oedipus and the Rape of Proserpina[18] must be mentioned. These are treated in a style based on the alternation of lights and darks, and were apparently chosen as funerary subjects suitable for a necropolis. Other schemes must have included the myth of Orpheus and that of Leda, but no vestige of these has survived from this period. Hercules must have been held in no less honour, but only a single high relief representing him can be cited, belonging to a private collector.

PLATE P. 76 Two themes used in tapestry-weaving fall naturally into this group. One of these displays beautiful yellow fish, their body-colour varied with numerous supplementary colours, swimming across a uniform green background. The deep green shadows cast by the fish stand clear, under their bodies, in the manner to be seen in Pompeii, in the house of the Vettii, and in various mosaics, such as that

FIG. II of Daphne, in the Louvre. Originally from Antinoë, this tapestry is now divided between the Textiles Museum (Musée Historique des Tissus) of Lyons and the Louvre.[19] To render the modelling the weaver has here used the technique of

Portrait of a woman. Tapestry. Ninth century. Size 21 × 19.5 cm. Paris, Louvre, Christian Antiquities.
Photo: Max Seidel.

Dancers (fragment). Tapestry. Twelfth century. Size 58 × 40 cm. Paris, Louvre, Christian Antiquities.
Photo: Max Seidel.

hatching with coloured threads characteristic of the Graeco-Roman period.[20] Subjects based on plant motifs naturally enjoyed great favour. These appear frequently and in diverse settings, for example, in painting at Tunah el-Gebel or in tapestry in the Berlin Museum.[21]

Other themes appear to have been translated directly from those of ancient Egypt, without even having left the country of origin. Yet transformed they are, both in spirit and in style. These are the Osirian themes. Under this head we must include the motifs concerned with the Egyptian gods Osiris, Isis and Horus. Even the outward appearance of one or the other was frequently modified at this time. On many of the painted burial cloths Isis is represented in the guise of a Roman matron, sometimes in regard to the costume but always to the features.[22] Bronze statuettes of Horus, dressed as a Roman soldier, exist in a number of museums.[23] By the same token, the workmanship is no longer pharaonic, but Graeco-Roman. However, the transformation goes further: a syncretism was established between Osiris and Dionysus, between Isis and Aphrodite and between Horus and Harpocrates, on the basis of their similar roles in the rebirth of nature and of individuals. This syncretism is often rendered literally, in the numerous terra-cotta representations found in Alexandria, and also in the Hellenistic towns of Egypt.[24] However, it retains only the general idea of the myth peculiar to Egypt, favouring rather those of Greece and, even more so, those of Neoplatonism and of the religions of mysteries and, equally, the concepts of Gnosticism. This appears frequently, alongside many other syncretisms, in the so-called Gnostic intaglios which have been found in great numbers in Egypt, and in which the symbolism is most often of a magical variety.[25]

FIG. 1

Another group of themes taken over from pharaonic Egypt and passed down to Graeco-Roman Egypt is that of Nilotic subjects. In these a no less profound transformation may be seen – to the extent that at times one must wonder if some of them have not abandoned Egypt with little hope of return! This could well be our reaction, for example, to the large Palestrina mosaic, in which a landscape, conventionally Nilotic in its lotus, provides a setting for the gambols of amorini around the Nile god among crocodiles, the whole in a purely Graeco-Roman style.[26] It is possible that the original model for the subject had been elaborated for a mosaic in Alexandria itself, but no evidence has been adduced for this. It should be compared with the mosaic, originally from Constantine and now in the Louvre, representing the Triumph of Amphitrite, in which she is accompanied by the Nile god and surrounded by water-borne amorini.[27] Many other objects, decorated with analogous subjects, are known. There is, in particular, a group of two complementary tapestries, one representing the Nile god and preserved in the Pushkin Museum in Moscow, the other representing Earth and to be found in the Hermitage Museum in Leningrad. They can be very precisely dated to the end of the second century by the detail, and by the style of the decoration, if one may judge from the treatment of details, similar in every respect to that of mosaics from Antioch dating from that time. To these precise indications must be added that afforded by the treatment of the faces of the two personages, and that of the

FIG. 5

Nile god's pectoral muscles, rendered in skilful gradations of tone using the hatching technique typical of an art tending towards the Hellenistic.[28] We may compare with it, since it is identical in decoration and in the realism of the style, the scene of two Cupids paddling a boat, which forms the subject of a piece of loop-weaving in the British Museum, and the representation of a quail within a crown which ornaments a square of woven material in the Berlin Museum. The first of these compares precisely, as to the style, with similar subjects – notably some scenes with Cupids – of the fourth century, to be seen at the Episcopal Museum of Trier in Germany.[29]

FIG. 6
FIG. 7
To the same tendency belong what are known as the Faiyum or Antinoë portraits and masks, and the standing figures, painted on burial shrouds, of the same provenance. Although these are Egyptian, indeed pharaonic, by virtue of their place on top of the sarcophagus – and the purpose for which they were intended – in style, in the details of the costumes, and in the shape of the faces they are Roman. They are distributed in date between the first and fourth centuries, and were used by the Romans settled in Egypt. For the most part they bear witness to a fusion between pharaonic elements and a spirit and style which are clearly Graeco-Roman.[30] The type was later to be revived by the Christians, to judge from the painted fabric from Antinoë, now in the Louvre, which shows a woman

FIG. 8
holding the *ankh*, or *crux ansata*, against her breast.[31]

Techniques
The techniques of this period, in their turn, offer an extremely varied field of study, since old methods were perpetuated or new ones introduced.

In building construction, the Roman occupation had considerably extended the use of baked brick. Only a few examples of this survive from that time in Egypt: the wells and certain tomb houses at Tunah el-Gebel. We can be sure, however, in view of its frequent use in Coptic architecture, that many more existed.[32]

In sculpture, the progressive abandonment of the full-round in favour of relief is manifest. This may take the form of high relief, of which there exist – outside Egypt – numerous examples, in particular on the triumphal arches of the emperors. In Egypt, mainly because of the destruction of contemporary monuments, very little remains. One may cite, as an example of Roman art, though very probably carved in Egypt, since even the stone came from there, the porphyry group of the First Tetrarchy in the exterior side-wall of St. Mark's Cathedral in Venice.

FIG. 9
The same can be said of a relief on wood, now in Berlin but originally from Ashmunein, depicting the relief of a beleaguered city.[33]

It is at this time that we frequently find the rock-drill being used alongside the chisel for hollowing out the lower level of the relief. While the latter tool was well-suited to handling the reliefs and for subtle gradations in the purest Hellenistic style, the former – faster-working but more brutal in effect – led to simplification, and consequently towards direct transitions from one level to another, giving the effect of two contrasted levels. Here again, in Egypt itself from the period in question, examples in stone illustrating this are lacking. They do exist, however, quite nearby, in the temple of Leptis Magna in Libya. In Egypt, on the other hand, the so-called Gnostic intaglios present an analogous effect, in concave form, carried out in this case with the graver. In certain ivory plaques, which originally served as the components of small coffers, we find a technique resulting again in somewhat analogous effects; the subjects – usually amorini – are treated in relief, in the Hellenistic style, and the contrasts further accentuated with black ink.[34]

In the arts of colour, the range is very varied. Painting, whether in Alexandria, in the tombs of Anfushi or Kom es-Shugafa, or at Tunah el-Gebel, was carried out in patches of light and dark tones.

The arts of colour

Mosaic, a Greek or Near Eastern invention, does not seem to have flourished extensively in Alexandria. It may be that the burial of the ancient town beneath layers of modern building accounts for the paucity of subjects treated in this technique that have been found there, though it was certainly known. It does not appear to have been used in Upper Egypt.

The part played by Alexandria in the early development of manuscript illumination is more generally recognized. The papyri of pharaonic times certainly seem to have been the only ones in the antique world to include, at rare intervals, little panels of painted scenes, boxed in the text. It can hardly be doubted that the techniques persisted in the Ptolemaic period, to be taken up again by the Byzantines, with Alexandria as a point of departure. Nothing dating from Roman times remains of this. One of the oldest of illuminated manuscripts may be that of the Topography of Cosmas Indicopleustes, written in the middle of the sixth century, in Alexandria.

The origin of tapestry-weaving in colours remains in dispute. It is generally attributed to the Hellenistic Orient, possibly reflecting influences from the Orient proper and of even earlier date. Pharaonic Egypt of the New Kingdom had provided us with a few examples, notably two pieces found in the tomb of Thutmose IV, under the name of Amenhotep II;[35] the famous dalmatic of Tutankhamen;[36] and a piece in the tomb of a noble, preserved in Turin. The extreme rarity of tapestries in pharaonic art – so prolific in all other art media – coupled with the presence of these few specimens from the New Kingdom, leads rather to the supposition that they may have been imported, possibly from that part of the Orient into which the rulers of the New Kingdom had penetrated so deeply in their conquests; an area of civilization close to Egypt itself.

Although nearer to the Roman period, at Palmyra there are figures depicted on the buildings, whose garments are ornamented with bands of decoration.[37] Also at Palmyra, and dating from the third century, ornaments resembling plant motifs have been found woven into fabrics.

We know, from the scenes painted on funerary urns, that the weavers in ancient Greece made use of the technique of the high warp loom, as had those of Egypt from the time of the New Kingdom. They do not appear to have used coloured threads for the weaving of motifs, either animate or inanimate. Two processes must, in any case, have been used from Graeco-Roman times onwards to obtain the same effects: the flat tints found on Greek vases of the third century B.C., and the modelling achieved in mosaics of the Alexandrian period. We owe the sole

FIG. 10
PLATE P. 77

FIG. 11

surviving examples to the extreme dryness of the Egyptian soil. The oldest of these are, on one hand, the large *orbicula* reproducing in tapestry those painted on Egypto-Roman burial shrouds,[38] and on the other the small *orbiculum* in the Moscow Museum, representing the head and shoulders of the Nile god. In the first group a flying shuttle duplicated the work of the weft shuttle and defined the outlines of the flowers or geometric motifs. In the second, the effect of modelling was given by hatchings produced by wefts of unequal length.

In this context we must not omit to mention the so-called Faiyum portraits, painted on wood, and usually in encaustic.[39] This technique may have been derived from analogous methods used in Roman mural frescoes of the first and second centuries. Egypt, however, appears to have been the only country to have used it in this manner, no doubt because of its funeral rites, which were often adopted in turn by the occupying race.

This brief survey of programmes, of architectural ornament, of themes and techniques, indicates the range of possibilities available, in Egypt and in the adjacent countries, to that art which, under the name of Coptic art, was to flower in the valley of the Nile.

IV. THE AWAKENING: PROTO-COPTIC ART

(end of the third century – first half of the fourth century)

The beginnings of an art, particularly when it succeeds another, are always difficult to detect. Still veiled in the trappings of the earlier art, the first manifestations of the new vital force will appear somewhat at random. Its characteristics will make themselves felt not so much on their own account as in comparison with the preceding art. It is an awakening, with all that this implies in uncertainty and timidity about progress forwards – at some times backward-looking and at others, on the contrary, brutal in its novelty, but displaying, in any case, a naive purity in its inventiveness.

In the case of Coptic art the difficulty of the task is accentuated by the conditions into which it was born. Such fairies as may have bent over its cradle would appear, in defiance of normal custom, to have been more concerned in suffocating the infant in its swaddling clothes than in dispensing any pledges to ensure its happy development!

CONDITIONS AT THE BEGINNING

It seems as though, at the beginning, and for long afterwards, the hand of fate was against it. The entire country groaned under the yoke of the conqueror. Thus, from the start, freedom was lacking; that liberty which, as one knows, is a prerequisite for the free play of activities which allows the spirit to rise above the mere necessities of life.

A country under foreign occupation

One of the richest countries in the world at that time, Egypt's entire wealth was siphoned off and, bypassing even the capital, channelled to Rome, and later to Byzantium. The state of luxury upon which it should have been able to count, and which is normally an essential for the flowering of an art was, and would ever remain, lacking. The mere mention of luxury becomes absurd in a context where the bare means of subsistence were themselves burdened with taxation – the heaviest of its time – and where the collection of taxes was often of the most arbitrary kind.

A picture of Egypt in Roman times would show a people, almost without exception bent double over the soil in the effort to extract from it the maximum yield. If one of these should raise his eyes, dimmed by the blazing sun and blurred with sweat, it was only to see the fruits of his labour, down to the very scrap he might try to raise to his mouth, snatched away, to disappear down the Nile, to follow a well-guarded route leading to the imperial treasury. Had he cherished the smallest hope of straightening his back, and whiling away a moment of leisure in imposing upon some object a form going beyond that of mere utility, he would hardly have known how to go about it. This could not be expected of the fellaheen, chained to the soil—the pariahs of society. And how, at first sight, could it be expected from the artisans or small landed proprietors, almost equally subject to taxation? The rare privileged individuals who had managed to acquire knowledge, and doubtless also well-being, in Alexandria, could but aspire to escape the fate of their less fortunate brethren and, in order to safeguard their privileges, to link themselves ever more closely to the way of life and the culture of the masters of the hour. *Trahison des clercs* indeed. Betrayal of the Egyptian people by their own élite, who thus deprived them of a leadership – if not that of a court, at least of an aristocracy; a betrayal all the more damaging in a country where art had always been aulic in inspiration, and at a time when, elsewhere, it had not ceased to be so. In theory, Rome – and later Byzantium – should have performed this function. But how could they be concerned to encourage, direct and bring to flower the art of an enslaved people, bent over the sod, from whom, moreover, they lost no opportunity for extorting the last drop in the way of tribute? From imperial Rome such a thing was out of the question. The Byzantine government might well have felt some qualms concerning a people comprised more and more of Christians. No doubt one is justified in seeing signs of this in the building of a church, later followed by others, in the imperial style, on the site of Abu Mina, near Alexandria. The legend – however exaggerated – which attributes the building of numerous churches to St. Helena, the mother of Constantine, and a Byzantine influence perceptible in the reliefs, particularly those on the friezes and capitals, may also be adduced in support of it. But these examples remain sporadic. Nothing, either in these beginnings of Coptic art or later, bears the marks of an overall direction of effort emanating from a court; a court, in any case, too distant, whose patronage could never be on a scale commensurate with the size of Christian Egypt.

Social diversity
The cohesion of the people inhabiting Egypt, already weakened to some extent by political and economic factors, suffered no less from differences of race, culture and religion.

In addition to Roman high officials, occupying the important administrative posts in Alexandria and in the larger towns, and to more numerous minor functionaries, one must also distinguish from the indigenous population the Greeks, established in Egypt before the Ptolemies, and the war veterans, often of diverse origins, to whom lands had been granted. Some of these latter, at Faiyum or Antinoë, may have been Romans; others – as, for example, at Ahnas el-Medineh in Upper Egypt – originally came from Palmyra. All brought with them their own customs, and doubtless their own religions, which can be identified, even when they became integrated with the religions of the country, as is evident at Ahnas el-Medineh.[1] Among them, according to the class to which they belonged, we find various levels of culture, including even the most mediocre. Syncretism in thought and in religion is not calculated to abolish – even if it attenuates – differences, and the survival of Gnosticism as far south as Chenoboskion in Upper Egypt, as late as the fourth century, bears witness to the diversity of religious and philosophic concepts, even in the most cultivated circles. The propagation of Christianity did nothing to simplify matters. In the third century, and even in the fourth, it constituted one force among others, and was far from having eliminated the remnants of the pharaonic religion from among the pagan Egyptians, who had by no means adopted an Egypto-Greek syncretism. The pagan population, including those adhering to the autochthonous religion, was still relatively large.

Apart from foreign elements, which were far from negligible at the beginning, and even during the course of the period, the mass of Egyptians was therefore composed of pagan Copts at least as much as it was of Coptic Christians. But of liberty, affluence, an aulic or aristocratic direction, unity – the conditions normally accompanying the flowering of an art – not one made its appearance.

Given such a state of destitution, one can understand the difficulty sometimes felt by scholars in conceiving that a Coptic art could have seen the light of day. On the other hand, when the facts speak loud enough to make the conclusion inescapable, as they do here, we can but accept with added wonder that Coptic art, probably alone among all the known arts of the world, could possibly have overcome such obstacles, and at times even turn them to its advantage. Indeed, the spectacle of Coptic art making a way for itself through these most unfavourable conditions is extremely moving. In fact, any other example of an enslaved people which succeeded in forging an art of its own would be hard to find. We must emphasize the point that the Copts, pagan or Christian, using that merest fringe of liberty left to them, must have been equal to the task and have laboured towards aesthetic ends. It is equally a fact that from their meagre resources they managed to spare what was needed to build and to decorate temples, and later churches and monasteries, as well as to provide for themselves a decent burial and ornamented clothing for the dead.

Somewhere among their number must be found those who were capable of it, and above all the élite which was capable of channelling their efforts in a given direction. *Evidence of an élite*

At this point we must introduce a fact of history, long consigned to oblivion; ignorance of which explains in some measure the prejudice against Coptic art.

The term designating the Copts, because of the tax burdens which fell on them, and which must not be minimized, almost invariably evokes the image of a mass of unskilled labourers, whose condition was worse than that of the slaves in Rome. The concept is not wrong, if one is thinking of the great majority of them, who were in fact fellaheen. These men, it is only too clear (though the point has never been stressed), cannot be regarded as responsible for Coptic works of art, even of the most inchoate variety.

But, while admitting this, one must make an exception in respect of the minority among them: a minority relatively large, however, consisting of artisans whose condition was, by definition, slightly better than that of the fellaheen, both as to their skills and their resources; for a middle class of small town and country tradesmen and, finally, for the Egyptians dwelling in the monasteries.

The existence of a class of small tradesmen or landowners is attested by the documents and is, at the same time, apparent from numerous other indications. We know of this, for example, from papyri of Hermopolis Magna (Ashmunein) and Oxyrhynchus, dating from the first century B.C.; later from the fact that officials, sometimes quite senior, were selected from among the Copts; and finally from the social status of certain Copts, such as Anthony – a small landowner on the outskirts of Beni Suef until his retirement into the desert. This middle class into which, from the beginning of the Roman occupation, were grouped the small shopkeepers or officials of the towns and the small landowners outside them, embraced two communities, the indigenous and the foreign. A fusion took place between them, although in varying degrees. There is no doubt that the immediate distinguishing mark of this middle class was hellenization; naturally enough, since this was the prerequisite for survival in a milieu where the framework of social life was, in style and language, Greek. But the basis of it was quite as much Egyptian and Egypto-Greek or Egypto-Roman as it was Greek or Roman,[2] even to the extent – as in the case of Anthony, which can hardly have been an isolated one – of knowing no language other than Coptic. In this very fact we have the elements of artistic guidance: one which could not pretend to the quality, nor in particular to the unity, of guidance emanating from a royal court or from an aristocratic class. It could only function at its own level. But it made use, according to its lights, of craftsmen who had their own techniques. It provided the basis for a patronage more conscious of its purposes, with coherent ideals and aims in church decoration, and of relative affluence – of which the source was the Christian monasteries.

Monasticism came into being, in effect, during the first half of the fourth century. As we know, it spread very rapidly, all the more so in that it provided an escape from taxation and even enjoyed certain subsidies. It was the monasteries that came to the aid of the first propagators of the Gospel, enabling them to Christianize the most distant parts of Middle and Upper Egypt. Placed as they were on the dividing line between the desert and the cultivated lands, the monasteries exercised an unprecedented influence on the peasants in the villages. In fact – on the strength of their spiritual renown, of the modestly higher cultural level needed for the practice of the liturgy and of the relative affluence, in real terms, which they derived from the product of the lands in their possession – they exercised a certain power over the authorities,[3] no less than over the common people. The monks themselves, stemming largely from the peasant class, necessarily remained in touch with it, as we know from monastic documents – for example, the Lives of St. Pakhom and St. Shenute – and for this reason enjoyed all the more influence. Many of them were masons[4] and were entrusted with the building, repairing and embellishment of the monasteries. Their labours were particularly directed towards the care and decoration of their own churches. From this a profound and more coherent influence – even if exercised in varying directions – must have made itself felt on an artistic movement which already existed in rough and ready form.

The forces which helped to chart the first outlines of Coptic art can thus be defined: a Christian architecture which had made its first options; colouristic arts in which, over the entire period, we find a breaking away from the art held in respect up to that time; and, particularly, the existence of a small élite of the lower middle class which, under the most unfavourable conditions, had managed to survive and which, expanding with the monastic movement, oriented itself, and with it the entire mass of the population, in a direction of which it became ever more conscious. Examples are not lacking in history of a lower middle class

Birth of Aphrodite. Tapestry. Sixth century. Size 27 × 26 cm. Paris, Louvre, Christian Antiquities.
Photo: Max Seidel.

Nile god. Tapestry. End of second century. Diameter 25.5 cm. Moscow, Pushkin Museum. Photo: Max Seidel.

◀ Tapestry with fish design (fragments). Antinoë. Second-third century. Height 44 cm, width 33 cm. Paris, Louvre, Christian Antiquities. Photo: 'La Photothèque' (Paris).

Goddess Gaea. Tapestry. End of second century. Diameter 25.5 cm. Leningrad, Hermitage.
Photo: Max Seidel.

which succeeded in pushing its best elements towards artistic creativity. This is known to have been the case with the middle class in Flanders in the fifteenth century. Within its own limitations, this is also the case with the Coptic lower middle class.

At the commencement of this period, the end of the third and the beginning of the fourth centuries, no more pharaonic temples were built. In those already built, and particularly those constructed in the time of the Ptolemies and at the beginning of the Roman occupation, the kings – later, the emperors – are portrayed in scenes depicting the adoration of the pharaonic gods. But although these were also widely disseminated in Upper Egypt, they remained alien to the Egyptian people. Their architecture is turned in upon itself, offering less and less encouragement to the faithful to frequent the temple: the priests themselves were involved in religious currents of Greek origin; the people, in a religion which had lost its keystone, responded only to magic and superstition and became an easy prey to any of the new cults. Construction of new pharaonic monuments had long since ceased. No doubt shrines of a new type, closer in style to the Greek, were appearing: a Serapeum at Memphis, another in Alexandria, and these were probably frequented up to the end of the fourth century, but of their design we know nothing. No more is known of the pagan religious buildings which still existed at the beginning of the fourth century at Oxyrhynchus, Ahnas el-Medineh and Antinoë. Nothing remains but decorative fragments—elements which we must however take into account, since they accrue to the oeuvre of the pagan Copts.

We are scarcely any better informed regarding the beginnings of Christian architecture, and must await the commencement of the fourth or even the fifth century for the appearance of any reasonably firm data, and for a few actual surviving monuments.

Certain 'holy places' confiscated from the Egyptians by the emperor Valerian (253–60) were restored to them by his successor, Gallienus, according to a rescript addressed by him to Dionysius of Alexandria and his colleagues in the episcopate.[5] Thus we know that, before the middle of the third century, in Egypt, apparently in Alexandria and the Faiyum, the faithful congregated in buildings belonging, not to individuals, but to the Christian community. Two churches dedicated to Mary, built in Alexandria, may be dated to this time. One of these was built by the bishop St. Theonas and the other by St. Peter the Martyr. The bare mention of these, which we owe to historians such as Eutychius, provides no information as to the architectural design of the monuments. The mention by John of Nikiou[6] of a martyrium in honour of St. Mark, erected near the coast to the east of Alexandria, permits of no more than the supposition – based on the connection with Rome – that its plan was either circular or octagonal.

The use of pharaonic palaces and of old temples, and their transformation into churches, widely practised later in Upper Egypt, started at the beginning of the fourth century in Alexandria, according to St. Epiphanius, under the aegis of Constantine himself and at the expense of the Caesarium which Cleopatra had begun to build in honour of Caesar and of Caesarion.[7]

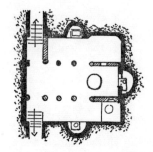

FIG. 12 – *Plan of crypt of Abu Sarga, Old Cairo. After A. Butler, Ancient Coptic Churches of Egypt, Oxford, 1884, p. 200, fig. 12.*

The construction of churches properly so called, in Alexandria and in what is now Old Cairo, was not long delayed, according to the same sources, which cite the names of numerous churches in the two cities. Here again there is a lack of information on the plan adopted. As some of these were martyria, such as the shrine in honour of St. Metra in Alexandria,[8] we may venture the guess that in this, as in other analogous cases, a circular or octagonal plan was used. In fact, if it did exist, which seems probable, it has nevertheless left no trace. Not a single Egyptian martyrium has survived, even in ruins. We only know of those mentioned without description in the texts. In the matter of churches, on the other hand, if one may judge from the consistency with which all the known later churches utilized the basilican plan, one is justified in assuming that this plan predominated in the earlier ones.

For evidence of these, it seems we must look to Old Cairo. The dating of them is, however, uncertain. The tradition according to which one of them, the crypt of Abu Sarga, was visited by the Holy Family, cannot be upheld, but at least certain indications militate in favour of a dating within the period under review.

We cannot base this entirely on the considerable difference between the level of the crypt and that of the present-day ground-level, which may have been formed at a time much nearer to our own day. The certainty, or even the probability, of this dating can only be based on systematic excavations carried out over a wide area and at different levels. In the meantime this difference in the levels does provide a clue which must not be ignored.

Situated in Old Cairo, the crypt of Abu Sarga (St. Sergius)[9] extends below a present-day, and much later, church of the same name which owing to the rising of the ground level in the interim had to be built over the top of the original chapel which thus became a 'crypt' as it is today. The plan is that of a basilica roofed with three flattened vaults and comprising a nave and two side-aisles,

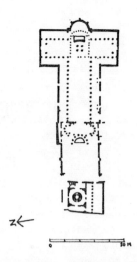

FIG. 13 – *Plan of basilica of Arcadius, Abu Mina. After R. Krautheimer, Early Christian and Byzantine Architecture, Harmondsworth, 1965, p. 85, fig. 31.*

separated from each other by two rows of columns. It measures 3.50 metres in length by 3 metres wide and is nearly 3 metres high. A projecting apsidal niche prolongs the nave at the east end. Two further projecting niches, facing each other, are hollowed out of the middle of the north and south walls. A nook in the north-east angle contains a basin and may well have served as a baptistery in times past. The columns, apart from one in granite, are of marble and one of these is very classical in style. The use of this material, and the style, in a building substantially below ground level inclines one to attribute the building, not to the troubled era of persecutions, but rather to a period when Constantinople was lavishing gifts of new shrines upon the most renowned Christian sites.

It is possible that a building, placed on the same level as the present-day church of El-Adra el-Mu'allaqa, formed part of the oldest church of the same name, but too little now remains for us to reach any definite conclusion on this. The only other church one could, with due reservations, consider as contemporary with the 'crypt' of Abu Sarga is that known as Mari Mina (St. Menas')[10] situated between Cairo and Old Cairo and dedicated to St. Menas, the soldier-martyr, who is buried, according to legend, in the Maryut desert near Alexandria. Alexandria also raised a church in his honour at the end of the third century, which is mentioned by the historians. This fact, and the proximity of Old Cairo, could provide clues as to the antiquity of the church. Furthermore, although it was restored in the fifteenth century, the simplicity of the plan is a fact of some significance. We find once again the rectangular basilican plan with three naves, of which the wider central one is separated from the other two by two rows of square pillars. The east end was taken up with three returning apses, their widths corresponding to those of the naves. These were headed with arched vaults in brick.

Clearly, we must await further discoveries, or excavations, before we shall be able to establish with certainty the plan of the churches of that time. But we must take account of the historical fact of their existence, and their number; of the plan of those which seem to be the oldest, or which can reasonably be attributed to succeeding periods; and finally, of the closeness of those of Abu Mina, compared with those of Alexandria – of which we shall have occasion to speak later. The cures effected by the tomb of St. Menas in the Maryut desert near Alexandria, and those attributed to the waters of the miraculous springs running close by, established the fame of this site from the late third century onward. The water was collected by pilgrims in the 'ampullae' they carried with them for the purpose and thence transported to the remotest parts of the empire. In fact, the fame of the site was comparable to that of Lourdes in our own day, and touched even the imperial court. Tradition, in effect, attributes to Constantine the foundation of a basilica over a crypt containing the martyr's remains. As the number of pilgrims increased, the Emperor Arcadius, at the end of the fourth century, extended this

FIG. 13 with a basilica measuring 67 metres by 52, the atrium of which rested on the tomb of the saint. Inaugurated by his successor, Theodosius II, in 412, it is now in ruins. The transept and the chevet, or projecting choir, give it a cruciform appearance. Internally, the very wide nave is separated from the aisles, and right round the transepts, by colonnades. The richness of the materials used – as regards the revetments, perhaps even richer here than in Constantinople itself – confirms that this was an imperial commission. The tomb, and probably the semi-dome of the apse, were embellished with mosaics; the limestone walls were covered with marble plaques; the columns bore capitals with a double range of acanthus; and the plan was cruciform, analogous to those of St. John of Ephesus and Gaza, the indirect source of which would seem to have been that of Constantine's church of the Apostles in Constantinople. Such a combination of features is foreign to what later, as we shall find, constitutes Coptic architecture. It may, however, have served to reinforce the Copts' preference, in church building, for the basilican plan.

The church forms part of a complex of buildings designed for the accommodation of pilgrims: a complex which includes baths, a secular basilica of baths with two apses facing each other, dating from the end of the fifth century, a pilgrims' shelter and a cemetery. Near the cemetery is a basilica with the centre nave prolonged by a returning apse. This detail hardly exists anywhere else, except in certain churches in North Africa or central Syria, but, while becoming more elaborate, will continue to be almost invariable in the architecture of Coptic churches, as we can indeed see near Old Cairo at Mari Mina.

We must also exclude from Coptic architecture, properly so called, two chapels, one known as the chapel of Peace and the other as the chapel of the Exodus. These form part of a funerary group of much later date, at El Bagawat in the Kharga oasis, situated in the western desert at the latitude of Luxor. These square constructions,[12] of which the façades have blind arcades on colonnets, are each surmounted by a low cupola; they are of very modest dimensions (2 × 2 and 5 × 5 metres respectively), and reveal an interior arrangement that justifies their classification as churches. They may be regarded as the prototypes of devotional chapels of the same shape and approximately the same dimensions, such as we shall find later at Bawit in Middle Egypt. But the paintings on the cupola do not in the least accord with what we shall have occasion later to define as Coptic.

Funerary architecture is very poorly represented. Those tombs in which bodies we may assume to have been Christian have been found, are completely below ground level, as for example at Antinoë – the tomb of the matron with the *ankh* (*crux ansata*), of which the decorated lintel is in the Louvre.[13] A notable exception is the catacomb of Karmuz near Alexandria, long since destroyed, of which we now have only drawings.[14]

The little that remains of religious architecture of the proto-Coptic period is rather disappointing. The churches still standing that may be cited are rare and their dating conjectural. It is particularly unfortunate for this study that one of them, the large church built by a successor of St. Pakhom in the fifth century in his monastery at Pbou, in Upper Egypt, should have been destroyed in the eleventh century, by al-Hakim. We can only guess, from the preceding indications, what church architecture during the proto-Coptic period was like.

Apart from imperially commissioned monuments at Maryut and in Old Cairo, too little remains to justify any attempt to define its characteristics. All the same, the basilica does seem to emerge as a highly favoured plan in Egypt at a time when elsewhere it was strongly rivalled in popularity by the octagonal plan and the square plan. One example of the cruciform transept which exists on the soil of Egypt will remain unique, and this is only found in a complex of buildings commissioned by the emperor at Abu Mina. This exclusive preference for the basilica was, however, already typical. Taking the facts established so far as a whole, this is as far as one can go for the present. If an explanation is to be found, more facts are needed. Doubtless the Coptic period proper, richer in monuments and in firmly established data as it is, will provide it.

Under this head may be grouped those Coptic works belonging to the arts of sculpture and of colour. Throughout the proto-Coptic period an evolution made itself felt which will become clearer when we examine the works themselves. Meantime, taking them as a whole, what permits of their grouping here is a sort of 'disengagement' in relation to pre-Coptic art, i.e. in relation to the art which prevailed at that time, and which we may classify in its entirety as an art with Hellenistic leanings.

DECORA-TION

During this period of transition, themes of Coptic origin are rare, if indeed they exist. This must be freely admitted. The creation of artistic themes is only possible in the favourable climate of complete autonomy, with an effective expansion in all fields. Furthermore, under ideal conditions – such as the lost ones of ancient Greece, or even of pharaonic Egypt – borrowings from earlier or contemporary civilizations are in fact constant. Coptic Egypt, particularly at this time, when its own élite was only painfully extricating itself from the mass of the people, enjoyed too narrow a measure of liberty for the elaboration of new themes. Mercilessly held down to the common task, Egypt could not commune deeply enough with

I. Themes

FIG. 14 – *The Nile god and Euthenia. Tapestry. Seventh century. Diameter 13 cm. Paris, Louvre, Christian Antiquities.*

FIG. 15 – *Nereid with cruciform nimbus. Tapestry. Ninth century. 14 × 17 cm. Paris, Louvre, Christian Antiquities.*

its own soul to search for original themes. On the other hand, she did succeed in rising above her misfortunes sufficiently to select from among the themes immediately available, and to transform them in accordance with her own concepts of reality. This, as we have said, was not the work of the fellaheen, totally immersed as they were in daily toil, but of two groups sprung from their ranks which enjoyed a certain degree of affluence, although still strictly limited. The first was a group of minor officials, small landed proprietors and artisans; the second included churchmen, and in particular monks. The first group, still heavily burdened with taxation, were able, as a result either of their earnings or of the return on their properties, to assure themselves both leisure and a modest financial independence. The second group, over a long period, escaped taxation and succeeded, as much by function as by vocation, in raising themselves, through prayer, above manual work, from which their status alone did not emancipate them. These two categories must therefore be regarded as responsible for Coptic art, as much in its inspiration as, very often, in its execution. The direct Christian inspiration must have chiefly been the work of churchmen, and not least, of monks, who did not systematically reject the themes currently in favour, but rather Christianized them. The laity continued to provide a more profane – indeed at times a frankly pagan – source of inspiration and, according to circumstances, artisans, monks or laymen might undertake the execution of such works.

It should be remembered that the mass of Copts, whatever their social class, was still to a great extent pagan. Christianity was still in a period of expansion, rapid

though this was, and the tide was only just beginning to turn in its favour. Because
of the very limited freedom they enjoyed, and because of their origins, the field
from which members of the élite could draw their themes proved very limited.
Pharaonic art, with the figurations proper to it, was too distant from the Egyptians
of that time, and Christianity had no inclination to revive it. There for the taking
were themes in which pagan and Christian Copts alike were steeped, as were their
contemporaries.

Most of these themes were of Hellenistic origin, although already coloured by
Alexandrian speculative thought – preoccupations, as one knows, which ranged
beyond Graeco-Roman mythology in search of profounder meanings, frequently
of an esoteric order. Often these themes were invested with particular traits of
pharaonic origin. It is sometimes difficult to tell whether these details were added
in response to the Alexandrian syncretist tendency, or by Copts – even Christian
ones – who were still under the influence of their origins or of their pharaonic
environment. In any case, even in an ensemble thus transformed, both externally
and internally, the Copts – either answering to their own imperatives or to those
of Christianity – exercised a deliberate choice, a point which it is important to
stress.

One might have anticipated that Gnostic representations, such as those engraved
on intaglios, would have been adopted by the Copts. Certainly Gnosticism flourished in their midst. The Gnostic library discovered in 1946 is comprised of
papyri collected in volumes. These were stored in jars buried at Nag Hammadi

in the very heart of Upper Egypt, at a site in close proximity to the first Pakhomian monasteries. Dating, in general, from the fourth century, they were contemporary with them. Among the intaglios there are even many dating from the same period. None, however, display the characteristics of early Coptic art. Except in certain magical papyri, none of the subjects represented figures, either at that time of later, in the other techniques used by the Copts, particularly the principal ones – reliefs on stone, on ivory or in bronze; nor do they appear in the colouristic arts of painting, tapestry or ceramics.

In Roman Egypt several of the pharaonic gods, due to popular magical beliefs, survived: Bes, Thueris, Bes Pantheos, and the god Horus in his alternative form, as Harpocrates. None of these appear in Coptic representations, even pagan ones. In the same way, there was in Alexandria a whole group of subjects, very well known, the 'grotesques', the majority of which are found on ceramics: an extremely inexpensive technique and a kind of subject well within the popular range.[15] These will be sought in vain in Coptic art.

However, another category, dear to Alexandrian artists, remains foreign to Coptic art, even in its beginnings: draped women, ephebi and melephebi, groups of men and women and individual animals.[16] Many mythological subjects are also absent. Of the cycle of the first Olympians, children of Cronus, only Demeter is to be found. But this is also true of many of the sons and daughters of Zeus as, for example, Athene, Ares, Hephaestus and the Muses, despite the frequency with which they appear in Alexandrian art, and their origin, which brings them closer to the mortal world.

It remains a fact, nevertheless, that the themes treated were numerous. Several of those transmitted through Alexandrian art made only isolated appearances, either on episodic occasions or in close association with a particular place. Among the former may be counted Artemis, Hermes, Pasiphae, Pan, Hercules and the Graces, while among the latter are Leda and the swan, Daphne in her tree and Orpheus with his lute—representations of which are frequent at Ahnas el-Medineh.

Most of the themes which are of Alexandrian origin are centred around a few cycles: Dionysus and his train of bacchantes; the birth of Aphrodite and her

FIG. 17 – *St. Menas flanked by camels. Terracotta. Abu Mina. Sixth-seventh century. Height 10 cm. Louvre, Christian Antiquities.*

86

Amorini boating. Fabric. Fourth century. London, British Museum.

Nereids in high-relief. Limestone. Ahnas. Fourth-fifth century. Height 60 cm, width 52 cm. Trieste, Museo Civico di Storia ed Arte.

Horus mounted. Sandstone. Fourth century. Height 49.1 cm, width 32 cm, thickness 7.8 cm. Paris, Louvre, Christian Antiquities. Photo: Max Seidel.

Abraham's sacrifice, Adam and Eve. Painting. Kharga (Egypt), Chapel of Peace. Fourth century.
Photo: P. du Bourguet.

entourage of nereids and tritons; the Nile god and his followers in the form of
amorini; the Parthian horseman or hunter; the *imago* (or portrait) enclosed in a
crown of laurels supported by Victories, or indeed framed; the Seasons; and,
finally, bucolic subjects.

In these cycles the subjects are varied. Dionysus may be accompanied by Ariadne,
or shown in his car; he may appear with a follower or leaning against a column, or
among ruins. Aphrodite may be shown emerging from her shell or at her toilette;
the Nile god may have Euthenia at his side, be supervising the nilometer, or   FIG. 14
emerging from the waters. The presence of these central figures was not in fact
always considered necessary, no doubt on the grounds that this was sufficiently
clearly implied by showing one of their known companions or attributes: dancers,
nereids, shell, amorini, dogs and game, or shepherds.

The outward aspect of these themes and cycles, however, serves only to evoke
more profound truths. These truths were well known in other contexts, and are
generally concerned with the idea of rebirth, which was the prevailing preoccupation throughout the area dominated by Alexandria at that time.

These same themes, however, once selected, took on a truly Egyptian significance.
Thus Dionysus is a new personification of Osiris, and Aphrodite of Isis; and the
two cycles have indeed a tendency to become intermingled.[17] The Nile god,
after having been adopted in Palestrina, in Italy, slipped back easily enough into
his old role in the valley of his origin. The *imago* had seen its purpose 'Egyptianized'
in the funerary portraits on sarcophagi. The hunt seems to have assimilated Horus,
now in the guise of a soldier, as well as the Parthian horseman. Only the pastoral
scenes and the Seasons found no corresponding figuration in pharaonic Egypt,
but they represented subjects which had formed part of the agricultural civilization
of Egypt since the beginning.

These assimilations, in each given case, must have been effected, particularly in
the first instances, in Alexandria itself. Dionysus/Osiris and Aphrodite/Isis are
found again in the Alexandrian terra-cotta figurines of the two first centuries,
which reflect those mystery religions so dear at that time to the city founded by

Alexander.[18] But if we compare these cases with all other instances of thematic modification, it is impossible to ignore both the convergence of symbols and the 'naturalization' of these themes in Egypt. It is difficult not to see in this a preference exercised by the Egyptians themselves, and finally by the pagan Copts.

Is it likely that, among these latter, those who became Christians would abandon these themes? Such a hypothesis is almost impossible to credit, for the immediate past is never abandoned entirely: it is transformed.

This is exactly what happened during this period and the following one. The proof lies in the outward Christianization of one or another of these subjects. We see it, in this fourth century, in the linen cloth from Antinoë in the Louvre, upon which is painted a woman clasping to her breast the ansate cross, reminiscent of the *ankh* symbol of the pharaonic epoch, and previously reserved to the gods who held it, the arm rigidly extended at the side.[19] We shall recognize it again, a little later, in Sabina's Shawl, where, within an ornamented frame, Daphne is depicted imprisoned in her tree and offering to Apollo a flower in the form of a cross, held out at arm's length,[20] or again in a tapestry in the Louvre portraying nereids, the head of one of them encircled by a cruciform nimbus.[21]

APPX. PL. 7

FIG. 15

Daphne's very gesture shows that we should not be content to see here merely a superficial application of the cross. The subject, already charged with meaning in pagan symbolism, readily enough bore this same meaning when transposed to a Christian level. It was enough that the idea of rebirth be shifted into a new perspective: that of Resurrection through the Cross.

Thus, in the same way that an appropriation of certain Alexandrian cycles by the pagan Copts took place, so also these latter, on becoming Christians, found no difficulty in retaining them, without even feeling obliged to mark them with the sign of the cross. This explains why most of them were to be indefinitely perpetuated in Coptic art.

These themes of Alexandrian origin are the ones most frequently met with in Coptic art. This is not surprising since the latter, at first pagan, became progressively Christianized, and in doing so did not find it necessary to abandon them. In this period a few themes of Christian origin were just beginning to appear.

One of these was to become common in Coptic art: the *Virgo lactans*. It will not be out of place, after what has been said above, to draw attention to the fact that the group of Mary and Jesus in this pose is closely reminiscent of that of Isis nursing Horus. This Christian theme may well have first seen the light on the banks of the Nile.[22] In the catacomb of Priscilla in Rome, it is true – in the chamber of the Velatio – we find depicted a seated woman breast-feeding a child, but it is very doubtful if this represents Mary, who is, on the other hand, often portrayed in the Roman catacombs, seated and holding the Infant Jesus to receive the Magi,[23] in an attitude doubtless equally inspired by that of Isis, whose cult was disseminated all round the shores of the Mediterranean, and particularly in Rome. There can be little doubt that in Egypt, in any case, the ever-popular devotion to Isis, which had become even stronger during the Late Kingdom, transformed itself easily enough into a devotion to Mary.

FIG. 16

FIG. 19 – *Capital from Gethsemane. Limestone.* A.D.
390. Jerusalem.

A saint who achieved early popularity in Egypt, and whose iconography was equally rapidly established, was St. Menas. We find him placed between two camels,[24] in memory of those which, according to legend, had borne his body FIG. 17 into the desert until they reached a suitable place for the erection of his shrine. The reference is doubtless rather to his calling. This group obviously recalls that of Daniel among the lions. Some have preferred to see in it a modified representation of Horus-Harpocrates straddling the crocodiles. This hypothesis has little FIG. 18 to recommend it. At the most, the introduction of a subject with symmetrical elements might, in this way, have been facilitated. If this is the case, it would bring us back, through Horus-Harpocrates, to a derivation from a theme linked with the Osirian cycle, which in Egypt was outwardly linked to the Dionysian cycle.

Such are the themes employed by the Copts during this period. The choice exercised, and the continuity of themes of Alexandrian origin, certainly make it appear that from the pagan Copts these themes passed in due course to the Christians. The rare Christian themes are themselves at times not unrelated to certain of the Alexandrian cycles and, at least occasionally, to subjects originating in Egypt itself.

It is in sculpture that the breakaway from current art is particularly noticeable, *2. Plastic arts* because it is in this technique, and more especially in stone sculpture, that one can base one's argument on solid points of comparison. It will be best, if we are to proceed on a firm footing, to begin by focussing attention on these points.

FIG. 20 – *Capital from the Golden Gate. Limestone.*
A.D. *425–430. Church of the Golden Gate, Istanbul.*

FIG. 21 – *St. John the Baptist capital. Limestone.* A.D. *450–460. Church of St. John the Baptist, Jerusalem.*
FIG. 22 – *Ahnas capital. Limestone. Ahnas el-Medineh. Fourth century. Old Cairo, Coptic Museum.*
FIG. 23 – *Oxyrhynchus capital. Limestone. Oxyrhynchus. Fourth century. Alexandria, Graeco-Roman Museum.*

Here credit is due to E. Kitzinger.[25] Starting from an examination of the groups of detached fragments of decorative sculpture recovered from Oxyrhynchus, now in the Graeco-Roman Museum in Alexandria, and those excavated at Ahnas el-Medineh, mainly displayed in the Coptic Museum in Cairo – in respect of which there was a total lack of precise chronology – he proceeded to isolate the capitals, and to search throughout the Middle East for dated elements to compare with

FIG. 19   them. As a result, he was able to pick out three capitals, the first from the church of Gethsemane in Jerusalem, dating from 390, the second from the church of the

FIG. 20   Golden Gate in Istanbul, dating from 425–30, and the third from the church of

FIG. 21   St. John the Baptist in Jerusalem, dating from 450–60. In comparison with the classic Corinthian capital, these capitals were characterized by three peculiarities: the disintegration of the upper zone to the extent that the volutes were covered over by the leaves of the second zone; the sharp and elongated appearance of the acanthus leaves, and also the reduction in the number of their points from 4 to 3, no longer directed upwards but to the side; finally, the regular, conventionalized, almost abstract appearance of the foliage. All these characteristics are more pronounced on the later capitals than on the first.

Exactly the same accentuation of the traits observed here is again found in a

FIG. 22   capital from Ahnas. In addition, in this instance the zones are separated in the height, the second springing from a large boss. We even find a small boss, slipped between the interstices at the base of the leaves, which is also found in the capitals of the church of St. John the Baptist in Jerusalem.

We have, then, at Ahnas – if we group together the capitals of this kind found there – an ensemble belonging to this *accentuated* style, which Kitzinger calls the '*rude*' style.

FIG. 23   In contrast, the ensemble of capitals from Oxyrhynchus, with its straight and slightly rounded leaves, is close to the capitals at Gethsemane. Thus the author was in a position to distinguish three periods: one, the 'soft' style, corresponding to the end of the fourth century; a 'rude' style corresponding to the middle of the fifth century; and finally an 'accentuated rude' style corresponding to the end of

FIG. 24 – *Child-follower of Isis in a niche. Painted limestone. Antinoë. Fourth century. Height 41.5 cm. Munich, Aegyptische Staatssammlung.*

the fifth and to the sixth century. Into the first category one may put the group of sculptures from Oxyrhynchus and part of the group from Ahnas; into the second, another group from Ahnas, and in the third the 'ruder' ones recovered from the monasteries. It goes without saying that each style gradates imperceptibly into the succeeding one, as in every normal evolution. But the distinction is sufficiently marked to permit classification of the groups. The terms 'rude' and 'soft' were not chosen at random. The first style retains something of Alexandrian naturalism, while already conventionalizing it; the second eliminates it more rigorously while conserving some naturalism in the proportions, but the third has no compunction in sacrificing both entirely.

It is the first, so-called 'soft', style which relates to the proto-Coptic period.

At Oxyrhynchus and at Ahnas, this is naturally not limited to the capitals.

We find, at both sites, decorative broken pediments which originally surmounted niches. Here they are rounded in the intermediate section and more accentuated on the sides than in the temple of Bacchus at Baalbek, which, being dated in the second century, is antecedent to them, thus providing confirmation of the hypothesis. On the friezes of interlacing acanthus stems the leaves go to the side, one in number and then two, as at Chaoura in Syria, which is also of the late fourth century.

The human figure takes an honoured place, and it is upon this that the decorative motifs converge, serving to enhance it, while the ordered effect retains much of Hellenistic equilibrium. One relief in particular, belonging to the Trieste Museum, as it were, sounds the chord which announces a new measure to the dancers.[26] It shows two nereids above a dolphin, astride which is an amorino. The gracefulness of the bodies, their elegance, the dancing movement of the legs, all still bear the imprint of Hellenistic harmony. But the faces, although still gentle and smiling, are conventionalized, and indeed the dimensions of the collar and of the jewel attached to it are out of proportion. We are entering upon a new style.

The tendency developed very rapidly. A case in point is the Aphrodite, still cradled in her shell, in the Coptic Museum in Cairo, and another, the Dionysian

Human figure

PLATE P. 88

PLATE P. 24

figure in the Louvre, both of which are in high relief, and were mentioned earlier in the context of our imaginary exhibition. Both, while still cast in Hellenistic form – the first with more grace, the second with more vivacity – nevertheless represent a breakaway, in their rejection of natural proportions and in the stylization of the features; both these features serve to express the new idea, in a harmony superior to that generally in favour. They rank, by this very fact, among the key works of an art that is already Coptic.

Ahnas, surprisingly enough for a town somewhat far away in the southern part of Middle Egypt, was influenced by Palmyra to a degree not found elsewhere. The fragment of a pilaster(?) in the Coptic Museum in Cairo bears, on its principal face, a bust[27] which it has been possible to identify as representing the Nile god, by comparing it with another, belonging to the Brooklyn Museum, which is easily identifiable as such by the amorini borne on each shoulder and by the exaggerated pectoral development, perhaps intended to suggest the breasts of the god. The torso, on the other hand, is narrow, and this characteristic reminds one

FIG. 26 – *Nereids in relief. Ivory. Third century. 9 × 2 cm. Paris, Louvre, Christian Antiquities.*

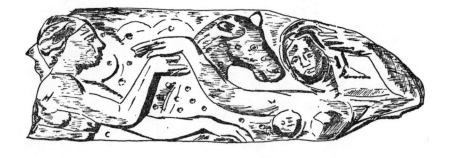

FIG. 27 – *Ceramic decoration. Terracotta. Antinoë. Fourth century. Height 12 cm, max. diameter 14 cm. Paris, Louvre, Christian Antiquities.*

of the Dionysian figure in the Louvre. But many of the details, and these among the most characteristic, show a direct Palmyrene influence. The nose, widening out under deeply cut, arching brows, in an oval face, is indeed Mesopotamian, as is also the hair, with its tightly rolled curls like a chain of beads, and the regular succession of snail-shaped curls edging the beard. But above all it is the band of the diadem and the ribbons which ornament the left side, passing over the arm and then below the waist, which present a range of alternating motifs: rosettes, joined by interlacing. All this is directly imported from the ornamental bands on Palmyrene robes of the second and third centuries A.D. The pose of the god, the upper part of his body inclined forward to emphasize the idea of abundance, is indicative of his personality. These three streams, reunited in a representation of the Nile god – Egypto-Hellenistic as regards the person of the god and the highly evolved nature of the representation; Palmyrene in the treatment of the head and of the decoration – justify the assumption that there lived in Ahnas retired legionaries, or in any case artisans, of Palmyrene origin, converted to the syn-

FIG. 28 – *Geometric and rosette designs. Tapestry. Hawara, Faiyum. Fourth century. After Sir Flinders Petrie, Hawara, Biahmu and Arsinoë, London, 1889.*

FIG. 29 – *Decorative leaf. Wool weaving. Dura Europus.*

cretism of the Nile valley and already caught up in the movement towards a Coptic style.

FIG. 24 To these reliefs must be added a few stelae found at Antinoë – rare in comparison with those elaborated and Christianized in recent times for commercial purposes – consisting of a carved niche within which, framed, as it were, in stone, the figure of a child is sculptured in relief. The child squats on the ground, holding in one hand a sprig of greenery and in the other a bird. The figure has been correctly identified as a follower of Isis.[28] The shape of the face links this with the 'soft-style' Aphrodite in the Coptic Museum in Cairo.

With these pieces we find ourselves face to face with figures which have undergone a transformation, firstly in spirit, through the new importance given to the symbol, and then in treatment, through the mobilization of the various elements in the service of the symbol, at the expense of realism. They remain no less pagan, and thus emanate from the pagan Coptic population that inhabited Egypt at that time, concurrently with the first Christians and in close contact with them.

From the same milieu, though doubtless a little later in date, towards the middle of the fourth century, comes another sort of relief. This is the decorative fragment in sandstone, now in the Louvre, which represents the god Horus transfixing a PLATE P. 89 crocodile with his lance. The god is identified by his falcon's head, but portrayed as a Roman cavalryman[29]. The symbol of Horus-Harpocrates trampling crocodiles underfoot is common in pharaonic mythology, and signifies essentially the triumph of Good over Evil. Under the last dynasties of the Ptolemies it had become even more popular, and its magical power had been reinforced. Already in the second century A.D. Horus is often thrust into armour, in the guise of a standing Roman soldier. Here the scene illustrates his role in more vigorous form, while at the same time exalting the idea of triumph through the representation of the god as a mounted soldier: typically, the victorious emperor.

This attitude, the three-quarter view of the horse's fore-quarters, its head turned towards the rider, creating a movement in depth, suggests irresistibly a link with the emperor portrayed on the Barberini ivory to be found in the Louvre. The rendering, on the other hand, is rather crude, partly because of the material. But the great interest of this relief lies in its position at a point of transition between the high reliefs, sculptured in terms of volumes, which we have just been examining, and the Coptic reliefs which were soon to gain the ascendant. Here the effect is produced less by the volumes than by differences of level. This appears clearly in the treatment of the horse's head which, although turned three-quarters towards the rider, is contracted into the neck and withers, instead of projecting forward naturally; and in the position of the torso of Horus, seen full-face beneath a head in profile, yet with the left arm pressed flat against the body. The aim here has been to give greater prominence to the ensemble, rather than the details, which are all on the same level of relief. The effect is achieved by simple contrast of the ensemble, thus high-lighted, with the background, which remains in shadow. It is difficult not to be reminded of pharaonic reliefs in which parts of the body are arranged perpendicularly to one another, and this similarity is worth noting. But now only

Biblical subjects. Painting. Kharga (Egypt), Chapel of the Exodus. Fourth century.
Photo: P. du Bourguet.

Parthian horseman. Tapestry. Fourth century. Size 19 × 18 cm. Paris, Louvre, Christian Antiquities. Photo: Max Seidel.

Head of a dancing girl. Tapestry. Fifth century. Height 42 cm, width 32 cm. Paris, Louvre, Christian Antiquities. Photo: Max Seidel.

Eagle with loop of ribbon in its beak (fragment). Tapestry. Antinoë. Fifth century.
Height 57 cm, width 37 cm. Paris, Louvre, Christian Antiquities. Photo: Max Seidel.

a short step was needed – the elimination, in the transition from the relief to the background, of what remained of the volumes – to arrive at the treatment which was to predominate in Coptic art. This work, which stresses the imperial majesty of Byzantium, relates to one of the pockets of Coptic paganism which remained in Egypt in the middle of the fourth century.

Were the Christian Copts still lagging behind? It would appear so, at least in the working of stone. There is, however, a stele in the Berlin Museum which originated in Faiyum, that is to say, in a region where, at the end of the third century, Christianity was already well established. This stele bears a figure of the *Virgo lactans* rendered in incised lines,[30] which must date from the proto-Coptic FIG. 25 period, if one compares it with a fragmentary plaque in the Louvre, of Crimean origin(?), depicting – also in incised lines – the miracle of the miraculous draught of fishes,[31] in which Christ has the same rounded shape of face as the Virgin in the former work. In this, the Virgin is seated on an upholstered folding stool. She holds the Child, to whom she is giving her breast, on her left arm, as in the statuettes of Isis holding the child Horus, which certainly provided the proto-type for this representation, and which became common all round the Mediter-ranean. The undulating folds of the draperies indicate an Alexandrian source as regards style and workmanship, although here simplified and stylized. But the shape of the face, the hair in tight curls and the high position of the breasts, are indications of a different style. The whole design emphasizes the concept of Divine maternity, to which Isis will, particularly at that time, have contributed her own human connotations, as well as providing the elements of the representation.

Evidently later than the stele, or even the relief of the mounted Horus, is the stone TITLE-PAGE plaque in the Louvre, originally from Erment, which portrays in high relief a fish passing in front of a cross; it was mentioned in connection with our imaginary exhibition. On this occasion, the uppermost level is flattened, and the relief stands out sharply from the equally flat background. The absence of volumes on the upper level is compensated for by incised lines – a type of work already anticipated in the stele of the *Virgo lactans*, the effect of which, as we shall see, is related to that of Coptic tapestries. This stylization, through the movement of the fish, inclined towards the Cross and touching the edges of the frame at points sym-metrical with it, bears witness to a fine sense of decoration and at the same time glorifies the idea of Christ the Saviour (Ichthus) through the fish.

To this period probably belongs a bronze in the Louvre[32] depicting Aphrodite flanked by an Eros on either side, in which the form of the body remains realistic, but with that elongation of the waist noted above with reference to reliefs in stone. Mention must also be made of numerous subjects in relief on ivory or bone. While Hellenistic in respect of such subjects as nereids or amorini, and by virtue FIG. 26 of a certain care for harmony of line, they yet exhibit a different, more simplified style in which, in the light of all that has been said in this chapter, we may recog-nize the work of pagan Copts.[33]

Thus the pagans or Christians of Egypt – all Copts, or at least 'Copticized', and distinguished from the Romans or Greeks, who were in any case far from numerous – achieved a transformation in sculpture which, allowing for variation of circumstance, reduced volume without sacrificing the depth of the relief and which, while preserving some degree of harmoniousness, modified certain natural proportions in the interests of expressing the content.

3. The arts of colour

At first sight, one would appear to be less well provided with works of any importance, belonging to this period, which derive from the arts of colour.

Mosaic

Mosaic does not seem to have appealed to the Copts. If one excludes from proto-Coptic art, as being an imperial commission, the churches on the site of Abu Mina in the Maryut desert, where fragments of work in this technique have been found, and also, if it is not earlier, a mosaic found at Sheikh Zueida in what was once a garrison, depicting – most unskilfully – the story of Hippolytus and Phaedra and certain of the Dionysiac mysteries, scarcely another example is to be found. Its total absence from later Coptic work allows us to conclude that it did not appeal to the Copts. Such a lack of interest cannot but provoke astonishment when one notes the considerable favour mosaic enjoyed in Byzantium, Antioch, Rome and North Africa, and the use made of mosaics in nearby Palestine in the middle of the fifth century—for example, in the church of the Multiplication of the Loaves and Fishes at Heptapegon (et-Tabgha),[34] executed by craftsmen who were no more skilled than were the Copts. Was it due to poverty? Nothing is less likely. However devoid of luxuries the life of the Coptic community may have been, mosaic – if one may judge from the use of other techniques requiring a certain financial competence, such as decorative sculpture, or even tapestry – should not have been beyond their means. We must therefore look for a more plausible reason. The future may hold some indication where we should look.

Painting

Contrary to first impressions, the same is not true of painting. For this period, there are doubtless no more paintings than mosaics which may be cited. But the great development of pictorial art during the Coptic period, properly so called, even before the period of 'the Copts', permits the supposition that it could not have been lacking during the proto-Coptic period. In the course of this era the craft must have been practised for it to have been in a viable state in succeeding periods. No reasons of poverty could possibly have applied, for this was an inexpensive technique, if ever there was one. On the other hand, we know, from records of excavations at Bawit, how fragile these became on contact with the air. We must therefore assume, not that the technique was rejected, but that evidence of it has disappeared.

PLATES PP. 90, 99

One might be tempted, it is true, to include in this period the paintings in the cupolas forming the roof of two chapels at Bagawat in the Kharga oasis, which bring together episodes, or allusions to scenes, from the Old Testament, with the inclusion of a very few personages drawn from the early days of Christianity. The fault would not lie in the dating, since they very probably are of the fourth century, but in attributing them to Coptic art.

Their presence in Egypt remains in the order of an accident: the more or less Egyptian costumes in the Allegory of Peace and the form of the Noah's Ark are purely superficial details; the outline of the ansate cross, reproducing the hieroglyph of Life, and the Coptic graffiti in one or other of the chapels are perhaps later additions. The differences between one and the other are marked. In the chapel of Peace the treatment, with the elegant bodies and harmonious drapery, is painstaking and evokes Greek or Byzantine models; in the chapel of the Exodus it is sketchy, without precise detail and very clumsy, even in those scenes by what is thought to be the earliest hand. In neither case does anything derive from Coptic art. If the style is just acceptable in the chapel of Peace, the manner is absolutely worthless in the chapel of the Exodus. The inscriptions which designate the personages or the places are in Greek. Everything here suggests a work carried out by Christian Greeks, probably from Alexandria and settled in this oasis, which is known to have been a place of exile for persons who had become suspect to the ruling power.[35]

The illumination of papyri might well have developed more fully than painting on stucco. It was in the direct pharaonic tradition and was effectively transmitted, if not by Ptolemaic papyri ornamented in this way, at least through small subjects ornamenting the walls of sarcophagi up to the fourth century A.D. However, the craft does not seem to have appealed to Coptic scribes, skilled as they were – whether pagan, as were some of those who copied the Gnostic books of Chenoboskion, or Christian, as were others, and certainly those who transcribed the Gospel of St. John at this time. One does not even find, during the period, the slight drawings which were soon to adorn Coptic manuscripts. In this case, we cannot postulate destruction. Should we rather envisage distrust in respect of a medium which had served up to that time mainly, and most recently, for the representation of the good and evil genii of the other world? *Illuminated books*

Erosion and wind are no doubt responsible for robbing us of the wall-paintings on stucco, which must have been far from negligible during the proto-Coptic period. The elements have not the same powers of destruction where pottery is concerned, with a coloured glaze fired on a clay base. If this could not escape destruction by breakage, at least fragments of it remain. These are by no means lacking, but they have not been collected in museums or in private collections with the same assiduity as have fragments of Byzantine or Arab pottery. *Pottery*

In the Coptic Museum in Cairo, however, and in the Louvre, we do find a fairly large number of vases or plates, decorated with vines or undulating stems, in which, however, the naturalism tends towards a certain monotony. Animals, particularly birds, and fish proliferate, but these are already stylized as regards their general form.[36] FIG. 27

In the arts of colour, the techniques so far examined within the framework of the proto-Coptic period leave us rather on starvation rations. Our hunger will be appeased by a technique of which it must be admitted that it enjoys exceptional good fortune as regards preservation: that of weaving.[37] Having been buried with the bodies they clothed, in the particularly dry sand of the Egyptian desert, textiles escaped the depredations of both clandestine and official searches almost to the end of the twelfth century. Once brought to light, the materials of which they were made, including the vegetable dyes used by the weavers, proved as impervious *Textiles* to air and light as they had been to the confined atmosphere in which they had spent so many centuries. This remarkable conservation of objects in universal use among both pagans and Christians for the entombment of their dead served to guarantee the survival, down to our own times, of a substantial number of examples. The technique of weaving had been learned and practised by the Copts, pagan and Christian alike, thanks to the Egyptian workshops distributed about the country, which were multiplied by the Ptolemies when they introduced wool to Egypt. We have already examined some specimens of work much influenced by the style with Hellenistic tendencies. It must be added that, in contrast with architecture and with the majority of the objects produced by other techniques, these tapestries – in the form of dalmatics or ornamented cloaks, wall-hangings or decorative panels – are not necessarily, or even most frequently, examples of religious art. Most of them were made for secular use, and many were ceremonial garments unconnected with religious ceremonies of any kind, even funerary ones.

It must be admitted that they are no more firmly dated than are any other Coptic art objects. Only two pieces, among more than 35,000 known examples, enjoy FIG. 28 a certain precision in this respect: one found with a piece of fourth-century coinage, and the other with a coin of the fifth century. The decorative elements of these unfortunately do not offer anything sufficiently characteristic to be very helpful. The first, however does allow us to place in the fourth century interlaced ornament which it would otherwise have been very difficult to date with such accuracy. FIG. 29 The occasional stylized leaf in a material in the Louvre seems to be copied from the same motif dating from the third century, found in the vicinity of Palmyra.[38] No doubt we must also assign to this period some series of canthari outlined on the inside of shoulder-bands.[39]

We are better placed with regard to representations of the human figure, or of vegetable or animal motifs, since we can compare them, *mutatis mutandis*, with points of reference established for sculpture.

Certain wall-hangings in the Berlin Museum, fragmentary yet reasonably complete, show male or female dancers, posed in a décor of plant-forms. One of the APPX. PL. 11 female dancers, her arm raised above her head, is shaking her castanets. A vertical line of trilobate laurel leaves divides the figures one from the other. Stylized in a somewhat monotonous manner, these leaves indicate a date later than the second century. The colours are bright, but being distributed in broad bands on the garments they move even further away from the delicate gradations of the Hellenistic style. The faces themselves are schematic to a degree which relates them to the high-reliefs mentioned earlier. The bodies no longer have the suppleness found in Alexandrian art, yet succeed in evoking the movement of the dance.

PLATE P. 100 A fragment of tapestry in the Louvre is very close to this one.[41] All that remains is a dancer's head and her raised arm, with the hand holding in the first two fingers the veil which in turn envelops the arm. The shape of the face, the noticeable schematization of the features, the outline of the eyes, the bandeau which holds back the hair, the ear-rings, and the gesture of the arm—all correspond to those

Portrait of Dionysus. Tapestry. Fifth century. Height 26 cm, width 23 cm. Paris, Louvre, Christian Antiquities. Photo: Max Seidel.

Portrait of Ariadne. Tapestry. Fifth century. Height 24 cm, width 22 cm. Paris, Louvre, Christian Antiquities. Photo: Max Seidel.

Page 110. Perfume-burner in the form of a human head. Bronze. Sixth century. Height 20 cm. Paris, Louvre, Christian Antiquities. Photo: Max Seidel.

Deir el-Abiad, Sohag. Fifth century. Photo: P. du Bourguet.

Fishing scene. Limestone. Seventh century. Height 17 cm, width 46 cm. Paris, Louvre, Christian Antiquities. Photo: M. Chuzeville.

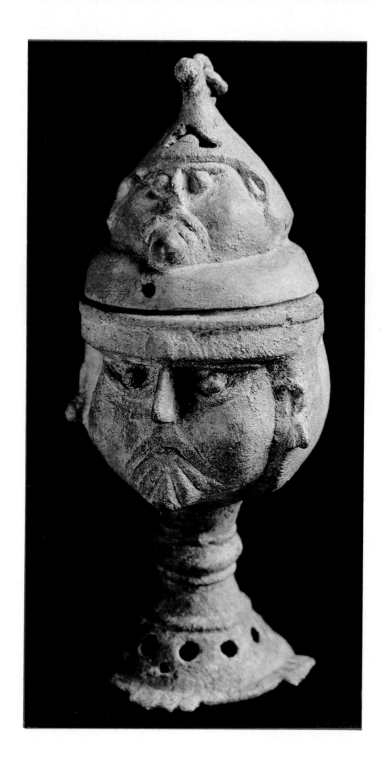

found in the Berlin hanging, despite some differences in the position of the head and the meaning of the gesture.

The two fragments of large shawls, one in the Berlin Museum, the other in the Louvre, must also be dated from the fourth century. The rather monotonous succession of flowers, the undulation in almost broken lines of the stems which extend from edge to edge of the inner frame, and which allows of leaves or bunches of grapes, each with its conventional high-light, filling the alternate spaces above and below – these features represent a break with the style of Hellenistic tendencies. The aim is clearly decorative, in an elaborately stylized direction. For all that, the effect remains no less beautiful. PLATE P. 54

Still later in this century must be placed a shoulder-square – or perhaps a cushion-cover, since it measures 20 × 20 cm – belonging to the Louvre Museum.[42] In an ornamental surround consisting of canthari alternating with rosettes, an inner square depicts a Parthian horseman above a dog, running in the same direction with its head turned to the rear. On the rearing horse, portrayed in good Hellenistic style, is the rider, his body presented full-face, with his cloak fluttering in the wind; his right hand is raised in the traditional gesture of blessing. In this small piece, we can distinguish, outlined in yellow thread – intended to suggest untarnishable gold – the horse's harness, the hair, the shoulder-straps, the belt, the shoulder-discs and the skirts of the tunic: all these details point to a dating in the fourth century at the earliest. Finally, the frontal view of the horseman's head and the absence of detail in the hand, the first two fingers of which should be extended, indicate a departure from the Hellenistic prototype. The technique, furthermore, is full of interest. Instead of proceeding by gradations of tone, as in the previously mentioned pieces, the details of the figure; the animals and the decorative elements, particularly the attachments of the bodies; the details of the rider's face; the swelling outlines of the canthari or of the rosettes – all are simply indicated, as in an over-printing, by the use of the flying shuttle. Here, therefore, we can see the first use of that means of suggesting volumes through the simple opposition of areas delimited by a line of thread, taken from the line drawings on Greek vases of the third century B.C. This must have begun to come into use, for purely decorative ends, in the interlacing ornament filling in discs, squares or bands, one of which, as we know, is dated. PLATE P. 101

Here we have the process which will predominate, without entirely excluding others. Examples abound in decorative pieces showing interlacings of plant-forms. We notice it particularly in a long band, decorated with bucolic scenes, belonging to the Louvre.[43] In order to fit the available space, shepherds, dogs and sheep alternate, from top to bottom. In a décor of plant-forms the shepherds, dressed in a sort of loin-cloth worn under an ocellated skin, stand with one leg crossed over the other, in a pose similar to that of Bacchus on the ivory on the pulpit (ambon) of Aix-la-Chapelle, playing the flute or the syrinx. The facial details, although simply sketched in, are clear. Like the details of the clothing or the musical instruments, the dogs' collars or the joints of the limbs, they are simply outlined with the flying shuttle. PLATE P. 56

PLATES
PP. 107, 108

PLATE P. 102

We find the same thing in the majority of the hangings, examples of which are to be found mainly in the Louvre or the Berlin Museum.

It is desirable, however, to draw attention at this point to two examples, both in the Louvre, which are still executed in the older procedure. Both are portraits, one of Dionysus and the other of Ariadne.

These two portraits, of Dionysus and of Ariadne,[44] correspond to one another; this is revealed in the movement of the heads which, although seen full-face, are slightly turned one towards the other. Within a framework of heart-shaped leaves, alternately pink and green, each personage stands out against a background of red-violet, and both are haloed. The torso of Dionysus is nude and crossed diagonally by a lanyard; that of Ariadne is clothed in a pink bodice. Dionysus' head is surrounded with trifoliate, stemmed leaves, while Ariadne's, her hair held by a bandeau, is surmounted by the turreted toque of the Tyche of Antioch. This is the head-dress worn by the season 'Summer' in the House of Gaea and the Seasons in Antioch, dating from the end of the fifth century; by a personage on a Coptic hanging in the Pushkin Museum in Moscow from the same era, and by Potiphar's wife in the sixth-century Book of Genesis in Vienna. Our two portraits are certainly older. Their appearance is markedly more naturalistic. It is, however, noticeable, although the eyes are strongly outlined, that the shape of the faces, in its simplicity, is reminiscent of the style of the fourth century. It is more squat, however, and furthermore the details of the torsos, apart from the nipples in the case of Dionysus, are practically blotted out. The monotony of the ornament, here even more accentuated, should also be taken into account. This time no use has been made of the flying shuttle but, instead, gradations of colour, though much less marked than in the past. The Hellenistic tradition endures, but we are now definitely in the soft Coptic style.

Lastly, in a decorative style of great beauty, although stylized as regards the position of the wings, is a red eagle, holding in its beak a loop of ribbon,[45] a motif probably of Iranian origin. The eagle stands out against a background of small flowers in very regular lines, in a manner absolutely parallel with that of the Phoenix, originally from Antioch and now in the Louvre. This theme is treated in a beautiful fabric in the Berlin Museum; an analogous fragment is also in the Louvre. Many other pieces could have been cited. We have contented ourselves with singling out the most typical in style and technique. We find again, in fact, the characteristics of workmanship and of inspiration which predominate in the other arts of colour, as well as in the plastic arts.

Not to labour the point, it will suffice to note, in conclusion, that certain choices are made during the proto-Coptic period: choices of techniques; choices equally in style, which begins to break with that current up to that time. A new orientation is clearly taking shape, while at the same time – whether in architecture, in decoration (plastic or coloured, according to the materials used), in the working of stone, ivory and bronze, in stucco ground and ceramic – craftsmanship is acquired and brought to the standard required for the following period, in which Coptic art proper was to become established.

V. THE ESTABLISHMENT: 'COPTIC ART'

(second half of the fifth century – end of the seventh century)

The date of the Council of Chalcedon (451) is decisive in the history of the Copts. *Birth of national consciousness* It turned them in a new religious direction: that of Monophysitism. Since it was the Copts who, in opposition to Byzantium and to the rest of the Christian world, took upon themselves the responsibility for this decision, and largely because they failed to make a sufficient distinction between religious and political matters, this date signalizes the birth of a national consciousness among them. It also coincides, in fact, with the establishment of the norms proper to Coptic art. Perhaps one should see rather more than a coincidence in this. Its inspiration, diverging more and more from the norms of Graeco-Roman art, and increasingly reluctant to come to terms on any plane with the Byzantine norms which had come into being in the previous period, had reached a stage at which the slightest shock would suffice to crystallize them about a new spiritual focus. Such a shock certainly appears to have been provided by the decision of the Council of Chalcedon condemning as a heresy the formula supported by Dioscorus, to which the monks rallied instinctively, bringing in their train the whole of the Copts.

For at this time the whole of the Egyptian middle class and the lower orders, whether of pure Egyptian stock or Greeks, or assimilated foreigners – the Copts, in other words – now formed a homogeneous mass. The only exceptions were the Alexandrian or Roman élite, a few leaders in the towns and a few pockets of incorrigible paganism, such as numerous tribes of nomads. The religious situation at the beginning of the preceding period, in which the pagans were as numerous as the Christians, had little by little changed in favour of the latter, as a result of the missionary activities of the monks. Coptic Egypt had now become Christian, and we can treat the whole of its art as Christian. No doubt from time to time objects of pagan inspiration slipped through, and there are also no doubt certain classes of artefacts, such as textiles, which because they were in everyday use belong to the field of secular art, despite the fact that many of them may include religious or even strictly Christian motifs. Coptic architecture, on the other hand, while the country was under an occupying power, had practically no concern with secular buildings and, following a long tradition in Egypt, attached no artistic importance to dwelling houses. Thus architecture was entirely religious, although decoration, whether in the plastic arts or in those of colour, might include profane elements.

In architecture, for the same reasons and to the same extent as in the proto-Coptic *ARCHITECTURE* period, we must immediately single out the churches commissioned by the emperor. These were, in any case, very few in number.

First, at the site of Abu Mina, in the Maryut desert, there is a building near the baths, probably secular, which it has been possible to date to the end of the fifth century by an examination of the decorative stonework.[1] It is a basilican con- *FIG. 30* struction, of which the plan is not without interest, in that, while consisting of three naves, it is closed at either end by an apse. This programme, which is not unique in Egypt – an example was the church at Erment, now destroyed – and which existed at the same time in Gaul (at Trier) and in north Africa, could, as we shall see, have exerted a certain influence on the architecture of the church at Dendera.

FIG. 31

By general consent, the great basilica of Hermopolis Magna (Ashmunein)[2] is given a dating in the middle of the fifth century. Its dimensions are impressive: 55 by 35 metres. Galleries encircle the end and the two sides, while the colonnades of granite-shafted pillars which separate these from the central nave are carried right round the side chapels in the trilobate chevet, terminating in front of the apse. If the dating is correct, this would constitute the first example of a trilobate plan for the chevet, and seems to effect the transition from the cruciform plan of transepts to the trilobate chancel which was to predominate in Egypt.[3]

The Coptic churches surviving from that time fall into three chronological groups: the second half of the fifth century, the end of the fifth century, and the sixth century. These we must now enumerate, before synthesizing their special features with a view to drawing some conclusions therefrom.

First stage

FIG. 32

The first stage offers two examples. One of them, it is true, – that of Deir el-Baqara (Monastery of the Pulley),[4] to the south of Samalut in Middle Egypt – owes its rather unusual form to its adaptation to the site. It is in fact a square basilica, partly carved out of the rock face and of which the chancel is entirely so carved, with a semicircular apse flanked by three rectangular niches, which opens on to two square chambers placed perpendicularly, while the body of the edifice, with its returning side-aisles, is built against the rock face of the mountain. Worthy of note, in passing, is the relationship borne by the general appearance to that of certain pharaonic temples, e.g. the Speos Artemidos in the immediate vicinity, and particularly the look of the side-aisles, which also call to mind the gallery of those courts, open to the sky, found in pharaonic temples, and which we shall find again elsewhere.

FIG. 33
FIG. 34

The second prototype is that of the basilica built on the ground. It is exemplified at Deir Abu Hennis (monastery of St. John) to the south of Antinoë in Middle Egypt, at Deir el-Abiad (White Monastery), and also at Deir el-Ahmar (Red Monastery) near Sohag, opposite Akhmim in Upper Egypt.

In the basilica of Deir Abu Hennis,[5] three naves end in a semicircular apse which prolongs the central nave. Three rectangular niches, with pilasters surmounted by a thimble-impost of Byzantine derivation, have been carved out of the enclosing walls. A central semicircular niche, flanked by two rectangular niches, is carved out of the apse.

PLATE P. 109
(ABOVE)

The church of Deir el-Abiad,[6] founded by Shenute in 440, thereby providing us with a precious dating, is contained within a walled precinct, planted with fruit-trees, in the manner of the pharaonic temples. Measuring 37 metres by 75, it is composed of three naves, separated by two rows, each of nineteen columns, and two narthex, one transverse and the other lateral. The trifoliate apse appears to

Bowl decorated with fish and birds. Ceramic. Seventh century. Height 9.5 cm, diameter 20 cm. Paris, Louvre, Christian Antiquities. Photo: M. Chuzeville.

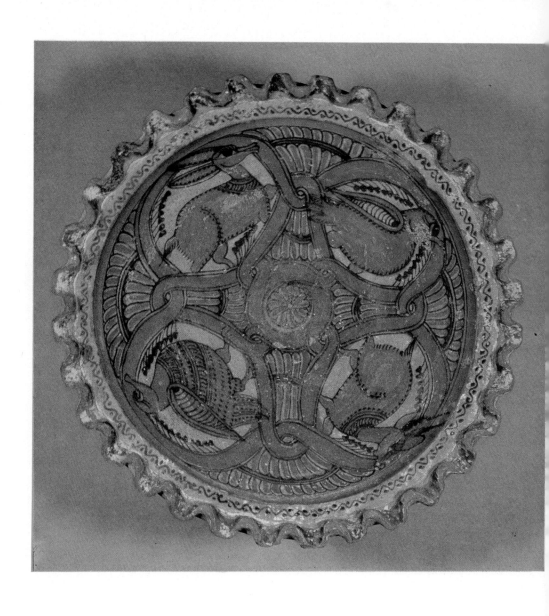

Bowl decorated with cervidae and birds. Seventh century. Height 16 cm, diameter 30 cm. Paris, Louvre, Christian Antiquities. Photo: M. Chuzeville.

have been inspired by that of the cathedral of Ashmunein. It is decorated with an assemblage of two superposed orders of five niches each, influenced by Hellenistic models.

The church of Deir el-Ahmar,[7] which is very probably contemporary, is comprised of almost identical elements.

At the second stage, we have again a church on the basilican plan. *Second stage*

In Upper Egypt, at Dendera, within the precinct of the temple of Hathor and PLATE P. 14 close to the *mammisi*, lie the ruins – the walls, however, still standing to a fair height – of the three-naved basilica we made use of to house our imaginary permanent exhibition. We will not return here to the plan or describe it again. All that is needed is to draw attention to the apsidal arrangement of the two extremities of the narthex, inspired perhaps by the bath-hall of Abu Mina in the Maryut desert, and to the secretive manner of the approach to the naves: entrance from the side and then only indirectly communicating with the naves. Despite its ruined state what we have here is still a very beautiful architectural ensemble.

At the third stage, we have chosen to group the churches belonging to the great *Third stage* monasteries.

There are, firstly, the two churches of the monastery of St. Jeremiah at Saqqara, not far from the ancient Memphis.[8]

The first of these is a funerary church, destined to house the body of the founder. FIG. 35 It was a basilica of three naves with returning side-aisles and a triumphal arch preceding the choir. This latter was a sanctuary chamber, with walls clad in marble. Apart from this rather luxurious detail – due, perhaps to the friendship linking the saint with the Emperor Anastasius (491–518), and which denotes a certain Byzantine influence – the remainder of the church is not rich. The walls are in red brick, resting at intervals on blocks the full length, as in Roman building.

The second church is in fact the principal shrine. Once again the plan is basilican, FIG. 36 with returning gallery, narthex on the façade and, on the south wall, an L-shaped atrium. Two apses have been built at different times, after the construction of the principal nave. The original apse, having columns with marble bases and capitals – thus inviting the same comment as in the case of the funerary church – has been prolonged, as it were, by the building of a second one, but this after the beginning of the eighth century, if one is to judge from the tombs between the two.

Another monastery, situated at Bawit, near Deirut in Middle Egypt, comprised two churches, of which that to the south doubtless played the principal role.[9] This FIG. 37 is again a basilica, though of small dimensions (10 by 14 metres), with three naves separated by pillars with capitals. The sanctuary is separated from the body of the church by a triumphal arch resting on two half-walls. The main walls were punctuated with a succession of transverse stone beams, supported by others of wood, all of them decorated. An archivolt on pilasters projects in relief from the back of the sanctuary, another at its inception, and finally another in the centre of each of the walls. Each of these compositions was flanked by two niches. Entrances were provided in the side-walls, the doorways confined by decorated door-posts.

A certain number of characteristics are common to most of these buildings. *Conclusions*

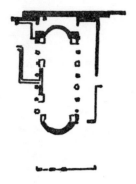

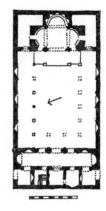

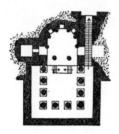

FIG. 30 – *Plan of basilica, Abu Mina. After A. Badawy, 'Les premières églises d'Egypte', Kyrilliana, Cairo, 1947, p. 349, pl. 6.*

FIG. 31 – *Plan of church of Dendera. After A. Badawy, ibid., p. 361, pl. 9.*

FIG. 32 – *Plan of church of Deir el-Baqara. After A. Badawy, ibid., p. 372.*

The three-naved basilica predominates in Coptic churches. We may regard this as a deliberate choice from what the previous period had to show, and which now achieved supremacy. In a country like Egypt, where pharaonic temples were everywhere to be seen, it is difficult not to recognize a relationship between these and the Coptic basilica.[10] There can be no question that the Copts could have been aware of the relationship, which certain scholars have been able to establish, between the hypostyle hall of the pharaonic temple, the Greek hall described by Vitruvius as the Egyptian house (*oikos aegyptiakos*), and the Roman secular basilica which may have been the origin of the Christian basilica in Rome, and later elsewhere. But we must not forget that, before becoming Christians, the Copts were pagans, that many of them remained so up to this time, and that before their conversion they normally frequented the pharaonic temples still in use. These were in any case dotted about the Egyptian countryside of the time in even greater numbers than they are today. Even when disused, or in ruins, their hypostyle halls remained standing. Was it not natural that they should have had some bearing on the exclusive preference shown by Coptic Christians for the basilica, when

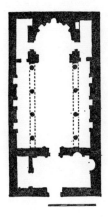

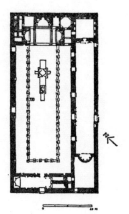

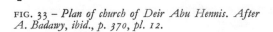

FIG. 33 – *Plan of church of Deir Abu Hennis. After
A. Badawy, ibid., p. 370, pl. 12.*

FIG. 34 – *Plan of church of Deir el-Abiad, near Sohag.
After R. Krautheimer. op. cit., p. 88, fig. 33.*

FIG. 35 – *Plan of church of St. Jeremiah, Saqqara.
After A. Badawy, op. cit., p. 362, pl. 10.*

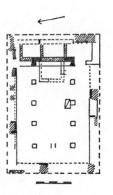

choosing from among the alternative programmes offered by other Christian
monuments within their orbit?

Apart from the general programme, there are certain details which force themselves on our attention in one church after another. Doubtless one could disregard
– even though examples are not lacking in pharaonic temples and tombs – the
tripartite division of the sanctuary at Deir el-Abiad or at Dendera, since we would
also have to consider Roman monuments such as the 'agora' at Ashmunein, which
could have served as models for this. But the outer court planted with fruit-trees
at Deir el-Abiad; the presence of a narthex both at Deir el-Abiad and at Dendera,
and particularly the screened passage, imposing indirect access on the entrant in
the latter; and the side entrances in nearly all of them: these are just so many
characteristic details which are found in conjunction with the choice of the
basilica as architectural programme. They orient the spirit in a single direction: that
search for seclusion, that secrecy, which is clearly manifest in Ptolemaic temples.
The Christian religion, however – except through force of circumstance in times
of persecution – does not in any way cultivate secrecy. In contrast with pharaonic

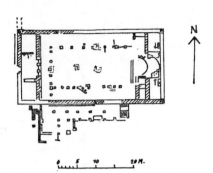

FIG. 36 – *Plan of main church, Saqqara.
After A. Badawy, ibid., p. 367, pl. 11.*

temples, the Christian church allows the whole body of the faithful access to the
divine mystery. But it does indeed seem that the Ptolemaic period was responsible
for deflecting in the direction of esotericism that quality in the pharaonic religion
which had encouraged a sense of the mystery of the divine majesty. This exaltation
of the mysterious, first by external isolation and then by certain 'hazards' interposed at the entrance, and finally by the solemn place reserved for it, beyond
the ranks of columns which advance towards the sanctuary as in a triumphal
march – could not this be the final explanation for the exclusive choice of the
basilica, and for details which would otherwise be adventitious, without any
purpose?

DECORA-
TION

It was in this great period of Coptic art, during which it became established,
that the main foundations were laid. It would, however, be contrary to nature
if it had not developed but had remained petrified throughout this period. No
doubt the 'rude style' predominated. But it did not supersede the 'soft style'
instantaneously. Before it took root in the beginning of the sixth century, there
was a transitional period between the two, which started in the fifth century.
We have here two phases, observable equally in the plastic and the colouristic arts.
It should perhaps be noted that, in contrast to what happened in Christian art
in Rome – particularly in reliefs on sarcophagi and often in paintings – the narrative style is almost entirely lacking. This is an astonishing fact in a country
which, in pharaonic times, had shown particular brilliance in this field, as much in
sculptured reliefs as in paintings. One would be inclined to seek the reason for
this in the lack of financial resources, which prohibited architectural decoration
on a grand scale. This latter, however, remains substantial, even if not on the
highest level. Should the blame be laid on the absence of great events, on the
atmosphere of general enslavement? But the Gospels, the Bible and the accounts
of the lives of the anchorites would have provided sufficient material, and the
Copts, so far as one can judge today, had no less taste and talent than their ancestors for composing scenes, and ones moreover in which humour is no more
lacking than in times past. Perhaps, in spite of their antagonism towards the
occupying power, we may detect in this something of Byzantine influence. One

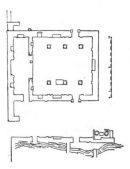

FIG. 37 – *Plan of church of St. Apollo, Bawit. After Chassinat, 'Fouilles à Baouît', Mém. I.F.A.O., Cairo, 1911, pl. VII.*

might prefer to see here another reason. This would be in line with the general orientation of the Coptic mentality, and we have already seen enough to appreciate the obedience they rendered to the fundamental imperatives of their art, which was more concerned with eliciting the significance of objects – their symbolism – than with observing their appearance in the concrete circumstances of life. Should we not therefore expect to find an insistence – analogous to that observable in the art of the present day – on the broad sweep, at the expense of detail? A mere hypothesis, but one which accords, not infrequently, with the tendencies discernible in every field of Coptic art.

During this period, in which the Christian Copts predominated numerically, one might expect that the same would be true of Christian themes.

1. Themes

This would be to forget that the fundamental themes of pagan origin – without even the need, from this time forward, to mark them with the symbol of the cross – had in Christian eyes already taken on, or were gradually coming to take on, a symbolic Christian meaning. This having taken place, there was no necessity for their elimination. Having become acceptable, they were accepted, and there was no call for their replacement with others for the purposes to which they had always been put, notably in decoration.

Themes of pagan origin

However, certain minor transformations are to be seen in them. The tendency to evoke the central figure by one or other of its known attributes increased. Thus the scallop-shell often appears in complete isolation. There is a tendency for amorini to take the place of secondary personages – nereids, victories or even hunters – disporting themselves, as it were, in every possible setting. In fact, in the majority of cases, one is tempted to wonder if the Christian significance itself had not become purely profane. It is doubtful if this was so in the case of stone sculpture, which, it would seem – since if is extremely probable that houses were not decorated – figured exclusively on the walls of churches or monastic buildings. Objects in current use, on the other hand, and items of clothing in particular, were ornamented with representations borrowed from cycles of pagan origin, and in their case there was no question of a liturgical use.

Christian themes, however, were becoming more numerous.

Christian themes

The first to appear was the ansate cross. This is the hieroglyph signifying 'life' which, according to Rufinus, the Copts consciously assimilated to the Cross surmounted by the crown of victory,[11] as a replacement for the images of Serapis, following the destruction of these together with their shrines. While these ansate crosses appeared from the end of the fourth century on Gnostic papyri, and in scenes in the chapel of the Exodus at Bagawat, its use as a Christian emblem only became general from the beginning of the sixth century, when it appeared in the design of woven materials, in illuminated manuscripts or accompanying engraved inscriptions on funerary stelae.

Christ   Christ is rarely represented, except with Mary and as an infant. This may have been due to the appeal of the more popular and human aspects of the Christian religion, as successor to Late Kingdom pharaonic representations, in which equally humanized myths of Osiris, Isis and Horus predominated. We must not, however, forget the very familiar, human form in which Christ is represented in

PLATE P. 43   company with St. Menas of Bawit.

From this time onwards representations of Christ in Majesty must also have existed, borrowed from Byzantine art: the prototypes for numerous paintings in the period immediately following this, which showed Him in His glorified aspect.

The Virgin   The Virgin provides the subject for numerous sculptures and paintings. The theme, however, has been diversified: instead of the *Virgo lactans*, we find the

FIG. 25   Virgin enthroned, and even scenes such as the Annunciation.

This followed from the definition, by the Council of Ephesus in 431, of the divine maternity of Mary. The protagonist of this doctrine, St. Cyril of Alexandria, was doubtless preconditioned for his part in this by a tendency proper to Christian Egypt, and already illustrated in the incised stele from Faiyum portraying the *Virgo lactans*. From this time onward, the tendency could not fail to develop further.

The saints   The saints now began to populate the iconographic field. One reason for this is that the influence of the great monastic figures was making itself felt – aided by time, which now favoured the Christian cause – to the point of becoming legendary. It is also probable that an element of popular devotion, more disposed to the representation of personages regarded as in the immediate orbit of daily life, contributed to their multiplication in the iconography.

The use of pagan themes by those Copts not yet Christianized, was not entirely eliminated. But the turn had definitely been made in the direction of Christian iconography: one, however, which was popular in character and which, when employing pagan themes, was in certain cases capable of reducing them to an aspect that was purely profane.

2. Plastic arts   Rather than group the objects into the two stages which divide this period, we shall endeavour – apart from stressing the development as occasion demands – to distribute them, according to the techniques, into two broad divisions: human figurations and purely ornamental motifs. It must not, however, be forgotten that, whatever importance we may attach to this distinction, sculpture was by and large used only in architectural decoration. Nevertheless, while human figures may appear in ornamental contexts, of which we shall not fail to take note, the purely ornamental subjects do possess certain characteristics which make it advisable to treat them separately.

A certain simplification of the facial features has been noted during the proto-Coptic period. This simplification forms part of a general tendency, due perhaps to the popular character of the style, but more probably, as we have remarked, to the emphasis on symbolism at the expense of concrete details. It is not impossible that this autochthonous tendency was accentuated by influence from a none too distant part of the Near East, or of an oriental art that was imported into Egypt itself in the course of the third century, or else quite simply of Roman art of the late third century; and that it may even have borrowed from one of these certain characteristic features which lent themselves particularly well to its own aims. A limestone relief, the style somewhat hellenized, dating from the second or third century and found in the Nabataean temple of Khirbet Tannur in Jordan,[12] has been thought to throw some light here. The subject is a bust of Atergatis-Tyche, Syrian goddess of fecundity and of love, wearing a crown in the form of a defensive wall (a reference to her role as patroness of towns), the whole enclosed in a zodiac. The conventional character, almost unavoidable in the portrait of a goddess, favours the expression of a style in which the details emerge almost spontaneously from the sculptor's chisel. Here not only is the face cast in triangular form – while yet avoiding rigidity – but the eyes, under clearly defined brows, are extremely prominent, their pupils filling out the area between the slightly stylized lids.

We have noted, in the proto-Coptic period, the direct influence exerted by Palmyrene art at Ahnas el-Medineh. The Nile god quoted in this context also had the triangular-shaped face, but the eyes, though deeply set in the sockets, were highly stylized.

The style is less subtly inflected as to the face in a standing portrait on a Roman stele originally from Kom el-Rahib, near Samalut, in the southern part of Middle Egypt.[13] The triangle of the face is more marked, while eyes like great globes start from the very lids, the latter being, as it were, merely stuck on, without the slightest attempt at pliancy of form.

Again, our attention is inescapably drawn to the faces of the Tetrarchs in the group of the First Tetrarchy in Venice. The porphyry block, and perhaps the workmanship, of this are of Egyptian origin—particularly so if seen in conjunction with the bust, also in porphyry, of Maximinus Daia[14] discovered near Athribis in Egypt. Apparent in each of these faces is the same treatment of the eyes as we found in the Atergatis bust in relief.

If to the above examples we add the stelae from Antinoë featuring children, followers of Isis, many of whom hold in one hand the same sprig of greenery as that held by the Roman personage on the stele from Kom el-Rahib, we can observe the emergence of a convention: a triangular-shaped face and spherical eyes between stylized lids, the latter either being applied to the surface of the eye-balls or allowing these to extrude between them. We shall see this again, stylized to a

Human figure (margin)

APPX. PL. 16 (margin)

FIG. 9 (margin)

FIG. 24 (margin)

FIG. 38 – *Leda and the swan. Limestone. Sixth century. 34 × 88 cm. Old Cairo, Coptic Museum.*

FIG. 39 – *Door panel. Wood. Church of St. Barbara. Fifth century. Old Cairo, Coptic Museum.*

more marked degree, in most of the human figurations of the Coptic period, particularly in stone, with which we shall deal first.

Two reliefs,[15] the first in the Louvre and originally from Bawit, the second in the Coptic Museum in Cairo, representing almost the same subjects, illustrate this well. In both two angels are portrayed, holding aloft a crown. In the first – a rectangular decorative panel – this crown encloses the bust of a Tyche; the angels supporting her are shown in three-quarter view, with the heads in profile, in the attitude of flight. They are winged but, though treated as male, their hair is rendered in feminine curls, according to the Coptic canon. The eyes, both of the Tyche and of the angel-victories, are spherical, with stuck-on lids. In the second – a subject under a broken arch – the angels, their hair treated in small globules, as is generally the case with personages of male sex, stand upright to lift the crown, which encloses a Greek cross. They are shown in three-quarter view with the heads full-face; their eyes start out from between lids with sharply pointed outer corners, and the head forms an equally sharply pointed triangle. The first of these reliefs has justifiably been compared with one panel of an ivory diptych, originally from Constantinople and now in the Museum of the Palazzo Sforza in Milan: the subject is approximately the same, and it is dated to the beginning of the sixth century. The two Coptic pieces, although the details are simplified, sometimes crudely so, and although they derive from a local and popular style, are in rather high relief in which the upper level is modelled to the extent of giving the limbs a chubby appearance. These are elements belonging to the 'soft style' which cannot be ignored. Therefore we must doubtless place both of them in the period of transition between the soft and hard styles, i.e. the end of the fifth and beginning of the sixth centuries.

The same may be said of a group of Pan with a bacchante[16] and of a bust representing either Earth or Plenty,[17] each of them placed in a broken pediment, decorated in the first case with acanthus leaves and with sea-lions on either side, and in the other with meanders arbouring rosettes, above a range of heart-shaped leaves. The rough character of the setting in the two pieces, the elongation of the waist and the stylization of the garments in the first and the simplification of the

bust in the second, should not mislead us into overlooking the attempt at modelling, clumsy as it is.

Two different poses of Daphne in her tree, in the Coptic Museum in Cairo,[18]   APPX. PL. 13
still retain, in common, an attempt at modelled form in fairly high relief. In the
first of these almost the whole body of the goddess is shown, while in the second,
under an arcade with a double range of egg and dart designs and scrolls, the body
stops short at the top of the legs. In this second example, however, the line of
scrolls is flattened. This places it closer in time to a third fragment in the same
museum, and of the same subject, but in which the modelling of the body is very
careless and almost flat in comparison with that of the face: characteristics which
should justify a dating later in the sixth century.

It is, in fact, in the second half of the sixth century that the treatment of the body
undergoes a great change, both in the modelling, which tends to disappear, and
in the facial features which lose some of their realism. This is clearly shown in two
monuments[19] in the Coptic Museum in Cairo: a group of Orpheus and Eurydice   APPX. PL. 14
in a broken pediment decorated with acanthus leaves, with sea-lions on either
side and, secondly, a scene, filling a panel, of the amorous conjunction of Leda   FIG. 38
and the swan, near a winged Eros. In both cases the elongation of the waist has
become conventional, like a tube, and even slightly flattened, retaining nothing
of the suppleness of the preceding period. Should we consider these to be purely
pagan themes, as the provocative nature of the Leda theme would lead us to
believe? It is not impossible that they may have been used in a pagan temple,
even at this late date, although the Christians of those days, less prudish than
ourselves, would have been concerned mainly with the symbol.

A rather amusing work, in this 'rude style' which still retains some modelling,
is a Birth of Aphrodite, originally from Ahnas el-Medineh, now preserved in the
Louvre.[20] In her shell, supported on one side by a nereid, on the other by a triton
– identifiable as such by the different treatment of the hair – Aphrodite, who stands
in the middle grasping a supporter by the hair with each hand, appears rather
dwarfed. We find once again the treatment of the eyes in which the eye-ball
stands out between stylized lids. This piece, in which the goddess is brought

FIG. 40 – *Liturgical comb. Ivory. Deir Abu Hennis.
Seventh century. 11 × 9 cm. Old Cairo, Coptic Museum.*

into the limelight, is particularly interesting because of the insistence, underlined by the carelessness of the workmanship itself, on the symbol. This, as one knows, is the birth of the soul. It is not unrelated – since in the Alexandrian tradition and later, up to Renaissance times it served to this effect – with the allegory of the birth of the Christian soul in the waters of baptism.

From the sixth century onward we may observe the phenomenon of a progressive flattening of the upper level of sculptured reliefs, the definitive establishment of which in the eighth century leaves no doubt as to its rapid development during the seventh. We have already seen some of the first tentatives in this direction.

APPX. PL. 15   A relief, originally from Ahnas el-Medineh and now in the Coptic Museum in Cairo, takes us a step further.[21] Beneath the arcature, decorated with acanthus leaves, of what must have been a broken pediment, Hercules(?) restrains a lion which is threatening another adversary. The personages are certainly in high relief and the limbs still slightly rounded, but they are attached to the background at the precise limit of their width.

A hunt for wild animals, depicted on the longer side of a panel discovered at Faiyum and preserved in the same museum,[22] constitutes, as it were, the culminating point of this tendency. On either side of a plant motif are two scenes of men in combat: on the right a hunter plunges his spear into the body of his opponent, while on the left his comrade raises a club to swing it against a bear which is following him. The hunters, their prey and the plant are compressed into the available space, their extremities touching the top and bottom limits of the frame. Most important, there is no longer any rounding of the limbs, which are flattened at the uppermost level, while a perpendicular and no less flattened plane unites them to the background. Here we have the end-product of the evolution which, from modelled high relief to flat relief, pushes to its logical conclusion the frank contrasting of two levels, i.e., of two surfaces, for the purpose of enhancing the

FIG. 41 – *Perfume-burner in form of a human head. Bronze. Seventh century. Height 30 cm. Berlin, Staatliche Museen.*

importance of the upper surface through the contrast of light and shade alone, while sacrificing every other indication of volume, and thus, to put it briefly, passing from naturalism or from realism to the abstraction of symbolism.

The process is the same in a small panel preserved in the Louvre,[23] on which is depicted a fishing scene. Boats and fishermen fill the allotted space to its extreme limits and, as in the preceding piece, nothing now stands out but the movement, with the protagonists merely indicated.

PLATE P. 109 (BELOW)

It would be worth following this evolution of style further in one particular material. But we may find it more easily in others, over which we shall have to pass more rapidly, chiefly because, being less durable, fewer works in them have survived.

In wood, one would like to be able to refer to the panels from a door belonging to the church of St. Barbara in Old Cairo.[24] But the median friezes – one probably representing Christ triumphant in a mandorla, and the other Mary seated, flanked by the twelve Apostles, and also those occupying the centre of the upper part, containing the image of Christ on one side and that of St. Mark on the other – are very worn, and barely identifiable. Furthermore, in the friezes from the upper part, in which a crown encircling a bust of Christ is supported by two angels, behind which stands an Evangelist, the workmanship is such as to suggest a relatively recent copy of the original subject. The same may be said of the panels bearing plant-form carvings, which furnish the inner surfaces of the doors. The subject of these latter, however, is related to those of St. Sabina, and inclines one to date the door, with its original panels, to the second half of the fifth century. Later on, very probably in the sixth century – if one compares it with analogous representations of the same subject in Syria, though the style is different – must be placed the relief on wood in the Louvre depicting the Annunciation. This, as we have seen in our imaginary exhibition, is a key work, which puts in the shade

Wood sculpture

FIG. 39

PLATE P. 42

objects of less good workmanship, as for example a panel representing an angel, in the Berlin Museum,[15] or, in the Louvre, a female figure in relief on a plaque of which the obverse bears, in high relief, the image of a flask.[26] It is quite normal that all degrees of quality in workmanship, the worst equally with the best, should appear in every period.

Ivory or bone   This is equally the case with reliefs on ivory or on bone. There is no lack of charming pieces, which can be dated to the second half of the fifth century. Among them are a Dionysus bending over a young follower, and a female figure, perhaps Aphrodite, both in the possession of the Walters Art Gallery in Baltimore,[27] although one might hesitate to place them so late in time. For the bodies are still very elegant, only barely revealing a certain lack of elasticity. But the over-blurred facial details are more or less repeated – though admittedly the general conformation is squarer and less harmonious – in an ivory belonging to the Museo Nazionale at Ravenna, representing the myth of Apollo and Daphne.[28] The movement of Apollo, bending backwards, does not eliminate, either in his body or in that of Daphne, who stands up to the ankles in her tree, their schematic aspect, which relates to the cylindrical form previously noted with reference to a relief on stone from the same period.

FIG. 40   Of much ruder aspect, with its flattened motifs and very restricted difference of levels, is the decoration of a liturgical comb,[29] in the possession of the Coptic Museum in Cairo. One side bears a Resurrection of Lazarus, and the other the triumph of a mounted saint, his arms raised in prayer, encircled with a crown of ivy carried by two standing angels, bending backwards. Everything about it is somewhat angular; the folds of the garments consist of series of incised oblique lines; the Apostle's hand is enormous. Despite the generally agreed attribution to the fifth century, it seems as though one should rather envisage the end of the sixth or even the seventh century.

FIG. 41   The same distinguishing traits between the second half of the fifth century and the sixth to seventh centuries are found again in two bronze perfume-burners, one
PLATE P. 110   belonging to the Berlin Museum,[30] the other to the Louvre.[31] The bodies of both are in the form of human heads. In the Berlin example it may be a woman's head; a man's head forms that in the Louvre. For the head-dress in the form of a triangular cap, with pierced openings to allow the smoke to escape, in the Berlin one, the Louvre example substitutes a different head-dress, in the form of a second human head. In the first, the chin is rounded and the face is modelled; in the second the whole effect is very angular, and even sharply so. This is what differentiates the two pieces, both of which display their Coptic authorship in the treatment of the eyes; the first of them, at least, is Christian, on account of the cross surmounting the bonnet and on the forehead; the second is very probably Christian as well. This form of perfume-burner, which is not unique, was doubtless borrowed from that of vases in the Hellenistic style, such as that found at Faras in Nubia,[32] belonging to the Khartoum Museum, which were intended for burning charcoal. In the Khartoum piece openings were also provided for the smoke to escape.

The elements used in Coptic ornamentation present an extremely varied range, which was often further augmented by combinations with human figures. To limit ourselves to the most important, in which can be seen the same distinction separating the two principal stages – second half of the fifth century and sixth to seventh centuries – we shall concentrate, in succession, on door-posts, on friezes on broken pediments with shell forms, and on capitals.

In an angle pillar found at Bawit, now preserved in the Louvre,[33] may one not see a survival of the 'soft style' from the end of the fourth century? Certainly, the draperies on both the angel and the Evangelist which, in a rectangular frame, decorate the summit, are handled according to the best canons. It is difficult, however, to accept a dating earlier than the sixth century, firstly because of the date of foundation of the monastery and secondly because of the decoration carved on two contiguous faces of the pillar; the other two faces are smooth, and were probably embedded in an angle of the wall. Beneath the Evangelist we find a succession of hexagons, each harbouring a rosette and, in one case, a cross alternating with an open flower with four triangular petals. Each detail of these motifs is itself ornamented with beads or rosettes, according to its position, either in the surround or in the centre. Here we are a long way from the simplicity of the fourth century, or even of the fifth, as exemplified, for instance, by the mosaics of Antioch. On the other face the interlacement of two branches which spring from a vase, even admitting the naturalism of the details, is too reminiscent of what one finds on objects of the sixth century to leave the question in much doubt.

Two pilasters from door niches, originally from the south church at Bawit, belonging to the Cairo Museum, commend themselves for simplicity of design.[34] On each face, a vertical panel has been carved out, leaving a raised band framing it on all sides. The stems and leaves are lightly incised in the centre. The intertwining stems constitute a sequence of elliptical forms from which spring on either side trilobate leaves which touch the frame with two lobes. The suppleness of the movement permits of a dating relatively early in the sixth century, while the regularity of this succession of ellipses and leaves, which fills the available space to the extreme limits of the frame, on either side of the continuous line, produces a decorative effect, unostentatious, but sure.

FIG. 42 – *Decorated pillar. Limestone. Bawit. Sixth century. 171 × 23 cm. Paris, Louvre, Christian Antiquities.*

Two further pilasters from door niches,[35] from the same source and structural position, perhaps later, having regard to their geometric character, are of outstanding quality. In their rounded form they resemble a column, whose entire surface is carved in relief in two registers, separated by a narrow band. Upon this, striated sepals follow one another, each touching its neighbour with base or tip, alternately. In the lower register we find two vertical zigzag lines, which at the top and bottom enclose a stylized leaf. At the top is a rich Corinthian capital with projecting acanthus leaves, which enhances the contrast with the flat application of these motifs on the engaged column.

The friezes give us some help with regard to the stages of evolution. One, which came from Bawit and is preserved in the Louvre,[36] appears to belong to the early part of the sixth century – if, indeed, it does not reflect the style of the second half of the fifth. From a vase placed in the centre a series of leafed scrolls branches out on either side and continues to the end of the space, where it curves back upon itself gracefully. At each incurvation a fruit is developed, doubtless a pomegranate, and a cinquefoil leaf. The elegance of the drawing and the naturalism of the details show that the artist derived his inspiration from earlier works, but this should not blind us to the slight flattening of the motifs, which brings us back to the sixth century.

From later in the same century are the broad friezes preserved in the Louvre, which no doubt ran high up along the walls of the south church at Bawit, and which were mentioned in connection with our imaginary exhibition.

From Bawit alone one is overwhelmed by the profusion and variety of decoration on the friezes, which begin in the early sixth century and continue far into the seventh. The oldest still have a naturalistic look about them in the treatment of the stems, and when these are 'inhabited', in that of the birds, animals, flowers or fruit embowered in them.

The foliated scrolls may be simple, giving the effect of a supple but regular undulation, the bellies and junctions of which harbour leaves or elements imported from outside. The most recent of these must be placed at the earliest in the seventh century – as even their position, on the outside of the walls of the south church, the decoration of which must have been carried out after that of the interi-

or, shows. They display 'inhabited' interlacings, but these describe alternately a circle or a square, and the stem is replaced by a band ornamented with strings of beads.

A fragment recently acquired by the Louvre, also clearly originating from Bawit,[37] falls opportunely into this period of evolution.

If the symmetrical grouping of the whole is what strikes us first, an analysis of the detail reveals, beyond this rather static impression, a tranquil force in motion: that of the leaves and stems which, in their curving growth, transmit the movement continuously from one to the other, until it dies out at the base of the central motif; they seem to be wafted along by a gentle breeze and to be urging the cross forward into the light.

FIG. 44

Broken pediments or niches with shell forms present an equally varied field.

Pediments and niches

The general form is borrowed from a model current in 'the art with Hellenistic tendencies'. But in Coptic Egypt, it is distinguished from second-century models, as for example that of the Temple of Bacchus at Baalbek, firstly by a wider separation of the broken elements and, secondly, by the development – without loss of the original angular form – of a second angle, often very large, in the space between the broken elements, or by the rounding out of this angle into the form of an arcature. All of these elements, moreover, were ornamented with acanthus leaves, or with egg and dart and bead motifs. The space provided within this interior angle, or arcature, might be filled with human figures like those considered above, or simply by a shell form.

FIG. 45

This latter, with its fan of elongated cells, was itself the subject of an evolution. It may remain close to nature, as is the case with several examples in the Coptic Museum in Cairo. Or it may be slightly elaborated in the form taken by the nub, with two volutes returning on themselves, as in the very fine broken pediment – originally from Bawit and now to be seen in the Louvre – which figured in our imaginary exhibition. Or else it may be stylized in the extreme, either by the complete rounding-out of the shell into a semicircular arch adapted to the form taken by the niche, as in the heading of a niche originating from Kom el-Ahmar, preserved in the Coptic Museum in Cairo, or again, as in those pieces in the same museum in which further rows of 'cells' are placed above and beyond the original shell, giving the effect of a peacock's tail.[38] In this evolution we notice the manner in which the natural motif comes to serve more and more as a mere stimulus to the decorative imagination.

FIG. 46

APPX. PL. 3

The cross is frequently incorporated, as for example in the broken pediment in

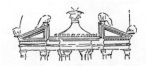

FIG. 45 – *Broken pediment.*
Limestone. Petra and Hilet.

FIG. 46 – *Shell motif. Limestone. Ahnas. Fifth-sixth century. 100 cm. Old Cairo, Coptic Museum.*

FIG. 47 – *Capital of a pilaster. Limestone. Saqqara. Sixth century. 43 × 41 cm. Old Cairo, Coptic Museum.*

APPX. PL. 3 the Louvre, where encircled crosses appear in both the angles formed between the peaks of the framing.

This observation is not without significance. It signals the adoption of the theme by the Christians. The theme, in fact, derives from that of the Birth of Aphrodite in her shell. Despite the absence of the goddess, it continues to evoke the rebirth of the spirit and, once adopted by the Christians, that of the soul in the waters of baptism and of grace. In its later forms we shall find that the cross, having replaced the nub of the shell, and at the same time Aphrodite, has given the theme its new meaning.

Capitals — Capitals, in their turn, present a very full range of variants which is no less suggestive. It will be necessary to distinguish between the capitals of columns and those of pilasters. In fact, the second category is modelled on the first. Three principal forms may be distinguished, the third of which, however, is of later origin and is only found in the capitals of columns.

In the first group we may place Corinthian capitals. These are extremely varied, as regards the proportions given to the three levels of acanthus leaves, the position of the boss according to the length of the stem, the carving, and also as to the FIG. 47 degree of suppleness and the angle of projection of the acanthus leaves.[39] This type of capital does not appear to have been decorated with the cross, despite its frequent use in the monasteries of Saqqara and Bawit. When surmounting a pilaster, a human figure may take the place of the upper range of leaves. This FIG. 48 is the case with an example originally from a monastery on the Red Sea and preserved in the Recklinghausen Museum,[40] in which, at the tip of the central acanthus leaf, we find the head and shoulders of a man, crowned with a fillet bearing the Greek cross, while on top of each of the outer leaves squats a bird. This elaboration of the ornament places such capitals in the seventh century, and this is confirmed by the style in which the bodies of such personages are treated. A second series may include those capitals which have been invaded by the ornament from top to bottom. The decoration was originally floral; on a piece FIG. 49 originally from Saqqara, now to be seen in the Cairo Museum,[41] the foliage is swept into a fine series of undulating curves, as though blown in the wind, in the manner of Syrian ornamentation. Again, the entire space may be given over to a

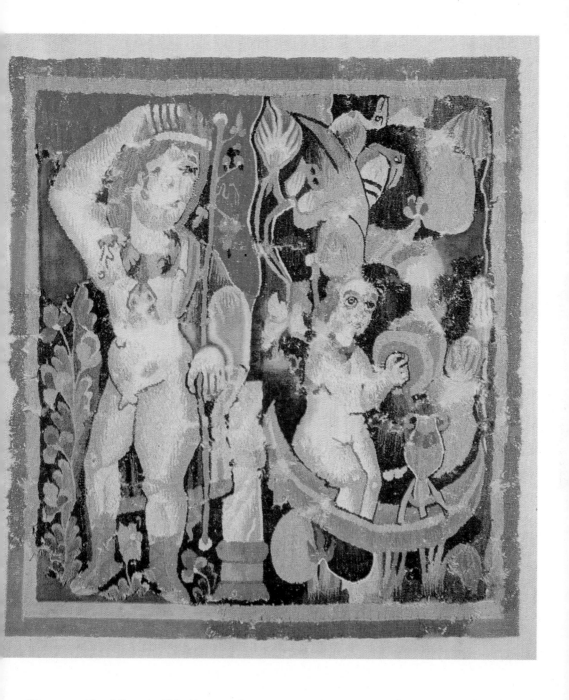

Dionysus with a follower of Isis. Tapestry. Sixth century. Height 58 cm, width 55 cm. Paris, Louvre, Christian Antiquities. Photo: Max Seidel.

Nereid holding a bowl in one hand. Tapestry. Seventh century. Height 65.7 cm, width 64.8 cm.
Cleveland (Ohio), Cleveland Museum of Art.

Pan and Dionysus. Tapestry. Sixth century. Height 37.5 cm, width 41 cm. Boston (Mass.),
Museum of Fine Arts.

motif involving human figuration, as in the example preserved in the Reckling-hausen Museum,[42] upon which is depicted a Birth of Aphrodite, in the hard style of the seventh century. The cross, as in the first example cited, appears frequently, placed at the summit.

The third series is comprised of basket capitals, the model for which must have APPX. PL. 2 come from Byzantium, although in Egypt it only displayed its immense variety from the seventh century onward. The surface in fact lends itself to every com-bination of band ornament, or leafed vine-stems, or acanthus while the upper part on occasion even presents motifs borrowed from the animal kingdom. In the decoration of capitals, wherever the 'basket' pattern flourished, it would seem that no one surpassed or even equalled the Copts in the matter of invention of motifs or in workmanship. In Egypt the earliest examples seem to be those from Saqqara, preserved in the Coptic Museum in Cairo,[43] on the surface of which the utmost variety of subjects deriving from plant forms are handled with a very sure decorative sense, while still remaining close to nature.

Thus far, we have been able to observe—in the various techniques and in their subdivisions, but particularly in stone, which offers more elements for its ex-pression – the establishment of a style and its particular orientation. Modelling, and in consequence the rendering of volumes, give place to the contrast between surface-areas and levels. The style expresses an insistence on the symbolic value at the expense of naturalism or realism. It becomes a setting, a vehicle in the service of the idea or the symbol.

As in sculpture – where, however, a few exceptions are to be found in the earliest *3. The arts* reliefs – so in the arts of colour, the Copts made no use of the narrative art of the *of colour* ancient Egyptians, nor even of what they might have gleaned from Alexandrian pictorial art. This is particularly true of their mural painting, at least in its early stages. The same reasons must have operated here. One must add that, where painting is concerned, in the Ptolemaic and above all in the Roman periods, the ritual pharaonic scenes bringing together a number of personages were entirely borrowed from the funerary books and had completely eliminated the great narra-tive and pictorial sequences of pharaonic Egypt, before they were themselves replaced by Greek mythology. The stages of this evolution can be reconstructed from the tomb of Petosiris at Tunah el-Gebel, where nothing survives in a pharaonic context but ritual scenes, and where pictorial and narrative scenes are treated in a Greek context; where, in a mural painting, one finds a woman dressed in Roman FIG. I fashion placed between the two gods, Anubis and Horus, the latter both still in Egyptian costume; where, in fact, in slightly later mural paintings, a Rape of Proserpina or the Oedipus myth have come to roost. In certain more recent arts, in particular mosaic, the narrative subject gives place more and more to the decorative subject, and human figuration is progressively reduced to the portrait.

Priest between columns supporting a pediment. Loop-woven fabric. Sixth century. Height 128 cm, width 94.5 cm. Boston (Mass.), Museum of Fine Arts.

137

FIG. 48 – *Capital with bust of an emperor. Limestone. Red Sea Monastery (?). Sixth-seventh century. 40 × 54 cm. Recklinghausen, Ikonenmuseum.*

This is not invariably the case, since in the fourth and fifth centuries Roman painting and sculpture frequently retain a narrative aspect.

Similarly, Byzantine art did not, in the earliest mosaics,[44] altogether abandon the narrative aspect. Its orientation, however, like the official Roman art in Santa Maria Maggiore, was towards a hieratic art. Coptic art, which had scarcely put in an appearance until the fourth century, in its proto-Coptic phase, does not appear to have made a start in painting until this era. It was at liberty, in accordance with the examples we have cited, to take up again the narrative vein of its ancestors, or the pictorial one to be found in Alexandria. It may be, as we have suggested, that any such attempts have disappeared. If they made no such attempts, apart from the catacomb paintings of Karmuz and Bagawat, which however are not typically Coptic, it would seem probable that, as we have seen in the case of sculpture, their natural inclinations bore them in the direction of decoration.

Painting It is also a fact, as we have seen, that there are no Coptic paintings available for study earlier than the sixth century. If this represents a break, it will be because the pagan Copts of the proto-Coptic period seem to have fallen out of sympathy with Greek mythology in its pictorial aspect, and to have retained rather the symbols, which we find expressed mainly in the presentation of certain mythological personages, together with their attributes. It is only episodically that a few of the scenes appear. If this explanation suffices to cover the facts, it will not be found surprising that the Christian Copts, who did not attain to any reasonable degree of affluence until the fifth to sixth centuries, should have waited until then to turn their attention once again to mural painting, nor that they should have used it only, at least in the beginning, either for a hieratic purpose, – when it contained human figuration – or for a decorative one.

Painting on wood It would seem, subject to eventual discoveries to the contrary, that mural painting was preceded, and prepared for, by the execution of small paintings on wood. It is in this way that the transition would have been effected from the Egypto-Roman portrait. Already this latter served to perpetuate the presence of the deceased's spirit by its position at the head of the sarcophagus, and even, through the attempt to achieve a likeness and through the intensity of the gaze, to make this presence felt. These mummy portraits were executed under the auspices of Osiris and the funerary gods and correspond to the Roman custom of casting a

FIG. 49 – *Foliated capital. Limestone. Saqqara. Sixth century. 43 × 42 cm. Old Cairo, Coptic Museum.*

death-mask and perhaps thereafter painting it. This presence, in the case of Christian icons, was to have a wider significance: that of giving rise to a cult. It is possible that the influence of this cult, as rendered to the emperor and to his widely disseminated images, may have functioned in this way. For this it was sufficient that the person represented by the Christians should be either a martyr, a saint recognized as such, or an angel. Not only the technique of encaustic, which was in any case soon abandoned, but also the symbolism of the portrait with a new content, seems to have passed from the Egypto-Roman portrait into the Christian icon.[45]

Thus an icon in encaustic, in the Coptic Museum in Cairo, bears the portrait of bearded Evangelist whose nimbus, however, has disappeared.[46] The features, though rather summary, are realistic enough in the treatment of the hair and the eyes and in the facial expression, managed by dint of a few lines. It should be added that in this we must have one of the earliest examples of the Christian icon in Egypt, dating from the beginning of the sixth, if not even from the fifth century. Recourse to another technique, that of tempera, can be seen in two other icons, doubtless of the seventh century. These originated in Bawit and are now to be seen, one in the Berlin Museum and the other in the Louvre. Both have already been mentioned in the context of our imaginary exhibition. They represent, respectively, Bishop Abraham and Christ protecting the abbot St. Menas. It is doubtless worth noting here that the name Menas is typically Egyptian, since it is extremely probable that it derives from that borne by numerous personages in pharaonic Egypt, notably the proprietor of a celebrated tomb of the xviiith dynasty at Abd el-Qurna in the Theban valley. It remains linked with the saint honoured at Abu Mina in the Maryut desert, and was common among Christians and monks, at Bawit as elsewhere. Here it designates, according to the inscription – repeated on the left-hand side of the panel – a *proeistos*, or prior, of the monastery at Bawit.

There is an evident continuity between the icon consisting of a single portrait and the more complex icon such as that in the Louvre. One comes to wonder if, with the Copts, it was not a direct step from the portrait, single or complex, to transposition to the wall. In any case, apart from exceptions at Karmuz and

Icons

FIG. 50

PLATE P. 43

FIG. 50 – *Icon of an Evangelist. Encaustic painting. Sixth century. Height 18 cm, width 11 cm. Old Cairo, Coptic Museum.*

Bagawat which are, moreover, hardly acceptable as Coptic art, narrative mural painting would appear to have developed at a rather late date.

Mural painting FIG. 51

The fact is that those mural paintings which may well appear to us the earliest retain this portrait character. We refer to a group, now no longer extant, which decorated the back wall of the sanctuary in the south church of Bawit, of which a photograph exists.[47] The decoration of this sanctuary, although perhaps the second in date, and the architecture of this apse, which ends in a flat wall clearly intended as the support for a painting, suggests that it was executed at the beginning of the sixth century. Now this group is composed of Christ and His Apostles, seated, all ranged side by side. The theme and its composition are pre-Byzantine and Byzantine, even imperial Roman, reminding one of the Christ enthroned among his disciples, again seated, in the apsidal vault of Santa Pudenziana in Rome, which dates from the beginning of the fifth century. The style, obviously, is entirely different. Gone is the realism of the faces and attitudes; gone, too, the freedom of pose and the superposed ranges of personages. In the Bawit paintings these are arranged on a single level, Christ alone being slightly raised. The folds of the drapery, reduced to mere lines – though these are disposed with precision – are treated in uniform fashion. The faces are round in form and smooth; in style as far from Graeco-Roman realism as they are from the elongation and the accentuated wrinkles of the Byzantine. Here we have, no doubt, the stylistic mark of the Copt: still firmly in the portrait continuum, but disposing the elements after its own fashion.

The principal characteristics are found again in a group discovered in the monastery of St. Jeremiah at Saqqara[48] in which a number of monks are represented, two of them holding the book of the Gospels; among them is St. Apollo, founder of Bawit, his arms raised as though in blessing, who seems to be particularly honoured in that a Coptic cross is placed on each side of his head, while a figure crouches at his feet. The date of this – quite apart from that of the foundation of the monastery, which is of the sixth century – would appear to be late, on account of the triangular faces of the two monks flanking St. Apollo, and in spite of the square form of the latter's face. Another painting from the monastery of Saqqara should more probably be placed in the seventh century. This shows the Virgin APPX. PL. 6 nursing the Child, flanked by two angels. The group occupies a coved and vaulted niche, the two angels being painted on the side- or returning-faces of the recess. The niche is crowned with an arcature ornamented with leafed interlacings and supported on two columns simulated in paint. The Virgin's face, by its shape, suggests a relatively early dating. But that of the Child is far from comely. Moreover the maternal breast has been almost conjured away. The rich Byzantine throne does not indicate an early date; the features of the angels, the leafed interlacings and the colonnettes are simplified. The theme, a basic one in Coptic art, perpetuates that already found in incised drawings of the fifth century.

The numerous little devotional chapels, forming so many separate buildings, in the Bawit monastery bear paintings of a whole series of votive subjects: a Triumph of Christ or of Mary, a scene commemorating some important event in the life of a Coptic saint, but most often groups of monks standing side by side. No archaeological element provides us with a fixed point for dating; we must content ourselves with differences of style, with general historical data and comparisons with the art of that time. The task is further complicated by the fact that there was no reason for the work to be completed within a limited time, so that it probably proceeded in stages, not only from one chapel to another but often in the same chapel over a period of one or two centuries. The *terminus a quo* most probably followed the building and decoration of the south church; the *terminus ad quem*, without going so far as the abandonment of the monastery in the twelfth century,[49] may well be the ninth century, since the Omayyad rulers did not hamper the activities of the monks; the isolation of their monasteries also enabled them to escape the full effect of whatever measures might be promulgated against the Christians. For various reasons, which we shall advance in due course, we may well be inclined to date the greater number of these paintings to the eighth century. Some of them, however, must date from the seventh century. A case in point is doubtless the eighteenth chapel, ornamented with bands of interlacement forming alternately a circle occupied by a portrait and a lozenge in which we find a bird with fruit. This repeats an arrangement used in the decoration of the south church of Bawit. A further case in point is probably that of the painting[50] covering the rear interior of a niche in the seventeenth chapel, which represents, in the upper vaulting, Christ enthroned and holding the Book, in a circular mandorla supported PLATE P. 53 by symbols of the four Evangelists and flanked by two angels, each above a portrait contained in a circle; in a register extending below this ensemble, lined up on either side of the Virgin, who stands with arms raised in the attitude of praise, are thirteen personages, six on one side and seven on the other, comprising the twelve Apostles and a figure which may be St. Paul or a monk. This painting, by the squatness of the bodies, by the facial contours of the youthful Jesus and of Mary, is related to the icons and paintings described earlier.

The subject is found again, in Bawit itself, a little later – doubtless in the eighth century – with one additional detail: the Virgin, no longer standing, is seated between two angels.[51]

FIG. 51 – *Christ and the Apostles. Mural painting. Bawit, south church, back wall of sanctuary.*

As we have said, the Coptic scribes do not seem, in the beginning, to have been concerned to enrich their manuscripts with illuminations. During the first few centuries these may, at the most, be ornamented – either in the margins or by emphasizing capitals – with ink drawings, and these moreover crudely executed, outlining either decorative motifs, such as interlacings, or occasional animal forms. It was not until the eighth century that the first important Coptic illuminations with drawings or paintings of human figures appeared. It would seem, therefore, that if this art came to them through Alexandria, it cannot have been until very late, after Byzantium had already again taken the lead.[52]

Nevertheless, an illuminated Greek manuscript preserved in Moscow has been attributed to a Coptic hand. This is a manuscript of the *Chronicles of Alexandria*, which can be dated palaeographically to the sixth century at the latest. Although drawn in black line, without use of colour, the figures here are of human beings, notably the Virgin and other holy women in the *'orans'* position, or the patriarch
Theophilus standing on the ruins of the Serapeum. While the garments are still well draped, the figures stand side by side in hieratic pose, their squatness of form contrasting with the Hellenistic or Byzantine manner.[53]

Possibly of the seventh century is a Coptic book of the Gospels, preserved in the Freer Gallery in Washington, in which we find drawings of the Evangelists, standing shoulder to shoulder. The style of this is close to that of the paintings at Saqqara.

FIG. 52 – *Organic motif from illuminated manuscript. After Maria Cramer, Koptische Buch-malerei, Recklinghausen, 1964, p. 19.*

Extremely rare though these specimens from this period are, they do nevertheless provide us with a starting-point.

Decorated ceramics, using the same colourings before, and occasionally after, firing, and broadly speaking the same procedure as that found in the manuscript illuminations of that time, display, in contrast, greater inventiveness.[54] The oft-recurring motifs of fish, birds, interlacings or plant motifs remain in favour. No less frequent are portraits, in which the shape of face and the rounded eyes are in the style of the period. The decoration of one of these vases, preserved in the Louvre, and which has its counterpart, found at Saqqara, in the Coptic Museum in Cairo, displays a quite attractive suppleness in the decoration. This consists of deer moving through interlaced ornament. In pursuit of his effect the artist has made excellent use, not only of the possibilities of drawing, but also of the curve of the vase.   PLATE P. 116

Coptic tapestry, during this period, was certainly at the height of its glory. In its   *Tapestry* evolution, the parallelism with that of sculptured relief is not difficult to establish. Freeing itself from the last ties that bound it to the 'soft style', it affirmed its originality, making use to that end of the richest of colourings. One may well suppose that, during the period of the final rupture, which corresponds to the second half of the fifth century and to the beginning of the sixth century, it could not have been a matter, as it was in the case of sculptured reliefs, of the elimination of all recourse to modelling. We have seen, however, that this latter could be obtained in tapestry by methods proper to the craft itself, which consisted of shadings brought about in the weaving through the stopping of coloured threads at decreasing lengths. This technique continued in use but not with the same deliberate purpose. This is apparent in a woven panel in the Cleveland Museum portraying a nereid raising a cup in her left hand. This is also true of the example   PLATE P. 134 in the Louvre portraying Dionysus with a follower, in an aquatic setting with plants and birds. Gone is the skilful separation of tones for the purpose of   PLATE P. 133 rendering the swelling muscles of the limbs or the prominences of the facial mask. The tones are now uniformly disposed, according to a sort of convention which by this very fact has lost all justification, on the outer edge of the limbs, the torso and the face. Moreover, while the broad aspect of the human body remains, the proportions, as can easily be seen, are constantly violated.

For all that, it is not totally lacking in effectiveness. In a variety of colours, among which only a few predominate, the vivacity of the tints, as fresh now as the day they left the weaver's hand, is a joy to behold. Furthermore, a contrast is estab-lished which brings out the tender, roseate nudity of the figures against the rich ground: that of the nereid is in violent opposition with the uniform blue ground; that of Dionysus and his companions is set off against a highly diversified background, in which a bright red sky is seen through an exuberant growth of green and yellow vegetation.

A further effect has been obtained here: that of depth, suggested by the juxtaposition of the compositional elements and by their respective dimensions. The very size of Dionysus establishes him as the principal personage, while the smaller size of his follower leads the eye to place her, the boat in which she sits, the fen upon which it lies, the surrounding flowers and even the birds above, at a distance – a distance which extends to the rear behind the pillar on which the god leans. These contrasts are entirely in keeping with an art which tends to exalt symbolism at the expense of the pictorial. Indeed, the symbolism here is striking, and has been brought about in a masterly way.[55] Dionysus is fused with Osiris, whom he recalls in his diadem, in the gesture with which his hand is placed upon it, the thyrsus he holds in his left hand, and by the pillar which recalls the tree-trunk in which, at Byblos, the god had been placed. The young woman striking the cymbals, one against the other, before a cantharus, is Isis in the funerary ship which floats on the marshy flats near the great Egyptian river, among the lotus and papyrus, accompanied by the cackling of the Nile geese. A syncretism, this, of the respective roles of Dionysus and Osiris, which blends the ideas of the rebirth of the god and of vegetation with that of the rebirth of the spirit after death.

Are these two panels Christian?

The nimbus which surrounds the nereid's head does not provide the answer. It is of pagan origin and serves only to emphasize a great personage. The presence of the laurel branch in the upper left-hand corner of the fabric is more positively suggestive. In the beginning it expressed the pagan idea of immortality, but already in the fifth century it had been adopted by the Christians. While more explicit, it is still not decisive. The treatment, by gradated tints, invites the

FIG. 53 – *Theophilus on ruins of the Serapeum. Illumination on papyrus. Fifth century. Moscow, Pushkin Museum.*

Decorative wall-hanging. Loop-woven fabric. Seventh century. Zurich, Collection Ch. Grand.
Photo: Grand.

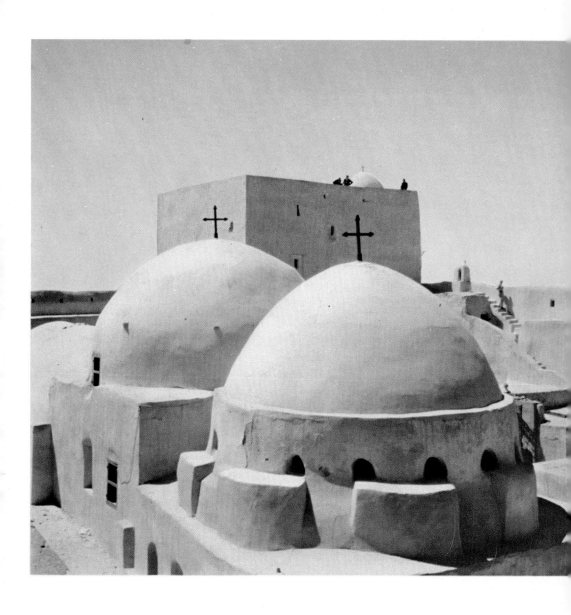

Church with cupolas. Deir es-Suryani, Wadi en-Natrun (Egypt). Photo: P. du Bourguet.

supposition that the material was woven in some originally Greek centre, but one which, as the style indicates, had become Egyptianized. This is clearly so in the case of the Dionysian subject. Paganism certainly still existed at the end of the fifth century, in the form of pockets of Egyptianized Greeks. The Coptic style of these two pieces makes it unnecessary to seek further.

This does not mean that themes of pagan origin, transformed by Alexandrian thought, had been abandoned by the Copts. The truth is quite the contrary. They persisted in even greater number than Christian subjects. But we must not forget that Coptic tapestries were not, in general, liturgical. Intended for secular use, they perpetuated themes of pagan origin while no longer attaching any importance to them. Furthermore, Alexandrian symbolism had been integrated without difficulty into Christian thought, which prolonged its significance on a new level. The Christians, in adopting the symbols, felt not the slightest need, for the sake of justifying themselves in the eyes of posterity, to add a distinguishing mark! We must therefore be content, particularly in this period, to examine Coptic tapestries from the standpoint of art history, and simply to recognize these distinctive Christian signs when they appear.

Among the themes are some which continue to appear in the fifth century and die out during the sixth. Others are found less frequently in tapestry. We shall content ourselves here with enumerating a few of the most typical ones in this period, making no attempt to exhaust the full range.

Nilotic subjects, taken over from Alexandrian or Graeco-Roman art, notably from *Nilotic themes* the celebrated mosaic of Palestrina, flourished at this time. To some extent they derived, as we have seen, from the Osirian and Dionysian cycles. Moreover, they adopted without hesitation elements from parallel cycles, such as that of Aphrodite, who was, as we know, confused with Isis in the Graeco-Roman period. The Louvre collection is rich in examples of this. From this theme, for example, is derived the fragment known as 'Sabina's shawl', mentioned in our imaginary APPX. PL. 7 exhibition, in which we find scenes from Greek mythology treated in the Coptic style, one of which was Christianized by the plant transformed into a cross.

The departure from natural proportions has not been pushed as far, in the above example, as in a square panel belonging to the Louvre, in which they look as though intended to appeal to the child mind. In a Nilotic setting Aphrodite PLATE P. 24 appears between two nereids, emerging from her shell, which is supported by two tritons.[56] In style this subject is related to the other version, also in the Louvre and originally from Ahnas el-Medineh, treated in relief on limestone.

The eyes in this latter are spherical, but not enlarged to the extent of the square form seen in two small *orbicula* which, anticipating a little, are to be dated to the seventh century. In these latter[57] the Nile god and the goddess Euthenia are seen FIG. 14 seated among lotus, above a small nilometer flanked by two amorini, one of which is in a boat. The presence on the nilometer of the letters I H and I Z, corresponding to the figures 18 and 17, the best levels for the flood, suggest a magical intent, entirely admissable in the Coptic Egypt of that time.

Linked to the Dionysian cycle is a panel in the Boston Museum in which, within *Dionysian cycle*

147

a framework of stylized flowerets, Pan and Dionysus are seen shoulder to shoulder and designated by their attributes.[58] With this we are still at the end of the fifth century, as far as one can judge, not only from the freedom of movement in the torsos, but also from Pan's ill-set head and Dionysus' tube-like legs. Despite this all the characteristic features: Dionysus' hand gripping Pan's shoulder, the boxers' noses on both personages, the absence of neck on one and the other, Pan's head turned to the distance, the fixed and stony stare on the face of Dionysus, directed at the spectator – all these features evoke effectively two seasoned rascals, presented in a style not lacking in humour.

Cycle of Aphrodite

The cycle of Aphrodite, present in the above-mentioned square, may also lay claim to a square piece of material belonging to the Louvre, in which a female portrait, occupying the centre, dominates a scene of nereids disporting themselves on marine animals. As well as the decorative sense observable here one may

FIG. 54

further note a sense of symmetry, in that the four marine beasts correspond to their diagonal opposites; one pair is lion-headed and the other dog-headed. The spherical eyes and the distortion of the bodies are in the style of the late sixth century. To this cycle we must add, as being of the seventh century, an *orbiculum* in the Louvre, in which – though distorted to the extent of caricature – are portrayed the Three Graces,[60] standing in the traditional pose.

Pastoral scenes

Pastoral scenes, frequent in Mediterranean mosaics, especially in the fourth century, persisted in the centuries immediately following. They are to be found

FIG. 55

notably in a series of *orbicula*, in the Brooklyn Museum in New York, which came originally from Antinoë. Their numerous scenes drawn from the Roman bucolic repertoire have been compared[61] to the mosaics in the Great Palace of Constantinople and are reminiscent of the fifth century. Contemporary with them, perhaps, are two *orbicula* belonging to the Louvre, showing a woman occupied in milking a goat and another, seated, throwing grain to chickens.

Subjects of this kind are often used to indicate the Seasons or to accompany this theme. The latter, frequent in Mediterranean paintings and mosaics, is by no means absent from Coptic tapestries. It has even been claimed that the theme has been found repeated on very late pieces. However this may be, it can be identified on two *orbicula* which survive, together with shoulder bands from a dalmatic, belonging to the Louvre. These *orbicula*[62] both show a female bust. In addition to their appropriate attributes, an inscription in Greek on each of them enables us to identify the Season of winter and that of spring, the green garment of the one and the pink flesh-tints of the other contrasting vividly with the bright red of the background. The shape of the rather crudely drawn faces, the simplified yet sharply defined features, and the rather large eyes with their fixed stare mark them as products of the end of the fifth century.

Cycle of the hunt

An even more widely disseminated cycle than the preceding ones is that of the hunt. Its iconography may be very varied.

PLATE P. IOI

It may be a Parthian horseman, of which we have seen an example from the fourth century. Another, also in the Louvre,[63] must be dated to the sixth century for several reasons: the modification of the traditional gesture of the hand, which

FIG. 54 – *Portrait surrounded with Nilotic motifs. Tapestry. Sixth century. 31 × 29.5 cm. Paris, Louvre, Christian Antiquities.*

instead of being raised is extended with the arm extended sideways at shoulder level; the horse and rider are more stunted; both have large, almost square eyes; and there is a decor of open flowers, stylized in the form of cog-wheels.

In two other examples, again in the Louvre,[64] the gesture has reverted to the traditional one, but the head of the horseman is shown full-face and, most notably, the modelling is limited to large surface areas – a thoroughly seventh-century treatment.

FIG. 56

The hunter may equally well be on foot, as in the little shoulder square belonging to the Louvre,[65] in which, half-kneeling on the right knee, his back against a bush, he drives his spear into the neck of a wild beast as it springs, roaring, upon him with ravening open jaws, while his dog leaps forward barking. A scene in miniature, full of movement, it is firmly enclosed, leaving no empty spaces, within the confines of a small square, and the dwarfish proportions of the protagonists are typical of the sixth century.

APPX. PL. 5

One variety, no less ancient in origin, and which limits itself to a few elements only – dogs in pursuit of an animal, each enclosed in a leafed scroll – appears even more frequently. The stocky form of the animals, their eyes almost square, together with another detail, mark its sixth-century origin. This detail is the drooping

FIG. 55 – *Pastoral scene. Tapestry. First half of seventh century. Diameter 30 cm. New York, Brooklyn Museum.*

FIG. 56 – *Parthian horseman and 'inhabited'
scrolls. Tapestry. Sixth century. 22 × 21 cm.
Paris, Louvre, Christian Antiquities.*

three-quarter view of the scroll-leaves, after the manner seen for the first time in
the Church of the Nativity in Bethlehem, which dates from A.D. 550. This treatment of the leaves, stylized in accordance with convention, enables us to allocate
to the seventh century those examples which take this stylization a stage further.[66]

Portraits   The portraits would deserve a study of their own, but many of them form part
of subjects already dealt with. Dancers, whether individual or in groups of two
or more, or following one another through the successive bays of an arcade, must
not be overlooked, for this motif is no less frequently found. In these, too, one
can follow, from the fifth to the seventh century, the deformation of the limbs,[67]
the posture becoming more and more fixed, the contours of the face less and
less studied, the eyes more and more spherical and tending towards the square
form. They belong to the Dionysian cycle, and evoke its symbolism, even when
they break away from it and tend to take on a life of their own.

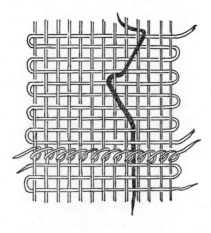

FIG. 57 – *Leaps and twists. Work with
the flying shuttle produces one sort of leap.
After P. du Bourguet, Catalogue des
étoffes coptes, I, Paris, 1964, p. 12,
fig. 9.*

St. Simeon's, Aswan. Photo: P. du Bourguet.

Christ mounted between two angels. Stone. Sohag. Ninth century. Height 42 cm, length 61 cm.
Berlin, Staatliche Museen.

Vase decoration (fragment). Ceramic. Size of vase: height 52 cm, diameter 35 cm. Paris, Louvre,
Christian Antiquities. Photo: Bulloz.

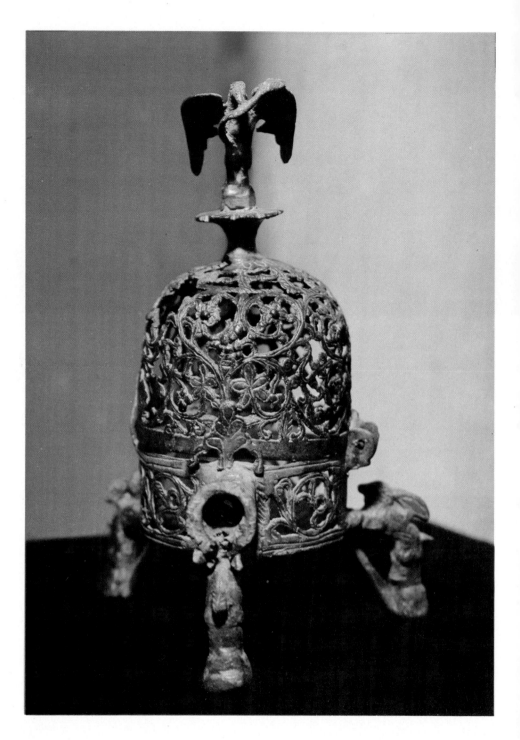

Here we must call a halt, although the elements used in ornament would have justified a study on their own: interlacings, flowerets, meanders etc. We have at least reviewed the principal themes with their symbolism, although of the latter it is not known how far, with the passage of time, an awareness of its meaning was still present.

The variations, as we have seen in the case of one or two examples, are infinite, and many have not even found a place here. The mere cataloguing of them will, however, have served to underline in passing the changes of style from the fifth to the sixth century, while occasionally also trespassing into the seventh.

The technique of weaving calls for a few words here. We have seen that, in the early stages of this development, two pieces show a continued adherence to the technique of hatching, doubtless inherited from the Greek workshops, but that this technique did not lend itself to the new style, which expressed itself more and more through the contrast of mass.[68] These masses are, on the contrary, emphasized by tapestry techniques which the Copts, from this time forward, made their own, with a view to obtaining the same effects as those achieved by the use of line on Greek vases of the third century B.C. These techniques consisted of lines and dots traced with the flying shuttle; a series of leaps in the direction of the warp; of a series of complete turns made around the warp threads while proceeding in the direction of the weft; of adding the product of so many extra weft-shuttles to the ground created by the regular weft on the warp – any or all of these being used whenever the occasion arose: for facial features, muscles, curls in the hair, folds in drapery etc. Already in use in the fourth century, these techniques became general and proved the perfect instrument of the new style – the style which is in fact the Coptic style – at least until the end of the seventh century.

Weaving technique

FIG. 57

These techniques thus came to dominate the field in the making of simple tapestries. But, in the course of these same centuries, tapestry was susceptible of further elaboration. This was accomplished with the aid of a method directly inherited from pharaonic Egypt: that of the *toile bouclée*, or looped weaving, which was in use at that time for bed-covers. It probably passed to the Copts through adaptation to cushion-covers, which were ornamented with a square of simple tapestry in the centre bearing a portrait or mythological subject, examples of which can indeed be seen throughout the 'Coptic' period.[69]

One example of this work has already been mentioned: the third-century wall-hanging in the British Museum depicting amorini in a boat. The process was to continue in use for a long time.

PLATE P. 87

There are two fine specimens from the fourth century. A hanging in the Boston Museum of Fine Arts[70] represents, beneath a pediment mounted on columns, a priest, wearing a dalmatic and raising a vase with his right hand, while in the other he holds an incense-spoon. In another hanging, which belongs to the Detroit

PLATE P. 136

Brazier surmounted by an eagle. Pierced bronze. Ninth century. Height 28 cm, diameter 20 cm. Paris, Louvre, Christian Antiquities. Photo: Max Seidel.

Institute of Arts,[71] beneath an arcade, a woman dressed in a long robe and wearing a necklace with a large medallion, raises her arm in the *orans* gesture. In both fabrics the colours are bright, but they stand out all the more boldly by virtue of the fact that the tops of the loops are at a different level from the actual cloth.

PLATE P. 145 The relief effect is strikingly shown in a fourth-century hanging in the Charles Grand collection in Zurich,[72] in which bands of red-violet in simple weaving are set off by areas in tufted, unbleached linen thread. Thus we find in this technique, at one and the same time, the effect produced in reliefs carved in solid materials and that which allows of the contrasting of coloured areas.

The Copts did not abandon its use in the course of the seventh century. The PLATE P. 55 hanging in the Abegg-Stiftung in Berne is a magnificent specimen of it.

In this technique, clearly, we are mainly concerned with wall-hangings, or in any case with pieces used for secular ceremonial purposes, which may very well be of Christian origin.

The art of tapestry, or of weaving, appears to have held a high place among the Copts of that period which is eminently associated with their name. To the two dimensions of painting they managed to add a third, that of relief. Their craftsmanship displays a sureness without equal. They knew how to make colours sing, to create movement, to give full effect to the subjects treated; the style is their own, relying on the inter-relation of flat masses, either on a plane surface or on two surface levels.

This style is strikingly manifest, not only in tapestries but in all other techniques. It was poised for even greater successes, of a kind ideally suited to Christianity, of which the most perfect expression is the symbol, because by the visible it is able to evoke the invisible.

VI. 'THE ART OF THE COPTS'

(Eighth – twelfth century)

Brutal as had been the blow dealt to Christian Egypt by the Moslem conquest in 641, the vigour inherent in Coptic art enabled it to carry on for a long time under its own momentum.

Coptic art under Moslem domination

This was not at first, or for a long time afterwards, thought by archaeologists to be the case.[1] Recently one of their number has again gone back to the earlier view. Haunted to excess by a nostalgic and unavowed yearning for Hellenistic forms, and disappointed at not finding them in Coptic art, they seize quite arbitrarily upon the fact of Moslem domination as justification for signing, from that very moment, the death warrant of Coptic art, only allowing it, as a consolation, a century of slow death. In so doing they ignore, with superb complacency, the accumulation – too substantial for such a short duration – of Coptic productions of every kind after the Moslem conquest. There is too much evidence invalidating this judgement for its retention to be justified any longer. The actual conditions imposed on the Copts by the victorious Moslems, the number of monuments which must be taken into account and the differences of style which can be distinguished by anyone who really chooses to examine them; the fact that certain of these are dated, and unquestionably so, quite late in the period of Moslem domination; the evident relationship with certain monuments of Moslem art without any sacrifice of Coptic character; the evidence of Moslem inhabitants and travellers regarding the activity of Coptic artisans for several centuries after the conquest: all this – in short the results of recent studies – make it impossible for this attitude to be taken seriously.

It is too easily forgotten, in fact, that conditions, except by force of external circumstance – reduction in the number of Christians – proved no more unfavourable to the Copts than they had in the time of the Byzantine occupation. Despite the indignant remonstrances of the caliphs, the governors had recourse without hesitation to the services of middle-class Christians who were experienced in the administration of the country. In the course of time the conversion of Christians to Islam meant that the governors could rely on an increasing number of officials or craftsmen of the same faith as the conquerors. They never ceased altogether, however, to have recourse to the Christian Copts. These were always to retain a considerable number of posts, sometimes of high rank, in the collection of taxes; in weaving they were employed up to the eleventh century and a little beyond, and the craft of woodwork has remained their prerogative until the present day. Ostracism of the Copts was not laid down by decree until the end of the seventh century, and when it came did nothing to alter this policy. It is hardly likely that the Copts would have kept up any serious relations with Constantinople, at least in the course of the first two centuries after the Moslem conquest. Neither the Tulunids nor the Fatimids, who forged the official links

New social conditions

with the Byzantine court and Byzantine commerce, would have been very likely to permit this to the advantage of the Coptic community, however tolerant they may have been towards it. No doubt the Copts' resentment towards the previous occupying power must have weakened when the Moslem domination proved even more oppressive.

The seat of the Byzantine emperors was at that time the highest authority for Christian art of the Orient; simultaneously it was the nearest point of reference for Copts who sought moral relief from the often cruel grip of the new occupying power. The political struggles did not prevent the Copts from participating in this two-way current of exchanges. In another direction, Syria, whose art was particularly indebted to that of Byzantium, was close at hand, and one knows to what an extent, in the East, contacts were favoured by movements of individuals. Nevertheless, the exchanges which may very well have taken place could not have amounted to a Byzantine influence, except perhaps at certain moments. The breach with Byzantium, already virtually effective at the Council of Chalcedon, had become real and in practice definitive from the middle of the seventh century. The Coptic community, from this time forward, was sealed off; the sole influence which could exert itself upon the Copts would for a long time be that of Islam. But if the latter was to communicate artistic motifs and methods to the Copts, these first had to take form, if one agrees that Moslem art had first to borrow from all the countries conquered by the Crescent. Of this introduction of new themes and processes into Coptic art we must take due account.

Influence on the victors If this indeed happened, it is no less true that during the early centuries the Copts themselves exercised an influence upon their conquerors. The intermingling of Copts and Moslems clearly had much to do with this, and such reciprocal influence must be counted among the latent forces at work, of which the effects were by no means negligible. In any case Coptic artisans were employed from the beginning by their Moslem masters to exactly the same extent as were the artists, Christian or otherwise, in other countries which fell under their dominion. Furthermore, it must not be overlooked that at the moment of the conquest the Copts had already reached a stage of development at which they could command, in almost every technique – from monumental architecture to sculpture and painting, and including several minor arts – a real mastery, as well as an original vision. Their contribution to Moslem art extended even beyond that of skilled workmanship, particularly in the early days, while Moslem art was still finding its feet.

At the beginning, therefore, they were in a position of strength. This strength, during the time that Moslem art was coming into being, remained substantial, for, if Coptic artists, as has been stated, continued to work for Moslems, they had still to satisfy the demands of monasteries which as a result of their isolation

Portrait of a man. Tapestry. Ninth century. Detroit (Mich.), Institute of Art.

Dancing-girls (fragment). Tapestry. Twelfth century. Height 70 cm, width 11 cm.
Paris, Louvre, Christian Antiquities. Photo: Bulloz.

escaped the interdicts of the rulers. They had also, in periods of calm, to do the same for their principal churches. In this way they not only maintained and even renewed the quality of their art, but also preserved a religious inspiration that led to a uniform style. Thus Coptic art maintained its continuity up to the time of the Fatimids, during which the relatively consistent favourable atmosphere enabled artists, whether in the service of the Moslems or of their more prosperous co-religionists, to decorate their churches and monasteries in their own distinct style.

Coptic art thus preserved sufficient individuality that the new themes and new methods it borrowed, so far from submerging it, could be truly assimilated.

Thrown on their own resources within the narrow limits allocated to them, the Copts, during this period when their numbers were dwindling, closed their ranks vis-à-vis the Moslem power and rallied around their own pastors and their Christian faith. Their art therefore tended to be directed into religious channels, although productions of a secular nature were not excluded, for monasteries, and even private individuals, still enjoyed relative affluence.

In what fields, however, could they continue to work? The right to construct and restore churches and monasteries was only conceded after interminable representations, and in return for payment of special fees to the treasury. Refurbishing of the interior decoration of large monastery buildings remained possible because of their isolation. Liturgical objects needing replacement, the decoration of places of worship, the making of ceremonial garments for those of modest means or for the affluent: these were the only categories of artistic activity open to them. This activity – with certain admittedly numerous exceptions – could only take refuge in decorative art, especially during the iconoclastic crisis in Byzantium of which the Moslem rulers took advantage as a pretext to ban the human figure in Egypt, as elsewhere. Decoration, therefore, remained practically the only field open to Coptic art.

This was not enough to discourage it. Here, providentially, was an alternative which accorded with their own inclinations. A style which relies on the contrast between surface levels or areas of colour – in short on contrasts of mass – already engages in a certain stylization of the figures, and is by this very fact a decorative art. The Copts, past masters at this, threw themselves heart and soul into the task.

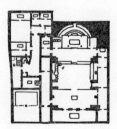

FIG. 58 – *Plan of church of Abu-'s-Sifain. Old Cairo. After A. Butler, op. cit., p. 78.*

This holds true in every field of expression. Indeed, the motif became in their hands more and more a mere support, when not reduced to the role of a pretext. The prolonging of the dominant compositional lines, the free play made with relative proportions, the cutting-up of the subject into masses, either to contrast with or to correspond with each other – all of which seldom failed in their object of enhancing the importance of the symbol – came, in the process, to lose sight of this object and to be employed for their own sake, in the most unexpected ways, and to the extent of pure fantasy. If certain productions here and there are mediocre, often strange, we witness in most of the others the flowering of a true inventive genius, of an astonishing exuberance: in short, the manifestation of a self-delight which renders this period one of unequalled originality – an originality which is no less essentially Coptic.

Outburst of originality Art in this last period, while it may represent a certain weakening, and doubtless a decadence in relation to the preceding period, commands attention by this outburst of originality which marks one step further along the path charted earlier. In the evolution of Coptic art, the 'art of the Copts' therefore has its place, and one no less deserving of interest than the other periods we have considered. It is in terms of abstraction from the subject that we may best classify the various phases of the 'art of the Copts'. Without their being in the least degree Moslem, but because of the interdependence of Coptic and Moslem art in Egypt, and because the art of the rulers necessarily occupies the forefront of the scene in the general history of art, these phases correspond effectively with the great Moslem periods of the first effectively with the great Moslem periods of the first seven centuries of the hegira, say, up to about the fourteenth century A.D. It is this order that we shall make use of in treating Coptic decorative art. A preliminary section, less sub-divided, will be devoted to architecture.

ARCHI-TECTURE
Coptic share in Moslem architecture
Rare as they have become, the Christian monuments of the proto-Coptic and Coptic periods are sufficiently numerous for us to be able to credit the Copts with technique and taste, not to mention the inspiration of which good architects are constituted. Even their absence, regrettable as this would be for science, would not have precluded our recognition of this talent among the Copts, for it is recorded in historical documents. According to Léonce de Néapolis, in 629 thousands of Egyptians had been sent to Jerusalem, to help rebuild the churches destroyed by the Persians in 614.[2] To judge from the number mentioned, we are doubtless justified in concluding that these were labourers, even slightly skilled ones, such as are still found in their thousands in Egypt today. Whatever the nature of the help provided by the Copts in reconstructing the Jerusalem churches, the Arab writers themselves render a more precise tribute to the qualifications of Copts in this field, with reference to one of the first Omayyad buildings: the mosque of Medina (707–9). According to Baladhuri,[3] the caliph al-Walid, in a letter to the town governor, enjoined him to demolish the existing mosque and to have it rebuilt, informing him of the despatch for this purpose of eighty Greek artisans from Syria and *Copts*. Samhudi,[4] citing Waquidi, and therefore referring to a date still very close to the building of the mosque, is more detailed: 'The

FIG. 59 – *Niche in Fatimid style. Wadi en-Natrun. Deir Abu Maqar, church of St. Macarius. Fatimid period.*

Copts', he writes, 'have built the sanctuary and the Greeks [from Syria] have worked on the sides and on the sanctuary of the mosque'. One may still quibble, and maintain that the Copts were only called upon to carry out the tasks of unskilled labourers under the direction of a Moslem clerk of works. A remark of As-Sonyuti's[5] in the fiftheenth century regarding this sanctuary settles all argument: 'At the beginning of the second century [of the hegira, i.e. A.D. 715]', he writes, 'it was forbidden according to tradition to make use of it [the sanctuary], since it was an ecclesiastical motif'. He is referring, obviously, to the *mihrab* in the form of a niche, which – as its origins were soon forgotten – owing to the veneration enjoyed by the mosque of Medina, soon became the traditional form for the sanctuary of a Moslem mosque. It is the product, not of the work of mere unskilled labourers, but of the calculations of an architect.

It has not escaped notice,[6] in regard to the trifoliate apse placed at the end of the hall in the Mshatta palace, undoubtedly built by al-Walid II in 743-4, that this architectural form, although it originated in Syria, is there preceded by a narthex only, while the placing of it at the end of a basilical hall appears to be of Egyptian inspiration. Here, surely, is the mark of a Coptic hand intervening once again, this time on the architectural level. As to the qualifications of the Egyptian workmen, still mainly Copts at that time, some papyri[7] of Aphrodite in Egypt, the first of which is dated 3 November 709, state: 'Pay as salary of one carpenter for work on the mosque of Damascus for six months not more than four nominal *solidi*.. for the maintenance of forty *skilled* workmen for the construction of Damascus…' The reference is to the Great Mosque of Damascus, erected by al-Walid I.

This documentary evidence of the activities of Copts outside Egypt is not without value. It confirms the esteem in which Coptic architects and craftsmen were held, well into the period following the Arab conquest. These skills could not fail to have been employed by them in constructing and maintaining their own churches, the security of which had been guaranteed under the treaty of surrender of 641, and whose eventual destruction only began to be envisaged as a result of the Abbasid caliph Mutawakkil's decree of 850.

Coptic churches

This period, therefore, remains rich in Christian monuments, but the data required for their precise dating are lacking.

Certain traditions, however, corroborate the references to churches made by Abu Salih in the twelfth century, and Maqrizi, historians of the Moslem period. We may accordingly consider, as being from the end of the seventh century, the church of Mari Girgis;[8] as from the tenth century, the churches of El-Mu'allaqa[9] and St. Barbara[10] in Old Cairo – all within the 'walls of Babylon'; as of the eleventh FIG. 58 century, and very probably even earlier, the church of Abu-'s-Sifain[11] in Old Cairo, and perhaps as of the ninth century, the church of El-Adra in Cairo.[12] Many monastery churches in Middle and Upper Egypt are doubtless contemporary with these, but more extensive studies would have to be undertaken to enable this to be proved for certain. On the other hand, it is remarkable that all these churches are basilican in plan, with a triple recessed chapel in the apse; they often have a narthex on the long axis and returning galleries and, as at El-Adra, in Cairo, access is gained from the side. Thus we find the principal characteristics of earlier churches re-appearing.

PLATE P. 12

It seems probable, however, that the method of roofing was something new. It consisted, for the most part, of a multiplicity of domes in single or double rank. This change was no doubt necessitated by the impossibility, for the Copts, of meeting the expense of a double-pitched roof, such as had been in use up to that time. The same economic pressure led to the adoption of a form of wall-finish utilized in Moslem buildings which the latter had in turn borrowed from the Byzantines while modifying its supports.[13] The adaptation was not difficult; it had the further advantage of offering, on the curved interior, a surface for painting, and examples of its exploitation in this way were not lacking among the Byzantines. These were borrowings, no doubt, but so far from disrupting the general arrangement they enhanced it and were intelligently assimilated.

Monasteries

The monasteries, more isolated than the village churches, particularly those of the towns, were doubtless rarely rendered safe by their enclosing walls from the PLATES PP. 12, incursions of pillaging nomads. This was certainly so in the case of the monasteries 146 of Wadi en-Natrun, which were several times destroyed between the fourth

FIG. 61 – *Enclosure wall. Ukhaidir, near Baghdad. End of eighth century.*

and the end of the eighth centuries by the Mazices – although this region, the Nitrian of ancient times, is half-way between Cairo and Alexandria. Attachment to their particular way of life, however, continually drove the monks to rebuild them. Such a rebuilding[15] took place in the ninth century, notably of the churches, which remained faithful to the basilican plan. In the course of time new details were added.[16] This is how, in the north sanctuary of the church of Deir Abu Maqar, a type of engaged arch comes to be directly comparable with that which ornaments the façade of the prayer hall in the mosque of El Azhar in Cairo.[17] Its style is of Fatimid origin, but the Copts found no difficulty in fitting it into the ornamentation of one of their monuments. In fact the arcade, or arcature, appears frequently in Coptic art. This one accords harmoniously with its general tendency and enriches the Copts' ornamental repertoire.

FIG. 59

FIG. 60

A further borrowing of an ornament, and one doubtless also brought in by the Moslems, is to be seen in the Christian necropolis of Bagawat in the Kharga oasis. The chapels here are contained within a long precinct wall upon which appears, in high relief, a succession of lofty blind arcades.[18] While the 'blind' aspect of the arcading may well be of Hellenistic origin, the repetition of the motif resembles so strikingly that prevailing at Ukhaidir[19] in the region south of Baghdad, that there must have been some connection whatever between them. But here again the broad aspect fits in quite naturally with the Coptic tradition of architectural ornament.

APPX. PL. 19

FIG. 61

Among the monasteries of this period it is also appropriate to mention that of St. Simeon, near Aswan, which dates, at the latest, from the ninth century and was abandoned at the end of the twelfth.[20] With its imposing dimensions, on two successive levels, and enclosing walls 6 to 7 metres high, in broken lines and furnished with turrets and watch-towers, it is one of the largest surviving from this time. The buildings are distributed around three courts. The cells here are contiguous, as is generally the case in Egypt. The church follows a basilican plan, with tripartite sanctuary and narthex. A long and lofty vaulted hall represents a magnificent development of the refectory halls usually met with in monasteries. Despite difficulties of all kinds, and even interdicts, construction on a grand scale remained in high favour among the Copts at least as late as the thirteenth

PLATE P. 151

FIG. 62 – *Liturgical patera. Bronze. Eighth century. Height 47 cm, width 34 cm, diameter 16 cm. Paris, Louvre, Christian Antiquities.*

century, as is clear from the last example cited above. The handiwork of artisans, either monks or laymen, its construction is inconceivable without the calculations of an architect. Historians, even Arab ones, recognize on occasion the existence of architects among the Copts, although not a single name of one survives. Art in those days was still anonymous. Architecture, more than in the other techniques, is the result of team-work, and the credit for it accrues quite simply to the Coptic community.

DECORA-
TION
1. Themes

It is natural that, in the course of this period, circumstances should have demanded the adoption of new themes, or a new way of interpreting those already in existence. In spite of, and perhaps also because of the diminishing size of the Christian population, Christian subjects came into greater prominence. These were Christ in Majesty, the Virgin with the Infant Jesus, Christ in Glory above the Apostles surrounding the Virgin, groups of monks standing shoulder to shoulder and, in general, the representation of those saints inscribed in Coptic martyrology: founders of monasteries, sanctified monks, foreign saints adopted by the Copts, saints on horseback etc. In painting, biblical and evangelical scenes appear sporadically. Their rarity is probably the result of acts of destruction which took place over the years.

This does not mean that the fund of Coptic themes, composed of subjects of pagan origin, rethought or not according to Christian symbolism, or moving little by little towards a secular plane, had been abandoned. But one of these tendencies was perpetuated through the amalgamation of Christian subjects with a principal subject of pagan origin. An example of this would be one of the frequent representations of a nude female dancer holding above her head a cross encircled with a crown. Another tendency, linked with that already existing in the period of Coptic art, and which became accentuated under the Moslem domination, consisted in isolating some detail or other from a theme. But as its meaning, even when Christianized, was gradually forgotten, the principal subject came to lose even its external form whereby it was immediately recognizable. Thus these themes of pagan origin – principal subject or details: Dionysian personages, dancing-girls,

nereids, shells, amorini etc. – persisted until at least the twelfth century. Such artistic continuity is a frequent phenomenon, and one exemplified by many of our present-day decorative motifs – derived from Renaissance models, themselves inspired by the antique. It could only mislead the least observant, and demonstrates the specious character of datings based solely on the themes represented.[21] Having passed into secular art in this way, these themes of pagan origin could with equal facility absorb those which the Moslem *ambiance* had to offer. These, as we know, are most frequently decorative ones. Under this aspect, which could not conflict in any way with the Christian spirit, they found their way quite naturally into the vein of Coptic decoration. For their assimilation, slight retouchings sufficed, and even these were not always necessary. In this connection, moreover, it must not be forgotten that the Copts, through their decorative themes, influenced Moslem art, and even that, during certain periods, art in Egypt was Copto-Moslem art. Among those themes taken or taken over by the Copts from the art brought in by the Moslems must be included the octolobate rosette, geometrical designs and, in general, the arabesque.

In the 'art of the Copts' therefore, we are faced with a very great wealth of themes; it now remains for us to see what use they made of them.

The decorative elements in use during this long period are numerous in most of those fields in which the Copts had already worked. They are centred upon a phenomenon which, as we have seen, did not run counter to the Coptic imperatives, but was liberated only as a result of particular circumstances. The blurring of lines in the subject is added to the liberties which had for long been taken with natural proportions in order to bring out more clearly the symbolic content. The process was rendered almost ineluctable through the canalization of Coptic art in the direction of pure decoration, as a result of the limitations imposed upon their architecture and figurative art. In the course of this period their ornamentation underwent an evolution, as a result of which the importance of the subject was progressively reduced. At the same time it remained linked to the normal development of Moslem art in Egypt, in which pure decoration plays an equally

2. Style

FIG. 64 – *Trellis-work design. Tooled and inlaid leather band. Ninth century. Cairo, Arab Museum.*

important role. The relationship was not one of dependence but of interdependence. The Copts, in conjunction with other peoples, provided Islam with motifs or workmanship, and for their part borrowed themes from Islam which their own art was still vigorous enough to assimilate. Coptic art, by its origins and its characteristics, was, in effect, no stranger to the return to naturalism – in such complexity as to become rather monotonous – which marked the Omayyad period, or to the marshalling of large masses so dear to the Tulunids, or again to the outburst of vivacity and intricacy which took place under the Fatimids. Each time the new orientation passed, without friction, into the mainstream of Coptic art.

If, during the period of the 'art of the Copts', there were changes of orientation, there was no break with Coptic art. While submitting to this constraint, Coptic artists continued to produce works in all the techniques they had forged, giving free rein to every fantasy which appealed to their imagination, and had no hesi-

FIG. 65 – *Monks ranged side by side. Mural painting. Bawit. Eighth century.*

FIG. 66 – *Parrots. Tapestry. Eighth century. 65 × 57 cm. Paris, Louvre, Christian Antiquities.*

tation in assimilating any motifs from Moslem art which appealed to them. So that it is purely for the sake of a historical framework, to obtain fixed points for purposes of comparison, that we shall have recourse here, for the classification of Coptic productions, to the broad divisions of Moslem history in Egypt.

Thus the logic proper to Coptic art continued to operate under the new conditions imposed upon it.

Contrary to what one sometimes hears said, Islam was not inimical towards the image, only towards its use in holy places.[22] In Omayyad palaces the human figure is frequently found in hunting or garden scenes. Without being favoured, we can be sure that it was tolerated in Coptic monuments. The fact is, however, that in these latter it became frozen and lifeless, while yet regaining a certain elegance. In sculpture, while the high relief may be said to have survived, modelling has disappeared, and these high reliefs have become the vehicle for a uniformly flattened decoration, to the extent that, apart from the design, nothing remains but the contrast of two levels, these being a more or less short distance apart. This can be seen in an archivolt, of unknown origin, exhibited in the Louvre, of which we made use in our imaginary exhibition.[23] The angel-musicians placed in the centre of the curve stand out in high relief against the rest of the decoration of the arcature, consisting of undulating stems, in very slight and flattened relief, but gripped by a mechanical movement foreshadowing that which is to be found again on ceramics from Nishapur in Persia, in the ninth century.

Elegance reappears in the stem of a patera, which, in one bronze piece in the Cairo Museum, and another which corresponds to it in the Louvre,[24] is in the form of a nude dancing-girl, holding over her head a highly composite cross. The follower in a Bacchic procession has thus been baptized, without a thought being given on that account to veiling her nudity. But if the body still retains a certain svelte quality, the legs have lost all their suppleness. While retaining a certain degree of modelling, they are crossed like a pair of rigid sticks. The 'frozen' look anticipates the extremes of stylization of the of the Tulunid period.

Omayyad period (658–750)

FIG. 67 – *Coptic floral design. Tapestry. Eighth century. 36.2 × 4.5 cm. Paris, Louvre, Christian Antiquities.*

FIG. 68 – *Moslem floral design. Mosaic. Jerusalem, Dome of the Rock. Eighth century.*

FIG. 69 – *Capital of pilaster. Limestone. Bawit. Eighth century. Height 56 cm, width 35 cm. Paris, Louvre, Christian Antiquities.*

In painting we see the same evolution which, on the Bawit site alone, runs through a whole group of paintings dedicated to David's youth. These once decorated one of the chapels;[25] photographs and reconstructions of them have been preserved, mainly of those which decorated the numerous other devotional chapels on the same site.

With the cycle of the youth of David, we are at the end of the seventh century, if not in the eighth. Here, in painting, narrative art seems to be stirring itself, though very tentatively, in that the scenes, instead of succeeding one another on one or more registers, are isolated from each other on self-contained panels. These portrayed, successively, Samuel's visit to Jesse, father of David; Samuel choosing David; the presentation of the young David to Saul; David playing the lyre while Saul threatens him with a spear; Saul encouraging David who, dressed in the king's armour, is going into battle; David, less heavily garbed, fighting Goliath; David's victory over Goliath; perhaps David's interview with the priest Abimelech; three paintings now destroyed; finally Jonathan warning David of his father's designs against his friend. Certain details date this ensemble. Among others, these are: the small pointed beard and drooping moustaches characteristic of the Arabs, here given to Goliath and to the spectators grouped in the upper corners of the picture; the Byzantine armour worn by Saul and David; the Persian costume worn by Goliath – a reference to the acts of destruction perpetrated by the Persians at the beginning of the sixth century, which doubtless became symbolic of the Copts' enemies – and, to separate the scenes, a decoration consisting of flowered trellis-work. The latter, though doubtless already extant in the Antioch mosaics of the fifth century, should in this case be compared with the same

FIG. 70 – *Pilaster with ornament of interlacing stems. Limestone. Bawit. Eighth century. 88 × 15 cm. Paris, Louvre, Christian Antiquities.*

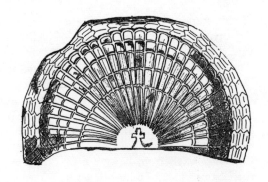

FIG. 71 – *Plant motif on ivory. Ivory relief. Eighth century. 8 × 3.5 cm. Paris, Louvre, Christian Antiquities.*

FIG. 72 – *Shell motif. Limestone. Eighth century. 65 × 100 cm. Old Cairo, Coptic Museum.*

decorative motif in the Omayyad pavilion of Qasr Amra[26] to the east of Amman in Jordan, or on wood-carvings encrusted with ivory,[27] dating from this time; finally, there is the use of the sunken panel as a framework for these paintings, comparable to that found at Khirbat el-Mafjar.[28]   FIG. 64   FIG. 63

The already extremely restrained movement to be found in these panels freezes up completely in most of the other Bawit chapels, which feature a row of holy monks standing side by side[29] or a subject used earlier, the Ascension of Christ above Mary flanked by the Apostles.[30] The bodies have regained a certain elegance in comparison with previous paintings, in which they were rather squat, and the faces are slightly elongated. In all these respects they have something in common with Byzantine mosaics, but the hieratic – or, more precisely – congealed aspect is even more marked, and the features are more simplified, while the general aspect of the drawing and of the colour endows these paintings with a tender quality which hardly exists in the Byzantine prototypes.   FIG. 65

This particular aspect is also found in textiles, as we have already noted with reference to the large, loop-woven wall-hanging in the Abegg-Stiftung. But in the decorative portraits executed in this technique and in ceramics the eyes become very square. Some of these figures are still surrounded by Nilotic landscapes,[31] while the dancers[32] become petrified, like the dancing-girl forming the handle of the patera mentioned above.   PLATE P. 55   FIG. 62

Furthermore, a complete décor, of rare colouristic quality, unfolds in the Bawit paintings[33] as also in the tapestries[34] – a quality which is to be found in Omayyad buildings as well. One thinks here of the parrots, either scattered about or in pairs facing each other, of the boxed leaves, such as we find in the Dome of the Rock in Jerusalem, or again of the decoration consisting of rows of open flowers or leaves, with, in the intermediate spaces, halves of these same leaves or flowers, placed opposite each other.[35]   FIG. 66   FIG. 68   FIG. 67

FIG. 69

PLATE P. 23

FIG. 70

FIG. 71

FIG. 72

FIG. 73

Architectural ornament, for its part, followed the evolution initiated in the seventh century. At Bawit, in the capitals of pilasters, one is struck by the rising of the caulicole.[36]

The basket capitals at Bawit, as at Saqqara, display their still fully robust exuberance in a movement which is consciously controlled. Among others of the same quality two capitals from Bawit, preserved in the Louvre and mentioned in the context of our imaginary exhibition, are both prime examples; the one as much for the effect of relief obtained as the other for its extreme stylization, amounting to a mechanical serration.

Certain pilasters from Bawit[37] exhibited in the Louvre call for comparison with the last-mentioned capital. In a vertical panel, two stems springing from a vase at the base interlace repeatedly as they are produced upwards, as in the case of a similar pilaster from Bawit, surmounted by the form of an angel, mentioned above. But a very rigid stylization is in force: the stems touch the border at regular intervals, encircling a vine-leaf, no longer – as in nature – one of five folioles, but here of seven and, moreover, deprived of the bunches of grapes which would have accorded with either a Dionysian or a Christian symbol, and thus passing into the sphere of pure decoration.

This monotony in the interlacing should be compared with a similar decoration on box-panels, carved on wood, bone or ivory. These have been justly compared[38] with an Omayyad carved panel from the mosque of El Aqsa in Jerusalem, presenting the same motif in the same style. Here it is difficult to decide in which direction the influence operated, but it would not be surprising if the influence had been that of the Copts on the Moslems, and not, as has been suggested, in the other direction. We need only consider the number and the variety of the supports; the continuity and evolution of the motif in Coptic art; or what is known regarding the participation of Coptic workers in the decoration of Moslem buildings, particularly at this time.

This rigidity affected, even more markedly, the numerous shell forms, originating from various sites and now preserved in the Coptic Museum in Cairo. The cells are laid out one beside the other, in lines straight from start to finish, with no reference whatever to the flexibility of nature and resembling rather shafts radiating from a hub, widening as they go.[39]

In this connection certain friezes from Bawit are worth attention. A complete evolution of the foliated scroll in the direction of pure decoration is noticeable in them. From the scroll hangs a fruit, sometimes double, which occupies the

FIG. 73 – *Foliated scroll with fruit. Limestone. Bawit, south church. Paris, Louvre, Christian Antiquities.*

FIG. 74 – *Scroll with swirling foliage. Limestone. Bawit, south church. Paris, Louvre, Christian Antiquities.*

centre. But from one frieze to the other one may follow the process whereby the fruit loses its natural appearance and, whether enclosed in a circle, replaced by a cross in a circle, or reduced to its simplest expression, no longer forms the termination of the branches and becomes the central point from which these latter spring, and then swirl around them.[40]

FIG. 74

These details have their importance, but they should not cause us to overlook a certain Omayyad exuberance, as witness the decoration of Mshatta.[41] This quite naturally invites comparison with the Red Monastery at Sohag,[42] and is a reminder that Mshatta had seen something of Coptic artisans.[43]

It would seem, to judge from their relative elegance – elegance which does not exclude a certain heaviness – that we should allocate to this period sundry candlesticks and bronze lamps. Some of the candlesticks rise to a considerable height, with a bulge or boss in the middle, from a splayed base resting on feet in the form of animals' paws.[44] The lamps, which assume various forms, including that of a dove with a lid on its back, common throughout the Mediterranean, are usually mounted on these candlesticks.

FIG. 75

Thus, in the Omayyad period, a slowing down of that evolution tending towards the rejection of natural proportions is noticeable. The Omayyad elegance may have been responsible for this, but without the Copts' orientation towards the purely decorative being lost in consequence. There was in fact a parallelism between the two arts, amounting almost to a pact for the acceptance of a quasi-mechanical monotony, particularly in respect of purely decorative motifs.

The evolution of Coptic art, in conformity with its governing imperatives, appears to have slowed down, without however coming to a halt, during the Omayyad period. Under the Tulunids, on the contrary, the movement recommenced. There seems to have existed, at several points, a complete accord between the two concepts of art.

Abbasid period (after 750); Tulunid period in Egypt (868–905)

It was from Samarra, the new Abbasid capital, situated above Baghdad on the banks of the Tigris, that in 836 Ibn Tulun was sent out as governor to Egypt. In the architectural monuments for which he was responsible numerous links with the art of Samarra have been noted. As an example one may cite the eight-lobed rosettes, enclosed in regular octagons, on the façade of the mosque of Ibn Tulun in Cairo.[45]

FIG. 76

The Copts themselves seem to have borrowed much from this art. There can be no doubt that Ibn Tulun's tolerance and the use he made of their talents could have acted as a stimulus. But the natural bent of their artistic concept must have contributed no less to this.

An illustration of this tendency appears in the monastery of Wadi en-Natrun, on the windows and doors of the haïkal at Deir Abu Maqar and, at Deir es-Suryani, on those of the church of El-Adra. They are ornamented, on stucco, with palmettes which, with their flat, clearly defined and considerably widened surfaces, look as though they were hacked out. Completely similar motifs, equally on stucco, are found at Samarra, notably in the Jausaq el-Khaqani, which date from 830.[46]

APPX. PL. 18
FIG. 77

On closer inspection the similarities multiply. At Bawit, on friezes now to be seen in the Louvre, foliated scrolls have been stylized to the appearance of groups of interlocking laurel leaves;[47] they are astonishingly reminiscent of the interlocked horns in an ornament from Samarra.[48] In other friezes from Bawit, also in the Louvre, the stems of interlaced foliated scrolls are embellished with a line of bead ornament,[49] of which examples abound in Coptic woodwork, such as one finds in quantity at Samarra.[50] Later on, in tapestry,[51] which was doubtless beginning to be introduced at this time, we shall find those eight-lobed rosettes enclosed in geometric octagons such as decorate the façade of the mosque of Ibn Tulun in Cairo, and which are already predominant at Samarra. In which direction is the influence operating?

FIG. 78

FIG. 79

Moslem tapestry, which, incidentally, flourished at this time, exhibits motifs and a style frequently indistinguishable from those found in Coptic tapestry. Portraits, dancing-girls, foliated scrolls and birds are woven into both alike, using a coarse thread and, in particular, a design in broad areas dominated by the colour yellow, which leaves us in no doubt regarding the dating.[52]

Should one conclude that Coptic art at this time had become a Christian art under Moslem influence? Yet we have often pointed out the intrinsically Coptic tendency to compose in terms of the equilibrium of masses, whether through the contrast of two levels, or of surface areas in relief or of colours, each mass defined by its common boundary with the others. Samarra or, more probably, Tulunid art, offered them a number of motifs the style of which tended in the same direction. In absorbing them, Coptic art had nothing to lose, particularly since it was quick to incorporate them in larger ensembles, which were specifically their own. In Moslem tapestry the nature of the themes is such that, in many cases, their source in Coptic art is evident. When one knows that the Copts were the weavers of that time,[53] it is reasonable to suppose that the influence, in this case, flowed from the Copts and not from the Moslems. Finally, apart from the themes – and we have, in any case, seen the extent to which these were used in common – it seems that apart from obvious copies it will always remain difficult in this period, to disentangle what belongs to the Copts and what to the Moslems.

Moreover, in those works of this period which, either because of their origin or of the use for which they were intended, can only be Coptic, the style follows on that of the preceding period while accentuating its characteristic tendencies. Certain features in stone- or ivory-carving will suffice to illustrate this.

We have seen, at an earlier period, dancing-girls whose legs are like a pair of diagonally crossed sticks, but which still retain some slight modelling. In a limestone relief in the Coptic Museum in Cairo,[51] a nude bacchante, provided with castanets, her over-large head crowned with a rounded mass of hair and wearing

FIG. 62

FIG. 80

FIG. 77 – *Reliefs on stucco. Stucco. North of Baghdad. Ninth century.*

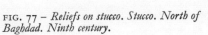

ear-rings, exhibits a much-shrunken torso and legs which, though less rigidly crossed, no longer possess even the shape of human limbs. Without going to this extreme, a small limestone panel in the Berlin Museum, originally from the White Monastery at Sohag, bears a relief of Christ, in the pose of the Parthian horseman,[55] mounted on an ass, between two standing angels. This is a clear case of the fusion of two themes, one of them pagan. However, in addition to the general flatness of the relief and the simplified and stereotyped facial features, the folds of the drapery, falling like organ-pipes, clearly invite comparison with those found in a Virgin Enthroned from an illuminated manuscript in the Pierpont Morgan Library in New York[56] and dated from the ninth century. From the aesthetic point of view this group is disappointing and explains the contempt often expressed for Coptic productions of this kind. But this contempt is misplaced and will, in any case, disappear completely when one examines the 'Virgin of tenderness', a sculptured relief on ivory, in the Walters Art Gallery in Baltimore, which was mentioned in the context of our imaginary exhibition.

The tendency reaches its climax, however, in the limestone panels in the Brooklyn Museum which treat, in relief, respectively the martyrdom of St. Thecla and St. Sisinnius.[57] In the first, which figured in our imaginary exhibition, as in the second, the flattening is complete, but the areas surrounding the bodies, plants or flames, and the lines expressing the details are gouged out, as in a woodcut, leaving the eye no point of repose within the frame; this has the effect, through juxtaposition and the difference of levels, of throwing the subjects into relief.

In plant ornament there is doubtless a relationship between the style found at Nishapur in Persia, which is of the ninth century,[58] and Coptic scroll work, for in both a mechanical movement is imposed on the undulating stems and their accompanying leaves. This is a by no means negligible aid in dating numerous Coptic reliefs on stone or wood.[59] So far as bronze work is concerned, it applies to a brazier in the Louvre, the lid of which is in the form of a dome surmounted by an eagle holding a snake in its beak, while the body is made up of a tangle of stems.[60]

PLATE P. 153

PLATE P. 44

APPX. PL. 12

PLATE P. 154

Baptism of Christ. Manuscript illumination. From a Copto-Arabic Book of Gospels. Thirteenth century. Paris, Institut Catholique. Photo: A. Held.

St. George and the dragon. Embroidery on fabric. Middle Ages. Height 155 cm., width
250 cm. Paris, Louvre, Christian Antiquities. Photo: Bulloz.

FIG. 79 – *Beaded ornament. Limestone. Bawit, south church. Sixth-ninth century. Paris, Louvre, Christian Antiquities.*

In tapestry, although only sporadic use continues to be made of the flying shuttle, it is not altogether abandoned. It no longer serves, in any case, for more than combinations of decorative lines, and has ceased altogether to delimit objects or to define limbs.[61] All now proceeds from the simple contrast of one coloured area with another. This holds good whatever may be the motifs: repeats of flower-buds, open flower alternating with two inverted halves of the same flower etc. Human figuration largely falls out of favour. The portrait, however, subsists. One of those belonging to the Detroit Institute of Art is typical of the style common to both Coptic and Moslem tapestry of the period.[62] Here, in an oval medallion, the space below which is filled by two stylized flowers, is the bust, in three-quarter view, of a bearded man holding a book. Not only is there a complete absence of realism combined with flat colours, but the features themselves result from the ordering of broad areas of colour. Slightly different in style, but not lacking in flavour, are a few examples of female portraits from the Louvre collection, of which we took note in our imaginary exhibition. The portrait is set off against a ground scattered with lozenges, and is enclosed in a broad and colourful rectangular frame. The body is stiff, clothed in a monochrome bodice ornamented with simulated precious stones, the outer edges of which are accentuated. Under a heavy head of black hair which encompasses it on three sides, the face is drawn out to a long rectangle; the nose and eyes are rendered schematically, and resemble a lorgnette, the handle of which is attached to the bridge connecting the two lens-frames. This elongation of the face and the features remains mechanical, but, quite apart from the accentuation of certain lines, is curiously modern.

PLATE P. 159

PLATE P. 65

Under the Tulunids, the most independent of the caliphs, Egypt's links with Constantinople were revived. It is extremely probable that these links had something to do with the style and quality of the paintings which decorate the apses in the El-Adra church at Deir es-Suryani in the Wadi en-Natrun, rebuilt in the ninth century. These consist, notably, of an Annunciation, a Nativity and an Assumption.[63] They can scarcely be credited to the account of Coptic art.
The same cannot be said of numerous tapestries featuring figures in long robes falling in folds and, it should be added, equally often others wearing wide baggy trousers after the Arab fashion.[64] But the folds often fall like organ-pipes, adhering to the treatment we have just been discussing, and have nothing in common with the skilful folds of draperies in Byzantine mosaics.

FIG. 81

Under Tulunid domination a new stage had thus been reached in Coptic art. No doubt, in some respects it represented a decline; yet this decline was marked by accomplishments on the part of the more gifted craftsmen, whose style enabled them to create the most delightful effects.

Fatimid period (967–1171)

The Fatimid period was a great era of culture in Moslem Egypt. The Fatimids, who belonged to the Shi'ite sect, of Persian origin, were disposed to favour works of a more naturalistic character. More tolerant in religious matters, and anxious to mobilize the entire forces of the nation in the service of a prosperity in which they themselves were interested, they made full use of the Copts – with some exceptions, for example under al-Hakim – for the tasks of administration and for the realization of artistic projects: tasks for which they found the Copts better equipped than anyone else.

One is also made aware, during this period in Coptic art, of dual tendencies. The first adapts itself to the views of the rulers, for whom the decoration of mosques and secular buildings is carried out. It does not differ from the official art, and may therefore be termed Copto-Moslem – so difficult is it to distinguish the Coptic contribution from the Moslem contribution. Refined and elegant, this manner

FIG. 81 – *Standing figure. Tapestry. Ninth century.* 10 × 7 *cm. Paris, Louvre, Christian Antiquities.*

FIG. 82 – *Portrait of Christ. Fragment of lustre pottery. Tenth century. Cairo, Arab Museum.*

will be found in the decoration of objects of small size, often with an exuberance of plant ornament: an exuberance, however, which retains a slightly mechanical look about it. The second tendency, while still permitting of an occasional influence from the first, marks one stage further in the evolution of Coptic art, and by this very fact allows of decorative subjects more in keeping with the style based on the ordering of broad masses. The first tendency, which is naturalistic, permits, even in Moslem art, the presence of human figures, which we thus find as isolated individuals or in groups, or else intermingled with plant-form decoration. Here the *horror vacui* principle manifests itself, so that the entire space delimited by the frame is filled in, either by an entanglement of lines of by compact masses. It is this fact, it is worth emphasizing, rather than the imposition of a sinuous curvature on the line, which is the true definition of the arabesque. It is readily identifiable in numerous wood panels, now in the Arab Museum in Cairo, which once formed part of the decoration of Fatimid palaces, or in decorative elements originally from the tomb of Salih Ayyub preserved in the Victoria and Albert Museum, London, or from the *minbar* of the Es-Salih mosque in Cairo.[65]

Decoration similar in every respect, but which may additionally – rare as this may be – include the presence of the Cross, is scattered throughout Coptic architectural monuments of the period. Some have thought to see in this a case of Moslem artisans working for the benefit of the Copts. The hypothesis cannot be taken seriously in relation to a country under Moslem domination, in which Christians might very well have been employed by the Moslems but the reverse is inconceivable, as much from the religious as from the social point of view. Wooden doors – among many other surviving elements – bear this sort of decoration. One of these commanded the entrance to the chapel of Mari Girgis in the church of St. Barbara, and others the entrance to the church of Abu-'s-Sifain, both in Old Cairo.[66] In both of these examples we find panels ornamented with foliated scrolls, 'inhabited' or delicately interlaced, with birds or ibexes; often prominence is given to a Greek cross. In the first case, certain panels bring together a group of personages which the condition of the panels, unfortunately,

APPX. PL. 22
APPX. PL. 21

FIG. 83 – *Portrait of a monk. Wood. Abu-
's-Sifain, chapel of St. John the Baptist. Tenth-
eleventh century. 14 × 11 cm. Cairo.*

does not enable us to identify; in the other we find monks or individual priests. The workmanship here is throughout as delicate as that found in specimens of Moslem art; here, in the same manner, every void is filled, and the figures, particularly in the first example, are treated as silhouettes rather than as undercut sculpture.

FIG. 82   Many other examples of Copto-Moslem art could be cited in the working of wood, as well as in other techniques. A case in point is the portrait of Christ on a fragment of pottery,[67] doubtless originating from Fostat and preserved in the Arab Museum in Cairo: the head and shoulders of Christ are in the Byzantine pose, but the eyes are distorted in the Coptic manner, while the stylization of the plant-stems which form the decorative setting seems rather to reflect Moslem influence. In glass, the bowl of a painted goblet belonging to the Louvre[68] is divided into a network pattern (réseaux), harking back to an earlier motif, but within these we find birds, simplified in a way reminiscent of that of ninth-century Moslem ceramics and Fatimid textiles.[69] The technique characteristic of the period consists of an application of painting to the interior and exterior surfaces prior to the final firing.

The second trend continues the Coptic tradition of decoration by means of large masses. En route it assimilates any related features of the Fatimid style, in particular the arabesque as we have defined it.

FIG. 83   In this way, on the portal of the church of Abu-'s-Sifain in Old Cairo, certain of the panels bear isolated figures of monks or saints.[70] The schematic rendering of features and proportions is not foreign to the Fatimid style, which we have already defined as Copto-Arab, but it is combined here with a weightiness more Coptic than Arab.

A fragment of painted glass, exhibited in the Louvre,[71] is no less typical. On it is painted a horseman in the same technique described with reference to the goblet *à réseaux*; the head and fragments of the lance, of the shawl and of the horse beneath its trappings, are all that remain. The facial features and the curly hair are related to those in a tapestry of the same period belonging to the Louvre.[72]

This trend finds a very wide field of expression in tapestry. The Coptic origin of numerous pieces which may be cited in this connection is beyond doubt. Most, if not all, have been found in Coptic tombs. Furthermore, they frequently bear the symbol of the Cross, not only as a decorative motif – which would allow an element of doubt to persist – but in a religious context, without, however, the question of liturgical vestments arising. The statement made by Nasiri Khusrau, an eleventh-century Persian traveller, to the effect that the craft of weaving was always the prerogative of the Copts in Egypt,[73] must not, in any case, be overlooked. This is another case of Copto-Moslem art, with an infusion of Byzantine style, but in which the element of Coptic style predominates. It displays, either together or separately, the following characteristics: a certain pliancy in geometric forms; use of the arabesque; and progressive distortion of the human figure, which follows the evolutionary line of the Coptic style. Contrary to what took place in Fatimid art – and this again is a Coptic hallmark – the themes favoured up to this time in Coptic tapestry, particularly motifs of Hellenistic origin, remained constant, although they became more and more deformed until they were barely identifiable.[74] The ground-colours might be either a washed-out violet or, using a dye extracted from an East Indian aphis imported by the Arabs, a deep red.[75] The *décor à réseaux*, elaborated in the tenth century, when the dividing

FIG. 84 – *Decorative design of flowers in réseaux. Tapestry. Tenth century. 50 × 13 cm. Paris, Louvre, Christian Antiquities.*

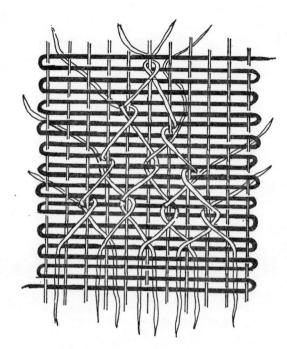

FIG. 84

PLATE P. 66

PLATE P. 160

lines were themselves transformed into 'inhabited' rectangles while retaining the same arrangement, combines with that in which a single open flower alternates with a pair of half-flowers cut by the border on either side of the design. One decorative motif complacently repeats octagons, each housing an octolobate leaf, with a Greek, Coptic or bifid cross in the centre, while the interval on the borders which separates the octagons is occupied by a triangle. This seems originally to have been imported into Egypt by the Tulunids, but its presence, with the same stylization, is confirmed in a Hispano-Moorish fabric of the twelfth century, preserved in the Arab Museum in Cairo. The bands, on which the motif is repeated in this way, frequently terminate in a line of boxed rectangles, framing distorted female dancers with heavy heads of curly hair falling to the waist, the latter being very short; the limbs are either separated from the body or, on the contrary, fall absolutely straight like the continuation of a rectangle; the whole design is expressed in a great variety and richness of colour. These dancers were preceded, in Coptic tapestries of the tenth and eleventh centuries, by others suffering apparent dislocation of the hip or looking like a child's 'tumbler' toy – a Humpty-Dumpty, identifiable by a big green and red necklace, or again, in the arabesque manner, filling the enclosing frame with large geometric masses.[77] During this same period analogous distortions affected the appearance of motifs surviving from Alexandrian art: nereids on sea-beasts, Parthian horsemen or hunters, Cupid holding a bird – but which came, in the process, to fuse with one another to the extent where they were recognizable only with difficulty.[78]

Weaving readily returned to the use of the flying shuttle, applying it, however, FIG. 85 to new purposes. Its most constant use was in outlining, – against the ground-colour, often red-violet – one after the other, the octagons and octolobate flowers discussed above, as well as the features of the dancers. Its use might be extended to the point of covering the ground inside the geometric figures with a very close nap of uncut loops. Original effects were obtained by crossovers with double flying shuttles, or even through the flight of four or more shuttles, the skilful compilation of these threads producing geometric-shaped voids on the coloured APPX. PL. 8 ground.[79]

Thus, alongside the elegance of stems and plants accompanied by a complexity of motifs reminiscent of fretted woodwork, we often find a bold separation of the elements in the motifs and a quite unconcerned filling-up of the frame in the arabesque manner, to the point where the subject becomes no more than a pretext for the balancing of colour-masses, or even for obtaining the effect of relief.

It is notable that wood sculpture and tapestry are the two techniques in which we can observe, still in great force, the main drives in Coptic art. In architecture, as we have seen, there was no revival, but the essentials of the craft were not lost, and could still find expression in monasteries, such as that of St. Simeon at Aswan, or in churches, such as that of Abu-'s-Sifain in Old Cairo. The Copts were still well able to assimilate borrowed ornament, as in the church of El-Adra at Deir es-Suryani in the Wadi en-Natrun.

In some of the other techniques, however, the Copts' artistic drive was clearly running out of energy. This we have seen, in the ninth century, in respect of the paintings in the church of El-Adra at Deir es-Suryani in the Wadi en-Natrun.

FIG. 86 – *Ascension. Carved wood. Thirteenth century.*
London, British Museum.

By contrast, in the field of manuscript illumination, even when appertaining to scenes from the New Testament, as in a twelfth-century Book of the Gospels in the Bibliothèque Nationale[80] and in another of the thirteenth century,[81] belonging to the Institut Catholique de Paris, the characteristics, like the costumes and settings, are almost entirely those of Moslem art.

PLATE P. 177

From this time forward, although work might still be carried out by Copts, there was to be no Coptic style in the true sense. Artistic production, necessary to the building and ornamentation of churches and monasteries, would still continue, but, now that the Copts lacked the strength to raise themselves out of their extreme poverty, these would be the work of mere casual labourers, devoid of any real craftsmanship or inspiration. In the thirteenth century Coptic art breathed its last.

SPREAD
AND
SURVIVAL
OF COPTIC
ART
Egypt

Before concluding, it remains for us to consider to what extent Coptic art, in common with other established arts, has survived and spread.

We need not look too far afield for continuations of Coptic art in the true sense of the term. On the banks of the Nile, a sort of Christian *koine* instals itself, in which the characteristics of this art are scarcely any longer to be found. The basilica remains the fundamental architectural programme, but in its simplest form and without any rethinking having taken place. Painting – the art of the poor – is almost exclusively the technique relied on; remains of it from the sixteenth and seventeenth centuries survive in the Wadi en-Natrun, in the monas-

St. Theodore Stratelates. Wall-painting. Church of St. Anthony-in-the-Desert. Thirteenth century. Photo: P. du Bourguet.

Page 188: Interior, Church of St. Sergius. Old Cairo. Photo: A. Held.

Church of Bieta Gheorgis, Lalibela (Ethiopia). Eleventh century. Photo: P. du Bourguet.

Page 189: St. Michael. Wall-painting. Faras. Eleventh century. Height 171 cm, length 199 cm. Khartoum, State Museum.

teries of St. Anthony and St. Paul, or in icons.[82] It borrows from all quarters, PLATE P. 187
notably from Byzantine and Armenian models, and is no longer, properly speaking,
anything more than the work of needy artisans. The same may be said of the
embroidered materials – liturgical vestments or decorative church hangings PLATE P. 178
– preserved in the Louvre,[83] or in the museums of Mainz[84] or Ann Arbor.
Parallel with this all-purpose style, another style, strongly influenced by the
Moslem milieu, was gaining ground. We find it in the wood panels of the Kevor-
kian Collection in New York representing, in relief, the Sacrifice of Isaac and,
in the British Museum, in those from the church of Sitt Mariam in which are FIG. 86
grouped several episodes from the life of Christ;[85] in bronze objects, particularly
perfume-burners;[86] in a number of icons from the seventeenth and eighteenth
centuries;[87] above all in illuminated books of the Gospels belonging respectively PLATE P. 177
to the Bibliothèque Nationale and to the Institut Catholique in Paris.[88]
Although situated immediately to the south of Egypt, Nubia was practically *Nubia*
untouched by Coptic influence. Evangelized, not by the Copts, but by the Byzantines, it only established relations with the Coptic community at a very late date,
when its own productions, notably the strange and beautiful paintings of Faras,[89] PLATE P. 189
Abu Simbel,[90] and Wadi es-Sebua were already in a markedly localized Byzantine
style.
In Ethiopia, and then only in certain of the rock-cut churches of Lalibela,[91] the *Ethiopia*
exterior form of which remains peculiar to the area, the painted decoration and PLATE P. 190
certain reliefs appear to be influenced by Coptic art of the Fatimid period. Here FIG. 87
again, despite the liturgical links and the veneration of Coptic saints, the art is
typically local in style.
Neither, despite tenacious beliefs to the contrary, does the West bear any marks *The West*
of it. The abstract nature of Merovingian or Irish art is not a hallmark of Coptic
influence. Neither the angular appearance of these two styles, nor the subjects,
the source of which is much more likely to be found in the Orient, are in any way
reminiscent of Coptic art. History, even in Ireland, and despite the establishment
of monasticism there, has not preserved a single trace of Coptic influence. One
Coptic theme alone – that of Christ in Glory supported by the four Evangelists and
placed above the Virgin surrounded by the Apostles – seems to have found its
way to the West: for example, from Bawit to la-Ferté-sous-Jouarre,[92] where it is
carved on a sarcophagus and, in painting, to Lavaudieu in the Auvergne, to Char- APPX. PL. 20
lieu in Burgundy and to Moncherrand in the Swiss Jura. The route may have lain
through the canal in Omayyad Spain on which Coptic artists are said to have been
employed.[93]
As it would appear from this last example, and as we know from any number of *Moslem art*
Moslem monuments, from Mshatta and the Dome of the Rock of Jerusalem to
Samarra, Coptic influence did indeed spread as a result of the efforts of artists and
artisans working for Moslem masters. It is here that we may find Coptic art,
which influenced that of the Fatimids as much as it in turn was influenced by the
latter.

**CONCLU-
SION**

For an art of a popular nature to survive ten centuries of foreign domination is a very rare, if not a unique, phenomenon.

Inspiration

Coptic art owes this long existence to a combination of circumstances which never became wholly unfavourable – except during its phase of decline – and particularly to the modest but continuing financial competence of the Coptic lower middle class and of an extensive monastic community. It owed its persistence no less to a force of inspiration in which one is tempted to see, subject to the variations dictated by circumstance, certain imperatives, originating perhaps in the distant pharaonic past; their successors served, albeit unconsciously, as a vehicle through which those imperatives could continue to exert a guiding influence.

Homogeneity

The fact is that Coptic art, in the period of its full flowering, displays traits of remarkable homogeneity. In this it stands apart from all the other arts of its time. These traits only manifested themselves gradually but, in this very progression, this struggle ending in victory, which one can hardly observe unmoved, Coptic art replaced, even while carrying on its traditional themes, the Graeco-Roman art which had possessed the field before it.

Once in full possession of its style and its professional skills, Coptic art might have risen to the level of a very great art, armed as it was with a vision of reality astonishingly well attuned to Christian symbolism. The Moslem conquest interposed an impassable barrier to this legitimate ambition. Far from withdrawing into itself, Coptic art directed its energies into the only channel which, among the range of possibilities proper to it, remained open: that of decoration.

Fantasy

Without ceasing to participate in the Moslem art of Egypt, it brought to bear in its works a fantasy that has perhaps no equal. It fell victim to its own enchantment, at the expense of subject-matter, and in this respect proclaimed allegiance to that quality which distinguishes the most successful examples of modern art.

N.B.1 – Full details of publications cited here will be found in the bibliography.

2 – Principal abbreviations:
B.S.A.C.: *Bulletin de la Société d'Archéologie Copte* (Cairo)
B.I.F.A.O.: *Bulletin de l'Institut Français d'Archéologie Orientale* (Cairo).

3 – Objects which have figured in the Essen exhibition (Villa Hügel, 1963) and the Paris exhibition (Petit Palais, 1964) will be indicated respectively by the words Essen and Petit Palais with the relevant numbers.
The catalogues of these exhibitions are mentioned in the bibliography. We shall not, therefore, reproduce here the bibliography relevant to these objects except, occasionally, the most important study.

I. HISTORY AND DISCOVERY

[1] G. Lefebvre, *Grammaire de l'Égyptien classique*, Cairo, Institut Français d'Archéologie Orientale, 2nd ed., 1955, p. 6, no. 3.
[2] G. Wiet, *Précis*, II, p. 268.
[3] F. W. Gravit, 'Peiresc et les études coptes en France au XVIIe siècle', *B.S.A.C.*, IV, pp. 1–22.
[4] P. du Bourguet, 'L'Apport des Coptes au patrimoine universel', *Mémorial du cinquantenaire 1914–1964* (École des langues orientales anciennes de l'Institut Catholique de Paris), Paris, Bloud et Gay, 1964, pp. 147–57.
[5] K. Wessel, *Kunst der Kopten* (Sammlung des Ikonenmuseums Recklinghausen), Aurel Bongers, 1962, p. 16. One must admit that the author has remained logical to the end, since his book *Koptische Kunst* (Eng. ed. *Coptic Art*, London, Thames & Hudson, 1965), which claims by its title to cover the whole of Coptic art, makes not the slightest allusion to the architecture of the Coptic monasteries and churches, although these are evident enough to tourists to this day, and sufficiently well known to scholars through specialized bibliographies.
[6] E.g., P. du Bourguet, *L'Art copte*, Petit Palais, no. 115.
[7] E.g., D. Talbot Rice, *The Beginnings of Christian Art*, London, Hodder & Stoughton, 1957, p. 43.
[8] Op. cit.; G. Maspero, *Guide du visiteur au Musée de Boulaq*, Cairo 1883, p. 128; A. Gayet, *L'Art copte*, Paris, Leroux, 1902, p. 41.
[9] J. Strzygowski, *Koptische Kunst*, p. XVI and E. Drioton, *Les Sculptures coptes du nilomètre de Rodah*, pp. III-IV, who gives in this one of the best definitions of Coptic art properly so called.
[10] J. Strzygowski, *Koptische Kunst*, p. XXIV.
[11] E. Drioton, 'L'Art copte au Musée du Louvre', *B.S.A.C.*, II, 1936, p. 7.
[12] K. Wessel, *Koptische Kunst*.
[13] K. Wessel, op. cit., e.g. in the French ed. (Brussels, Meddens, 1964), pp. 106, 165, 169, 170, 174, 180.
[14] According to inscription I, p. 105, in J. Clédat, *Le Monastère et la nécropole de Baouît* (Mém. de l'Institut Français d'Archéologie Orientale, vol. 12), Cairo, 1904.
[15] On the relations between the emperor Anastasius and St. Jeremiah of Saqqara, see *Chronique de Jean de Nikiou* (trans. Zoltenburg), Paris, Imprimerie Nationale, 1883, p. 368 (chap. LXXXIX). Friendly relations between important monks and imperial officials were frequent, even with characters as nationalistic as Shenute. See, among many others, P. du Bourguet, 'Entretien de Chenouté sur les devoirs des juges', *B.I.F.A.O.*, LV, 1955, p. 91.
[16] E.g., at Wadi en-Natrun, or in the monasteries of St. Anthony and of St. Paul in the Red Sea desert.
[17] E.g., in the French ed., pp. 164, 176 etc.

[18] J. Strzygowski, *Koptische Kunst*, p. XVI.
[19] See, e.g., P. du Bourguet, *La Peinture paléo-chrétienne*, (coll. Le Livre-Musée), Paris, Pont-Royal, 1965, p. 45.
[20] W. F. Volbach, *Elfenbeinarbeiten der Spätantike und des frühen Mittelalters*, 2nd ed., Mainz, Römisch-Germanisches Museum, 1952, no. 72 bis to 77.
[21] R. Rémondon, *Égypte Chrétienne*, col. 533.
[22] This task we set ourselves, beginning in 1948, in completely empirical fashion, with regard to one of the most important categories of Coptic production: textiles. The conclusions were inescapable. See P. du Bourguet, *Catalogue des étoffes coptes*, Musée du Louvre, I. The correspondences with other techniques, notably sculpture, impose themselves with equal force. See P. du Bourguet, 'Le Relief copte', *Revue des Arts*.
[23] On this section consult Paul Jouguet's two contributions cited in the bibliography.
[24] P. Jouguet, *Précis*, I, p. 344. The romanization introduced by Caracalla was not to begin its long course until the fifth century. Cf. J. Lallemand, *L'Administration civile d'Égypte de l'avènement de Dioclétien à la création du diocèse (284–362)*, Brussels, Palais des Académies, 1964.
[25] R. Rémondon, 'Le Régime des terres et l'évolution sociale dans l'Égypte Lagide', *Bull. de la Société Française d'Égyptologie*, 1962, nos. 34–5, pp. 30–1; Ch. Diehl, *L'Égypte chrétienne et byzantine*, p. 505.
[26] R. Rémondon, *Égypte Chrétienne*, cols. 533–4, which we have followed very closely here.
[27] P. du Bourguet, article 'Fayoum' in the *Dictionnaire d'histoire et de géographie ecclésiastique*, Louvain (to be published).
[28] On this section consult Henri Munier, 'L'Égypte byzantine de Dioclétien à la conquête arabe', *Precis*, II; Ch. Diehl, 'L'Egypte chrétienne et byzantine', G. Hanotaux, *Histoire de la nation égyptienne*, vol. III.
[29] H. Munier, *Précis*, II, p. 77.
[30] Ch. Diehl, 'L'Égypte', op. cit., p. 471.
[31] R. Rémondon, *Épgyte chrétienne*, col. 535. All necessary qualifications to this judgement are provided by the author in his article 'L'Égypte et la suprême résistance au christianisme', *B.I.F.A.O.*, LI, 1952, pp. 63 et seq.
[32] On Pakhom the documents have been made available thanks to L. Th. Lefort, *Les Vies coptes de Saint Pacôme et de ses premiers successeurs*, Louvain, Muséon, 1943. On the Kellia see A. Guillaumont, in C. R. de l'Acad. des Inscr. et Belles-Lettres, 92, 1963, pp. 218–25; F. Daumas, ibid., 93, 1966, pp. 300–9.
[33] On this section consult G. Wiet, 'L'Égypte musulmane de la conquête arabe à la conquête ottomane', *Precis*, II; L'Égypte arabe', *Histoire de la nation égyptienne*, vol. IV.
[34] The attitude of the Copts, apart from a few sporadic elements, was at first merely negative. Their support for Amr's army only became positive after the taking of Babylon and of Faiyum, and an armistice signed by Amr which promised the Christians freedom in the exercise of their religion.
In this connection see J. Tagher, *Coptes et Musulmans*, Cairo, 1952, pp. 46–9. See also R. Rémondon, *Égypte Chrétienne*, col. 544.
[35] *Précis*, II, p. 129.
[36] Ibid., pp. 132 et seq.
[37] On this section consult R. Rémondon, *Égypte Chrétienne*, cols. 532–48; H. Munier, *Précis*, II.
[38] J. Vergote, 'Clement d'Alexandrie et l'écriture égyptienne', *Muséon*, Louvain, 52, 1939, pp. 199–221.
[39] *Histoire*, II, p. 37.
[40] Consult P. du Bourguet, 'L'Égypte pharaonique' (Spirituality in Egyptian religion), *Dictionnaire de spiritualité*, pts. XXVI–XXVII, Paris, Beauchesne, 1959, cols. 501–31.
[41] P. du Bourguet, 'Fayoum', *Dictionnaire d'histoire et de géographie ecclésiastique*, Louvain (to be published).
[42] Consult A. J. Festugière, *Les Moines d'Orient*, I, Paris, Éd. du Cerf, 1961; L. Bouyer, *La Vie de Saint Antoine. Essai sur la spiritualité du monachisme primitif*. Abbaye de St.-Wandrille. Fontenelle, 1950. The severity of this judgement is mitigated in cases like that of Ammonius, regarded by Evagrius as both a holy monk and a thinker. (Cf. A. Guillaumont, *Les 'Kephalaia gnostica' d'Evagre le Pontique*, Paris, Éd. du Seuil, 1962, p. 56.) But even if the environment had not been against them, they do appear rather as exceptions.
[43] The writing in the Gnostic manuscripts of Nag Hammadi is of the fourth century.
[44] G. Wiet, *Précis*, II, pp. 132, 135.
[45] This follows from L. Bouyer's analyses in his *Vie de Saint Antoine*, previously cited.

II. AN IMAGINARY EXHIBITION

[1] *Late Egyptian and Coptic Art*, Brooklyn

Museum, New York, 1943; *Exposition d'art copte*, Cairo, 1944; *5000 ans d'art égyptien, mars-juin 1960*, Palais des Beaux-Arts, Brussels, 1960; *Christentum am Nil-Koptische Kunst*, Villa Hügel, Essen, April-October 1963; idem, Kunsthaus, Zurich, November 1963 – January 1964; *Frühchristliche und Koptische Kunst*, Akademie der bildenden Künste, Vienna, Feb.-April 1964; *L'Art copte*, Petit Palais, Paris, 15th June – 15th Sept. 1964.

[2] U. Monneret de Villard, *Les Couvents près de Sohâg*, I, pp. 48–55; S. Clarke, *Christian Antiquities*, pl. XLI, I; A. Badawy, *Les Premières Églises d'Égypte*, pp. 359–62. Petit Palais, nos. 82, 83.

[3] Petit Palais, nos. 82, 83.

[4] P. Lemerle, *Le Style byzantin*, Coll. Arts, Styles et Techniques, Paris, Larousse, 1943, p. 60.

[5] R. Krautheimer, *Early Christian and Byzantine Architecture*, pp. 85–6.

[6] Ibid., p. 218; J. E. Quibell, *Excavations at Saqqara, 1908–1910*, Cairo, 1912, pl. XXXII.

[7] Petit Palais, no. 54 (Essen, 102).

[8] There are frequent examples of this at Split, Jerash and Baalbek.

[9] Despite the mention of it by J. Graviers, *Inventaire . . .*, among the objects in the Louvre originating from Bawit. See also E. Drioton, 'L'Art copte', in *L'Art Sacré*, 1956, pp. 9–17; P. du Bourguet, in *Les Merveilles du Louvre*, Paris, Hachette, 1957, p. 201.

[10] É. Chassinat, *Fouilles à Baoût*, pl. LXXXV.

[11] U. Monneret de Villard, *La scultura ad Ahnâs*, Milan, Reale Acad. Nazionale dei lincei in Roma, 1923; J. Beckwith, *Coptic Sculpture*, pl. 62.

[12] P. du Bourguet, *Le relief copte . . .* pp. 9 et seq.; Petit Palais, no. 45.

[13] J. Strzygowski, *Koptische Kunst*, p. 37.

[14] P. Lemerle, in *Mon. Piot*, 43, 1949, pp. 98 et seq.; Petit Palais, no. 93 (Essen, 145).

[15] Luke I, 29.

[16] O. Wulff, *Altchristliche und mittelalterliche Bildwerke*, Berlin, Georg Reimer, 1909, I, p. 301, no. 1607.

[17] Petit Palais, no. 144 (Essen, 236).

[18] K. Wessel, *L'Art copte*, pl. II.

[19] Petit Palais, no. 89 (Essen, 136).

[20] J. Maspero, *Fouilles exécutées à Baoût*, Mémoire LIX of the I.F.A.O., Cairo, 1943, pl. XXI.

[21] Petit Palais, no. 186.

[22] W. F. Volbach and E. Kuehnel, *Late Antique-Coptic and Islamic Textiles of Egypt*, pl. 13.

[23] P. du Bourguet, *Catalogue des étoffes coptes*, no. A 19.

[24] Petit Palais, no. 152 (Essen, 329).

[25] E. Coche de la Ferté, *L'Antiquité chrétienne au Musée du Louvre*, Paris, Éd. de l'Oeil, 1958, no. 7.

[26] Petit Palais, no. 175.

[27] Petit Palais, no. 51 (Essen, 92).

[28] P. du Bourguet, *Catalogue des étoffes coptes*, I, no. F 230; compare ibid., nos. F 228, 229, 231, 233. See also Petit Palais, no. 252.

[29] *Ibid.*, I, no. I 30.

III. ON THE THRESHOLD: PRE-COPTIC ART

[1] For the beginning of this chapter, consult E. Drioton and P. du Bourguet, *Les Pharaons à la conquête de l'art*, Paris-Bruges, Desclée de Brouwer, 1966, chap. IX, 2. Périodes ptolémaïque et romaine.

[2] S. Gabra and E. Drioton, *Peintures à fresques et scènes peintes à Hermoupolis-Ouest (Touna el-Gebel)*, Cairo, Service des Antiquités de l'Égypte, 1954, pl. 25.

[3] J. Vandier, *Le Département des Antiquités égyptiennes*, Musée de Louvre, Paris, Éd. des Musées Nationaux, 1962, p. 15.

[4] P. du Bourguet, 'Médiation', *L'Égypte ancienne, Supplément au Dictionnaire de la Bible*, ed. L. Pirot and L. Robert, vol. V, cols. 991–7; Id., 'L'Égypte pharaonique', *Dictionnaire de spiritualité*, Paris, Beauchesne, 1959, cols. 501–31; E. Drioton and P. du Bourguet, *Les Pharaons à la conquête de l'art*, Bruges-Paris, Desclée de Brouwer, 1966; S. Morenz, *La Religion égyptienne*, Paris, Payot, 1962, chap. II; F. Daumas, *La Civilisation de l'Égypte pharaonique*, Paris, Arthaud, 1965, chap. IV.

[5] The documentation on this point will be found in P. du Bourguet, 'L'Égypte pharaonique', *Dictionnaire de spiritualité*, op. cit.

[6] E. des Places, *Les Religions de la Grèce antique*, p. 197; P. Fabre, 'La Religion romaine', *Histoire des Religions*, Paris, Bloud et Gay, 1956, III, pp. 416–17.

[7] J. Doresse, 'Le papyrus gnostique du Musée Copte', *Actes du XIe Congrès Intern. des Orientalistes, Paris, 1948*, Paris, Imprimerie Nationale, 1949, p. 365.

[8] J. Schwartz, 'Nouvelles études sur des fresques d'El-Bagawat', *Cahiers archéologiques*, XI, 1960, pp. 93–119.

[9] H. Torp, in *The Art Bulletin*, Sept. 1965, vol. XLVII, 8, no. 3, p. 361 B.

[10] K. Ronczewski, 'Description des chapiteaux conrinthiens et variés du Musée gréco-romain d'Alexandrie', *Bull. de la Société Archéologique d'Alexandrie*, suppl. to pt. 22, Alexandria, 1927, pp. 5–20.

[11] E. Drioton, 'De Philae à Baouît', *Coptic Studies in Honor of W. E. Crum*, Boston, Byzantine Institute, 1950, pp. 443–8.

[12] S. Gabra and E. Drioton, *Peintures à fresques et scènes peintes à Hermoupolis-Ouest (Touna el-Gebel)*, Cairo, Services des Antiquités, 1954, pls. 2–5, 19–20.

[13] E. Breccia, *Le Musée Gréco-romain d'Alexandrie, 1931–1932*, Bergamo, Istituto italiano d'arte grafiche, 1933, pl. XXXI-I.

[14] S. Gabra and E. Drioton, loc. cit., p. 15.

[15] A. Badawy, *L'Art copte, les influences hellénistiques et romaines*, p. 195.

[16] Notably at Deir el-Abiad.

[17] S. Gabra and E. Drioton, loc. cit., pp. 2, 3.

[18] Ibid., pls. 14–15.

[19] Petit Palais, no. 148. See, in the Louvre, the mosaic from Daphne, Department of Greek and Roman Antiquities, no. 3462.

[20] See fig. no. 11 and P. du Bourguet, *Illusion du modelé et tapisserie copte*, Mélanges Kazimierz Michalowski, Warsaw, 1967, pp. 37–40.

[21] S. Gabra and E. Drioton, loc. cit., pls. 2, 3; W. F. Volbach and E. Kuehnel, *Late Antique Coptic and Islamic Textiles of Egypt*, pl. 16.

[22] E. Guimet, *Les Portraits d'Antinoé*, Paris, Hachette, 1912, p. 34 and pl. XI.

[23] E.g. in the Louvre, see J. Vandier, *Le Département des Antiquités égyptiennes, Musée du Louvre*, p. 85.

[24] P. Perdrizet, *Les Terres cuites grecques d'Égypte de la collection Fouquet*, Paris, Berger-Levrault, 1921.

[25] Ph. Derchain and A. Delatte, *Les Intailles magiques gréco-égyptiennes*, Paris, Bibl. Nationale, 1964.

[26] Palestrina is twenty-five miles from Rome.

[27] Triumph of Amphitrite, Louvre (Greek and Roman Antiquities).

[28] P. du Bourguet, *Illusion du modelé et tapisserie copte* (see above, note 20).

[29] J. Beckwith, 'Tissus coptes', *Les Cahiers Ciba*, p. 6; W. F. Volbach and E. Kuehnel, *Late Antique and Islamic Textiles of Egypt*, pl. 17.

[30] E. Coche de la Ferté, *Les portraits romano-égyptiens*, Paris, Ed. des Musées Nationaux, 1952.

[31] Petit Palais, no. 25.

[32] A. Badawy, loc. cit., pp. 177–8.

[33] P. du Bourguet, 'Le relief copte...', *La Revue des Arts*, 9, 1959, pp. 9–14; Petit Palais, no. 16 (Essen, A X).

[34] J. Strzygowski, *Koptische Kunst*, pp. 176 et seq.

[35] H. Carter and P. E. Newberry, *The Tomb of Thoutmosis IV* (General Catalogue of Egyptian Antiquities of the Cairo Museum), Westminster, Constable, 1904.

[36] G. M. Crowfoot and N. de G. Davies, 'The Tunic of Tut'ankh-Amun', *Journal of Egyptian Archaeology*, London, 27, 1941, pp. 113–30; Ch. Desroches-Noblecourt, *Vie et mort d'un Pharaon*, Paris, Hachette, 1963, p. 266.

[37] R. Girschman, *Parthes et Sassanides*, Paris, 1962, p. 79, fig. 91.

[38] E. Guimet, *Les Portraits d'Antinoé*, p. 38 and pl. 72.

[39] E. Coche de la Ferté, *Les Portraits romano-égyptiens*, Paris, Ed. des Musées Nationaux, 1952.

IV: THE AWAKENING: PROTO-COPTIC ART

[1] E. Drioton, 'Art syrien et art copte', *B.S.A.C.*, III, 1937, pp. 29–40.

[2] See P. Perdrizet, *Les Terres cuites grecques d'Égypte de la collection Fouquet*, Paris, Berger-Levrault, 1921, p. XXX; R. Rémondon, 'L'Égypte et la suprême résistance au christianisme', *B.I.F.A.O.*, LI, 1952, pp. 63 f. Nothing is more significant in this connection than the collections of so-called Faiyum portraits, in which the Egyptian type of countenance is particularly frequent; this is a practice reserved for the well-to-do classes (e.g. nos. 3, 4, 7, 8 in E. Coche de la Ferté, *Les portraits romano-égyptiens*, Paris, 1952). It is important to remember in this connection the case of the Egyptian with the Roman name of Pollius Sôter, whose descendants with Egyptian names, e.g. Petemenophis, had sarcophagi constructed for themselves in the purest pharaonic tradition. Ibid., p. 13.

[3] The tone adopted by Shenute in addressing the imperial functionaries is significant in this connection. See, for example, P. du Bourguet, 'Entretiens de Chenouté sur les devoirs des juges' *B.I.F.A.O.*, LV, 1955, p. 91.

[4] It is clear that the Egyptian monks were from the beginning the builders of their own monasteries. One example among many is the construction by Pakhom himself and his monks of the monastery of Pbou, as related in L. Th. Lefort, *Les Vies coptes de Saint*

Pacôme, Louvain, Muséon, 1943, p. 115. The fact is attested in ibid., pp. 3, 95, etc. – Note also the profession of mason practised by several monks according to the inscriptions and graffiti at Bawit, in J. Clédat, 'Le Monastère et la nécropole de Baouît', Mém. de l'I.F.A.O., vol. 12, Cairo, 1904, I, p. 97 (inscription XII), p. 104.

⁵ Eusebius, *Hist. ecclésiastique*, VII, 13. For churches dedicated to Mary built in Alexandria, see *P.G.*, vol. CXI, col. 994 and vol. XVIII, col. 464.

⁶ *Chronique*, pp. 404, 428.

⁷ *P.G.*, XLII, cols. 204–5.

⁸ J. Faivre, 'Alexandrie', *Dictionnaire d'histoire et de géographie ecclésiastique*, 1914, II, col. 340.

⁹ A. J. Butler, *Ancient Coptic Churches*, I, p. 199; A. Badawy, *Les premières églises d'Égypte*, p. 376.

¹⁰ A. J. Butler, op. cit, p. 73; A. Badawy, op. cit., p. 377.

¹¹ R. Krautheimer, *Early Christian and Byzantine Architecture*, pp. 85–6; A. Badawy, op. cit., pp. 337–46.

¹² A. Fakhry, *The Necropolis of El-Bagawat in Kharga Oasis*, Cairo, Service des Antiquités de l'Égypte, 1951.

¹³ Petit Palais, no. 25.

¹⁴ Dom F. Cabrol, *Dictionnaire d'Archéologie chrétienne et de liturgie*, Paris, Letouzey et Ané, I, pt. I (1907), cols. 1125 f.

¹⁵ P. Perdrizet, *Les Terres cuites grecques d'Égypte de la collection Fouquet*, Paris, Berger-Levrault, 1921, pp. 160 f.

¹⁶ Ibid.

¹⁷ M. Th. Picard-Schmitter, 'Une tapisserie hellénistique d'Antinoé au Musée du Louvre', *Mon. Piot*, 52, 1962, pp. 27–75.

¹⁸ P. Perdrizet, op. cit., p. XXIII.

¹⁹ Petit Palais, no. 25.

²⁰ Petit Palais, no. 152.

²¹ P. du Bourguet, *Catalogue des étoffes coptes*, I, no. F 167.

²² K. Wessel, 'Eine Grabstele aus Medinet el-Fajoum: zum Problem der Maria Lactans', *Wissensch. Zeitschrift der Humboldt-Universität zu Berlin*, IV, 1954/5, pp. 149–53.

²³ P. du Bourguet, *La Peinture paléo-chrétienne*, Paris, Pont-Royal, 1965, pp. 24–5.

²⁴ H. Delehaye, *Les Légendes grecques des saints militaires*, Paris, 1909.

²⁵ E. Kitzinger, 'Notes on Early Coptic Sculpture', *Archaeologia*, LXXXVII, 1937, pp. 181–215.

²⁶ Petit Palais, no. 46 (Essen, 80).

²⁷ E. Drioton, *Art syrien et art copte*, p. 39; on the relief of the Brooklyn Museum see J. Beckwith, *Coptic Sculpture*, pl. 72.

²⁸ H. W. Müller, 'Grabstele eines Isis-Mysten aus Antinoé/Mittelägypten', *Pantheon*, XVIII, 1960, p. 267.

²⁹ Petit Palais, no. 7 (Essen, 77).

³⁰ K. Wessel, op. cit., pl. 6.

³¹ E. Coche de la Ferté, *L'Antiquité chrétienne au Musée du Louvre*, Paris, Éd. de l'Oeil, 1958, no. 2.

³² Compare with that in the collection of M. Bérard, Petit Palais, no. 114 (Essen, 172).

³³ J. Strzygowski, *Koptische Kunst*, pp. 183 f.

³⁴ A. M. Schneider, *Die Brotvermehrungskirche von Et-Tabgah am Genezaret und ihre Mosaiken*, Paderborn, 1934.

³⁵ H. Stern, 'Quelques problèmes d'iconographie paléo-chrétienne et juive', *Cahiers archéologiques*, XII, 1962, pp. 99–113; J. Schwartz, 'Nouvelles études sur des fresques d'El Bagawat', ibid., XIII, pp. 1–11.

³⁶ C. Neyret, *Les céramiques coptes du Musée du Louvre* (paper presented in 1966 at the École du Louvre).

³⁷ On the whole question see P. du Bourguet, *Catalogue des étoffes coptes*, Musée du Louvre, I, pp. 7 f.

³⁸ Ibid., no. A 4; R. Pfister, 'Les débuts du vêtement copte', *Études d'Orientalisme à la mémoire de Raymonde Linossier*, Paris, Leroux, 1932, vol. II, pp. 450–1.

³⁹ P. du Bourguet, *Catalogue des étoffes coptes*, I, nos. A 5 and A 6.

⁴⁰ W. F. Volbach and E. Kuehnel, *Late Antique-Coptic and Islamic Textiles of Egypt*, p. 5.

⁴¹ P. du Bourguet, *Catalogue des étoffes coptes*, I, no. B 22.

⁴² Ibid., no. A 7.

⁴³ Ibid., nos. B 19 and B 27.

⁴⁴ Ibid., nos. B 20 and B 21; see Doro Levi, *Antioch Mosaic Pavements*, Princeton, 1947, II, pl. LXXXI b; V. V. Pavlov and M. E. Matié, *Objets d'arts de l'Égypte ancienne dans les Musées de l'U.R.S.S.*, 1958, pl. 134; H. Pierce and R. Tyler, *L'Art byzantin*, I, pl. 196.

⁴⁵ W. F. Volbach and E. Kuehnel, *Late Antique-Coptic and Islamic Textiles of Egypt*, p. 20; P. du Bourguet, *L'Art copte*, Petit Palais, no. 156.

197

[1] A. Badawy, *Les premières églises d'Egypte*, p. 348.

[2] A. B. I. Wace, A. H. S. Megaw, T. C. Skeat and S. Shenouda, *Hermopolis Magna, Ashmunein*, Alexandria University, Faculty of Arts, publication no. 8, Alexandria University Press, 1959.

[3] R. Krautheimer, *Early Christian and Byzantine Architecture*, p. 88–9.

[4] A. Badawy, op. cit., p. 371.

[5] Ibid., p. 369; R. Krautheimer, op. cit., p. 218.

[6] R. Krautheimer, op. cit., pp. 88–9; A. Badawy, op. cit., pp. 351 f.

[7] R. Krautheimer, op. cit., p. 90; A. Badawy, op. cit., pp. 356f.

[8] A. Badawy, op. cit., pp. 364f; R. Krautheimer, op. cit., p. 218.

[9] E. Chassinat, *Fouilles à Baouît*, Cairo, Mém. de l'I.F.A.O., 13, 1911, vol. I, pls. VIIf.; H. Torp, 'Some Aspects of Early Coptic Monastic Architecture', *Byzantion*, 25–7 (1955–7), pt. 2.

[10] E. Drioton, *Art syrien et art copte*, p. 36; A. Badawy, *L'Art copte, les influences égyptiennes*, pp. 2, 3.

[11] J. Doresse, *Des hiéroglyphes à la croix*, Istanbul, Nederlands Historisch archaeologisch Instituut in Het Nabije Oosten, 1960, pp. 24–6.

[12] Petit Palais, no. 10 (Essen, 19).

[13] G. Duthuit, *La Sculpture copte*, p. 31 and pl. II c.

[14] Ibid., p. 32, pl. IV a.

[15] Ibid., p. 41, pl. XII b, a.

[16] Ibid., p. 42, pl. XXI a, b.

[17] Ibid., p. 42, pl. XXIII a, b.

[18] Ibid., p. 42, pl. XXII a, b.

[19] Ibid., p. 42, pl. XX c and p. 43, pl. XXVI a.

[20] Petit Palais, no. 47; W. S. Heckscher, 'The Anadyomene in the Medieval Tradition (Pelagia-Cleopatra, Aphrodite). A Prelude to Botticelli's "Birth of Venus"', *Netherlands Yearbook for History of Art*, 1956, pp. 1–38.

[21] G. Duthuit, op. cit., p. 43, pl. XXIV c.

[22] Ibid., p. 44, pl. XXXIII a.

[23] J. Vandier, *Le Département des Antiquités égyptiennes, Musée du Louvre*.

[24] J. Beckwith, *Coptic Sculpture*, p. 23; Petit Palais, no. 92 (Essen, 144).

[25] O. Wulff, op. cit., p. 120, no. 432.

[26] Petit Palais, no. 126.

[27] *Early Christian and Byzantine Art* (Catalogue of the Exhibition), Walters Art Gallery, Baltimore, 1947, nos. 176, 177.

[28] W. F. Volbach, *Elfenbeinarbeiten . . .*, no. 80.

[29] Ibid., no. 204.

[30] O. Wulff, op. cit., p. 205, no. 978.

[31] Petit Palais, no. 126.

[32] Petit Palais, no. 292 (Essen, 465); compare with Petit Palais, no. 293 (Essen, 466).

[33] Petit Palais, no. 55 (Essen, 79).

[34] G. Duthuit, *La Sculpture copte*, pl. XXXVIIIb.

[35] E. Chassinat, op. cit., pl. XXIV.

[36] G. Duthuit, op. cit., pl. LIV d.

[37] P. du Bourguet, 'Le Relief copte. À propos de deux acquisitions récentes', in: *La Revue des Arts*, 1959, pp. 12f.

[38] G. Duthuit, op. cit., pl. XXXVc; pl. XXXVIb (Petit Palais, no. 54); pl. XXXIVa; pl. XXXVa.

[39] E. Kitzinger, 'Notes on Early Coptic Sculpture', *Archaeologia*, LXXXVII, 1937, pp. 181–215.

[40] Petit Palais, no. 72.

[41] Petit Palais, no. 76 (Essen, 112).

[42] Petit Palais, no. 71 (Essen, 103).

[43] Petit Palais, no. 80 (Essen, 111).

[44] Likewise, moreover, among the most recent, cf. D. Talbot Rice, 'On the Date of the Mosaic Floor of the Great Palace of the Byzantine Emperors at Constantinople', *Karistérion eis Anastasion K. Orlandon*, Athens, 1964.

[45] E. Coche de la Ferté, 'Du portrait à l'icône', *L'Oeil*, no. 77 (Paris, 1961), pp. 24–31, 78.

[46] Ibid., p. 28.

[47] É. Chassinat, op. cit., pls. LXVII, LXVIII.

[48] J. E. Quibell, *Excavations at Saqqara (1905–1907)*, Cairo, Service des Antiquités de l'Égypte, 1908, pl. XLIV.

[49] H. Torp, 'La Date de la fondation du monastère d'Apa Apollô de Baouît et de son abandon', *Mélanges d'Archéologie et d'Histoire*, vol. 77, 1965, pp. 153–77.

[50] J. Clédat, 'Le Monastère et la nécropole de Baouît', pls. LXVII, XLf.

[51] Ibid., pl. XCVI.

[52] M. Cramer, *Koptische Buchmalerei*, Recklinghausen, Aurel Bongers, 1964. On the actual evolution of Coptic illumination, see P. du Bourguet's review of this book in *Bibliotheca Orientalis*, Leyden, XXIII, nos. 1–2, Jan.–March 1966, pp. 48–50.

[53] *Christentum am Nil-Koptische Kunst*, 1963, no. 623.

[54] Consult C. Neyret, *Les Céramiques coptes du Musée du Louvre*.

55 M. Th. Picard-Schmitter, 'Une tapisserie Hellénistique d'Antinoé au Musée du Louvre', *Mon. Piot*, 1962, vol. 52, pt. 2, pp. 27–75.

56 P. du Bourguet, *Catalogue des étoffes coptes*, I, no. 76.

57 Ibid., nos. D 36, D 37.

58 Petit Palais, no. 164 (Essen, 267).

59 P. du Bourguet, *Catalogue des étoffes coptes*, I, no. C 77.

60 Ibid., no. D 46.

61 G. Brett, 'The Brooklyn Textiles and the Great Palace Mosaic', *Coptic Studies in Honor of W. E. Crum*, Boston, Byzantine Institute, 1950, pp. 433–42. See, however, D. Talbot Rice, op. cit., G. de Francovich, 'L'Egitto, la Siria e Constantinopoli: problemi di metodo. L'Egitto', *Rivista dell'Istituto Nazionale d'Archeologia e Storia dell'Arte*, new series, vols. 11–12, 1963, pp. 83–229.

62 P. du Bourguet, op. cit., no. B 25.

63 Ibid., no. C 20.

64 Ibid., no. D 109.

65 Ibid., no. C 22.

66 Ibid., nos. C 70, D 140 and 141. On the 3/4 arrangement of the scroll leaf consult Doro Levi, *Antioch Mosaic Pavements*, II, pp. 506–7 and figs. 185 a, b.

67 For example, P. du Bourguet, op. cit., nos. B 17 and B 18, C 28 to C 34, D 43, D 58 etc.

68 P. du Bourguet, 'Modelé hellénistique et tapisserie copte', *Mélanges Kazimierz Michalowski*, Warsaw, 1967, pp. 37–40; P. du Bourguet, *Catalogue des étoffes coptes*, I, p. 12.

69 Ibid., p. 15.

70 Petit Palais, no. 165 (Essen, 277).

71 Petit Palais, no. 172 (Essen, 281).

72 Petit Palais, no. 181.

VI. 'THE ART OF THE COPTS'

1 Without denying this, but even postulating it (pp. 167, 186), K. Wessel in *Coptic Art* ignores this period of Coptic art and systematically places as before the eighth century works manifestly belonging to the Moslem period. Pls. XXIII, 172, 194, XX, 122, 125, IV, XVIII, 131, etc.

2 Cited in K. A. C. Creswell, *Early Muslim Architecture*, p. 43, n. 2.

3 Ibid., p. 43.

4 Ibid., p. 44.

5 *Rivista degli studi orientali*, IV, p. 246, n. 1.

6 K. A. C. Creswell, op. cit., p. 147.

7 Ibid., p. 45.

8 A. J. Butler, *The Ancient Coptic Churches of Egypt*, pp. 247f.; R. Krautheimer, *Early Christian and Byzantine Architecture*, p. 219.

9 A. J. Butler, op. cit., pp. 206f.

10 Ibid., pp. 235f.; E. Pauty, *Bois sculptés d'églises coptes (époque fatimide)*, Cairo, Publications of the Arab Museum, 1930, p. 17.

11 A. J. Butler, op. cit., pp. 75f.

12 Ibid., pp. 272f.

13 The nature of the roofing on Coptic monuments, none of which survives, remains controversial.

14 H. G. Evelyn White, *The Monasteries of the Wadi'n Natrûn*, III, pl. XXX.

15 Ibid., p. 35.

16 Ibid., pp. 90f.

17 Ibid., pp. 101, 102 and pl. XXXI.

18 A. Fakhry, *The Necropolis of El-Bagaouat in Kharga Oasis*, Cairo, Service des Antiquités d'Égypte, 1951.

19 K. A. C. Creswell, op. cit., fig. 38 a and p. 192.

20 U. Monneret de Villard, *Il monastero di S. Simeone presso Aswân*, Milan, Libreria Pontificia, 1927; R. Krautheimer, op. cit., pp. 218–19.

21 It is astonishing to find such illusory bases for dating still retained today by professionals in the field. See, for example, K. Wessel, 'Fragmente einer koptischen Tunika aus dem Besitz der Aegyptischen Staatssammlungen in München', *Pantheon*, 19, 1961, pp. 289–97.

22 We have only to refer to the decoration of Omayyad palaces and to miniatures.

23 See E. Drioton, 'L'Art copte', *L'Art Sacré*, 1956, pp. 9–17.

24 Petit Palais, no. 115 (Essen, 173).

25 J. Clédat, *Le Monastère et la nécropole de Baouît*, XII, pls. XVI–XIX.

26 K. A. C. Creswell, *Early Muslim Architecture*, Oxford, 1932, I, pl. 49.

27 Petit Palais, nos. 43, 44; see also M. Dimand, *A Handbook of Mahummadan Art*, New York, Hartsdale House, 1947, p. 125, fig. 69.

28 No doubt the 'caisson' was used in Byzantine art from the beginning, but it is associated with other motifs, Omayyad in style and origin, and the sum total of these indications cannot be ignored.

29 J. Clédat, op. cit., pl. LII and vol. XXXIX, pl. XIV.

30 J. Maspero, *Fouilles exécutées à Baouît*, Mém. de l'I.F.A.O., Cairo, vol. LIX, 1943, pl. XXXII.

31 P. du Bourguet, *Catalogue des étoffes coptes*, I, nos. E 28–E 31.

32 Ibid., nos. E 2, E 40, etc.

33 J. Clédat, op. cit., vol. XII, pl. LXXII.

34 P. du Bourguet, op. cit., nos. E 125, E 126, etc.

35 K. A. C. Creswell, op. cit., pls. 21–24.

36 É. Chassinat, *Fouilles à Baouît*, pl. XLV b.

37 Ibid., pl. XC.

38 H. Stern, 'Quelques oeuvres sculptées en bois, os et ivoire de style omeyyade', *Ars Orientalis*, I, Washington, 1954, pp. 119–32.

39 G. Duthuit, *La Sculpture copte*, p. 46 and pl. XXXV a; particularly p. 45 and pl. XXXIV b, p. 46 and pl. XXXVII d.

40 É. Chassinat, op. cit., pl. LXXXI a.

41 K. A. C. Creswell, op. cit., pls. 142, 150.

42 G. Duthuit, *La Sculpture copte*, pl. LI.

43 K. A. C. Creswell, op. cit., pp. 142, 150.

44 Ch. Boreux, *Département des Antiquités égyptiennes* (Musée National du Louvre, Guide-catalogue sommaire), Paris, Ed. des Musées Nationaux, 1932, I, p. 266, pl. XXXV.

45 P. du Bourguet, 'La Fabrication des tissus coptes a-t-elle largement survécu à la conquête arabe?', *Bull. de la Soc. Arch. d'Alexandrie*, XL, 1953, fig. 27.

46 H. G. Evelyn White, op. cit., III, pl. LXX a; K. A. C. Creswell, op. cit., pl. 58 b.

47 É. Chassinat, op. cit., pl. XXX.

48 K. A. C. Creswell, *Early Muslim Architecture*, Oxford, II, pl. 73.

49 É. Chassinat, op. cit., pl. XXVI.

50 K. A. C. Creswell, op. cit., pl. 74.

51 P. du Bourguet, op. cit., p. 29.

52 G. Wiet, 'Tapis et tapisseries du Musée Arabe du Caire', *Syria*, 1935; 'Les Tissus et tapisseries de l'Égypte musulmane', *Revue de l'Art*, vol. 68, 1935, pp. 3f; 'L'Égypte musulmane', *Précis de l'Histoire d'Égypte*, I.F.A.O., 1932, vol. II, p. 148.

53 Mukkadasi, 'Géographie', *B.G.A.*, vol. III, p. 213.

54 G. Duthuit, op. cit., p. 42, pl. XVII b.

55 J. Beckwith, *Coptic Sculpture*, pl. 126.

56 *Early Christian and Byzantine Art*, Exhibition catalogue, Walters Art Gallery, Baltimore, 1947, no. 745 and pl. CVI.

57 J. Beckwith, op. cit., pls. 121, 122.

58 There is, here, a continuity which one must take into account.

59 É. Chassinat, op. cit., pls. XL b, XLIV a.

60 Petit Palais, no. 127.

61 P. du Bourguet, *Catalogue des étoffes coptes*, I, p. 14.

62 Petit Palais, no. 201 (Essen, 342).

63 H. G. Evelyn White, op. cit., pls. LXI, LXII.

64 P. du Bourguet, *Catalogue des étoffes coptes*, I, nos. F 179–81, G 285, G 322–35.

65 See M. Dimand, *A Handbook of Muhammadan Art*, New York, Hartsdale House, 3rd ed., 1947, pp. 111–14.

66 E. Pauty, *Bois sculptés d'églises coptes (époque fatimide)*, pp. 27f.

67 G. Wiet, *Album du Musée Arabe du Caire*, Publications of the Arab Museum, 1930, p. 65. In the same album note the portrait enclosed in a scroll on tapestry, p. 79.

68 E. Coche de la Ferté, *Un fragment de verre . . .*, p. 269.

69 M. Dimand, op. cit., p. 253, fig. 164.

70 E. Pauty, op. cit., pls. XXXV–XXXVIII.

71 E. Coche de la Ferté, op. cit., p. 265.

72 P. du Bourguet, op. cit., no. F 227.

73 Nasiri Khusrau in the eleventh century. Cf. Ch. Scheffer, *Sefer Nameh*, Paris, 1881.

74 P. du Bourguet, op. cit., pp. 493f.

75 R. Pfister, 'Teinture et alchimie dans l'Orient hellénistique', *Seminarium kondakovianum*, VII, 1935, pp. 1–59.

76 P. du Bourguet, op. cit., nos. G 4–G 31.

77 Ibid., nos. I 22f.

78 Ibid., nos. H 137, 150, 170, 179, 196 etc.

79 Ibid., p. 15.

80 Petit Palais, no. 284 (Essen, 403); Maria Cramer, *Koptische Buchmalerei*, pp. 112f.; see also review of this work by P. du Bourguet in *Bibliotheca Orientalis*, Leyden, XXIII, no. 1–2, Jan.–March 1966, pp. 48–50.

81 M. Cramer, op. cit., p. 113.

82 H. G. Evelyn White, op. cit., pls. LXI, LXII; J. Doresse, 'Deux monastères coptes oubliés: Saint Antoine et Saint Paul dans le désert de la Mer Rouge', *La Revue des Arts*, 2, 1952, pp. 3–14. Petit Palais, no. 147 (Essen, 237).

83 Petit Palais, no. 211.

84 W. F. Volbach, 'Spätantike und frühmittelalterliche Stoffe', *R.G.Z.M.*, 10, 1932, 114, no. 286, pl. VIII.

85 J. Beckwith, op. cit., pls. 141–7.

86 Petit Palais, no. 128 (Essen, 203).

87 Petit Palais, no. 147 (Essen, 237).

88 See above, notes 80, 81.

89 K. Michalowski, *Faras, Fouilles polonaises, 1961*; Id., *Polish Excavations at Faras, 1962–1963*.

[90] A. Klasens, 'De Nederlandse opgravingen in Nubie'. For Wadi es-Sebua, cf. F. Daumas, 'Rapport préliminaire sur les fouilles exécutées par l'Institut Français d'Archéologie Orientale entre Seyala et Ouadi ès-Séboua en avril-mai 1964', *B.I.F.A.O.*, 63, 1965, pp. 255–63.

[91] L. Findlay, 'The Monolithic Churches of Lalibela in Ethiopia', *B.S.A.C.*, IX, 1944, pp. 5–58.
[92] P. du Bourguet, 'L'Art copte et l'Occident', *L'Art de France*, IV, 1964, pp. 272–4.
[93] Ibid.

Mme. Cl. Neyret, of the Louvre, has been largely responsible for the meticulous care needed in the preparation of the above documentation.

APPENDIX OF PLATES

1 – Archivolt with angel musicians. Limestone. Eighth century. Overall span 60 cm, width of carving 15 cm. Paris, Louvre, Christian Antiquities. Photo: M. Chuzeville.

2 – Basket capital. Limestone. Saqqara. Seventh century. Height 38 cm. Paris, Louvre, Christian Antiquities. Photo: A. Held.

3 – Broken pediment with shell form. Limestone. Bawit. Seventh century. Height 60 cm, width 87 cm, thickness 22 cm. Paris, Louvre Museum, Christian Antiquities. Photo: Photographic Archives.

4 – Frieze of foliated scroll ornament. Limestone. Bawit. Seventh century. Height 35 cm. Paris, Louvre, Christian Antiquities. Photo after E. Chassinat, *Fouilles à Baouît*, Cairo, pls. LXXXVI-I.

5 – Panther hunt. Tapestry. Sixth century. Height 9.5 cm, length 9 cm. Paris, Louvre, Christian Antiquities. Photo: M. Chuzeville.

6 – *Virgo lactans*. Niche painting. Saqqara. Seventh century. Old Cairo, Coptic Museum. Photo: E. Bazarghi.

7 – Sabina's shawl, fragment. Tapestry. Antinoë. Sixth century. Louvre, Christian Antiquities. Photo: Giraudon.

8 – Plants and animals in medallions. Tapestry. Eleventh century. Height 28 cm, length 24 cm. Paris, Louvre, Christian Antiquities. Photo: M. Chuzeville.

9 – Virgin and Child. Loop-weaving. Probably Sheikh Abada. Eighth-ninth century. Height 60 cm, width 40 cm. Paris, Chafik Chammas Collection. Photo: Louvre Archives.

10 – Saint on horseback. Painted glass fragment. Tenth-twelfth century. Height 7 cm. Paris, Louvre, Christian Antiquities. Photo: M. Chuzeville.

11 – Male and female dancers with castanets. Tapestry. Second-third century. Berlin, Staatliche Museen. Photo: after W. F. Volbach and Kühnel, *Coptic and Early Islamic Textiles*, pl. V.

12 – Martyrdom of St. Thecla. Limestone. Ninth century. Height 53.5 cm, length 58.3 cm. New York, Brooklyn Museum.

13 – Daphne in the tree. Stone. Ahnas. Fifth century. Height 40 cm, length 70 cm. Old Cairo, Coptic Museum. Photo: after G. Duthuit, *La Sculpture copte*, pl. XXIIb.

14 – Orpheus and Eurydice. Stone. Fifth century. Height 58 cm, length 132 cm. Old Cairo, Coptic Museum. Photo: ibid., pl. XXc.

15 – Hercules and the lion. Stone. Sixth century. Height 70 cm. Old Cairo, Coptic Museum. Photo: after G. Duthuit, *La Sculpture copte*, pl. XXIVa.

16 – The Nile god. Stone. Third-fourth century. Old Cairo, Coptic Museum. Photo: after G. Duthuit, *La Sculpture copte*, pl. VIIIa.

17 – Standing angel (detail of pillar). Limestone. Bawit. Sixth century. Paris, Louvre, Christian Antiquities. Photo: M. Chuzeville.

18 – Panel from a *haïkal*. Stucco. Ninth century. Deir es-Suryani; Wadi en-Natrun. Photo: after H. G. E. White, *The Monasteries of Wadi'n Natrun*, vol. III, pl. LXX, A.

19 – Surrounding wall of a Christian necropolis. Bagawat, Kharga oasis. Ninth century. Photo: P. du Bourguet.

20 – Ascension. Painting; Church of Moncherrand, Canton of Vaud, Switzerland. Photo: A. Held.

21 – Arched pelmet over a door (church of Abu-'s-Sifain). Carved wood. Fatimid period. Old Cairo. Photo: after E. Pauty, *Bois sculptés d'églises coptes*, pl. XXII.

22 – Corner-piece of a door-leaf. Carved wood. Fatimid period. Church of St. Barbara, Old Cairo, Coptic Museum. Photo: after E. Pauty, *Bois sculptés d'églises coptes*, pl. II.

5

10

ΗΚΕΗCΠΑΠΑΓΕωΡΓΙCωΝΤΑΔΙΑΚΥΝΙΕΡΗΜ

14

15

16

19

CHRONOLOGICAL TABLE

B.C.
2nd cent.
    First attempts to transcribe Egyptian with
    Greek alphabet result in Coptic language
  30 Egypt conquered by Octavian

A.D.

	33 Traditional date of death of Christ
45 Death of Philo the Jew	45 St Paul's first mission
	50 Beginning of commerce with India
	70 Destruction of Jerusalem by Titus
	105–106 Conquest of Nabataean Arabia
	107 Annexation of Dacia
	Trajan sends embassy to India
	110 Annexation of Palmyra
	114 Conquest of Armenia by Trajan
	115 Conquest of Mesopotamia
	117 Hadrian abandons eastern conquests of Trajan
	165 Persecution of Marcus Aurelius
	Teutonic invasion of Italy
c. 180 Foundation of Didascalium in Alexandria	172–80 Barbarian invasions of Spain
203 Origen in charge of Didascalium	193 Accession of Septimius Severus
204–269 Life-span of Plotinus	
	235 Persecution of Maximinus I
	242 Plotinus follows Gordian III into Persia
	Reconquest of Mesopotamia
	Accession of Shapur I in Persia
247–284 Episcopate of Dionysius of Alexandria	
250 Break-up of Merovingian kingdom	250 Persecution of Decius
251–356? Life-span of St. Anthony	255 Plotinus begins the *Enneads*
	256 Shapur seizes Antioch
	257 Persecution of Valerian
	260 Gallienus restores their churches to the Christians
270–275 St. Anthony retires to the desert	262 Odenathus rules independently of Palmyra
	272 Aurelian subdues Palmyra
	284 Accession of Diocletian
	293 Organization of the Tetrarchy
	after 297 Diocletian reforms provincial administration
305 St. Anthony organizes the monastic life	303 Beginning of persecutions of Diocletian
	305 Baptism of Tiridates, king of Armenia
	311 Galerius: edict of tolerance, death of Galerius
	313 Edict of Milan (?). Clergy relieved of civic burdens
318 Beginning of the preaching of Arius	
323 St. Pakhom founds the first monastery; Arius condemned	325 Council of Nicaea; exile of Arius
328–373 Episcopate of Athanasius in Alexandria	
330 Frumentius evangelizes Ethiopia	
	337 Founding of Constantinople
	Division of empire into East and West
	Baptism of Constantine

	India	China
		6 Arrival of first Buddhist monks in China
		8 End of Han dynasty
50	Beginnings of commerce with Rome	
		100 Invention of paper. Silk route reconnoitred by the Syrian Maës Titianus.
107	Embassy sent by Trajan	
		160 First Buddhist missionaries in China
		226 Roman merchants in Canton
290	Foundation of Gupta empire in Bengal	
		335 Buddhism officially acknowledged in China

Dates	Egypt	Rome and the Empire
		355 Invasion of Gaul by the Alamanni and Saxon Franks
		373–397 St. Martin bishop of Tours
381	Creation of diocese of Egypt	
385–412	Theophilus patriarch of Alexandria	
391	Theophilus destroys the Serapeum in Alexandria	
412–444	St. Cyril patriarch of Alexandria	
415	Murder of Hypatia in Alexandria	
		432 St. Patrick begins conversion of Ireland
444–451	Dioscorus patriarch of Alexandria	
		449 Attila in Italy
		469–476 Euric conquers Gaul
		480–547 Life-span of St. Benedict
		496 Conversion of Clovis to Christianity

355 Huns appear in Russia

380 Theodosius proclaims Christianity as State religion

391 Theodosius bans pagan religions

395 Huns reach Antioch

431 Council of Ephesus

451 Council of Chalcedon

453 Death of Attila

475 Peter the Fuller Monophysite patriarch

484 First schism in the East. Pope Felix III excommunicates Acacius of Constantinople

484 Christians of Persia adhere to Nestorianism

491 Anastasius succeeds Zeno. Monophysites in favour

512 Severus, Monophysite patriarch of Antioch

513 Severus condemns doctrine of Chalcedon at Council of Tyre

519 Deposition of Severus. End of Eastern schism.

526–546 Building of San Vitale in Ravenna

527 Accession of Justinian

529 Justinian recalls Monophysites from exile

534 Slavs cross Danube

Dates	Egypt	Rome and the Empire	Byzantium
			535 Anthimus Monophysite patriarch of Constantinople
			537 Proceedings against Monophysites Dedication of St. Sophia
538 Theodosius of Alexandria deposed. Egypt finally becomes Monophysite			
545–550 Cosmas Indicopleustes: Christian topography			
			550 Paul Monophysite patriarch of Antioch
619 Persians occupy Egypt			
			623 Heraclius proposes monotheism
629 Persians evacuate Egypt			
631 Cyrus Monothelite patriarch of Alexandria			
641 Arab conquest of Egypt			

552 Buddhism spreads from Korea into Japan

570 Birth of Mohammed

610 Mohammed begins preaching in Mecca

622 Flight (Hegira) of Mohammed to Medina

630 Taking of Mecca, followed by conquest of Arabia

632 Death of Mohammed. Abu Bakr succeeds him

636 Conquest of Syria

638 Taking of Jerusalem and Antioch

641 Omar I caliph

643 Conquest of Tripolitania

646–666 Conquest of Armenia

651 Conquest of Persia completed

Dates	Egypt	Rome and the West	Byzantium
655	Egypt revolts against Caliph Othman		
700		Latin ceases to be the language spoken in Gaul	
721		Moslems besiege Toulouse	
725		Moslems take Carcassonne and lay siege to Autun Pope Gregory II makes himself independent of Byzantium	
732		Spanish Moslems attack Aquitaine: Poitiers	
737		Charles Martel defeats Moslems at Narbonne	
741		Death of Charles Martel	
747		Pepin mayor of the Palace	
751		Pepin king	
754		Pepin crowned by the Pope	
764			Beginning of iconoclast persecution
771		Charles king	

653 Compilation of Koran of Othman

660 Mu'awiya caliph. Beginning of Omayyad
dynasty

661 Foundation of Kairwan in Tunisia and
building of Great Mosque

664–7 First raids in India

691 Completion of mosque of Omar in
Jerusalem

698 Arabs take Carthage

before 700 Weakening of Buddhism in India

705 Building of Great Mosque of Damascus

709 End of conquest of North Africa

711–13 Conquest of Spain

750 Beginning of Abbasid dynasty
Introduction of rag paper

762 Abbasids fix their capital at Baghdad

773 Introduction of Arab numerals

781 Nestorian inscription of Si-ngan-fu

786 Harun al-Rashid caliph

794 Revolt against Abbasid taxation

800 Imperial coronation of Charlemagne

801 Harun al-Rashid's embassy

802–829 New revolts

828 Transfer of ashes of St. Mark to Venice

868 Ahmed the Tulunid: governor

872 Ahmed the Tulunid: independent

886 Ibn Tulun recognized by Baghdad

905 Overthrow of Tulunids

911 Baptism of Norse chieftain Rollo

912 First Fatimid offensive

969 Fatimids conquer Egypt and take Syria. Beginning of their dynasty

973 Fatimids installed in Cairo

Byzantium	Islam	Orient
797–806 Monastic rule of Theodore of Studium	797 Frankish embassy in Baghdad	
	807 Harun al-Rashid recognizes special rights of Franks over holy places	
	830–1 Arabs take Palermo	
	836 Foundation of Samarra, new Abbasid capital	
	840–842 Arabs take Bari, Messina and Tarentum	
	842 Foundation of Great Mosque of Samarra	
843 Defeat of Iconoclasts		
	878 Arabs take Syracuse	
	889 Building of Mosque of Nishapur	
	902 Conquest of Sicily completed	
	970 Fatimids in Damascus	

Dates	Egypt	The West	Byzantium	Islam
996–1021	Al-Hakim caliph			
1054			Excommunication of Michael Cerularius. Schism between Rome and the Orient	
1095		First Crusade		
1100–1118				Reign of Baldwin I, first king of Jerusalem
1171	Saladin puts an end to Fatimid caliphate in Cairo			
1250	Battle of Mansura; capitulation of St. Louis Mamelukes masters of Egypt			
1270		Death of St. Louis in Tunis		

1 – Alexandria
2 – Abu Mina
3 – Wadi en-Natrun
4 – Old Cairo and Fostat
5 – Saqqara
6 – Medinet el-Faiyum
7 – Ahnas el-Medineh
8 – Monastery of St. Anthony
9 – Monastery of St. Paul
10 – Behnesa (Oxyrhynchus)
11 – Sheikh Abada (Antinoë)
12 – Ashmunein (Hermopolis Magna)
13 – Mallawi
14 – Deit Abu Hennis
15 – Bawit
16 – El-Bersheh
17 – Asyut

18 – Akhmim (Panopolis)
19 – Sohag
20 – Deir el-Abiad
21 – Fau
22 – Tabennisi
23 – Chenoboskion
24 – Dendera
25 – Thebes
26 – Luxor
27 – Erment
28 – Esna
29 – Edfu
30 – Monastery of St. Simeon
31 – Aswan
32 – Philae
33 – Monastery of St. Catherine
34 – Sinai

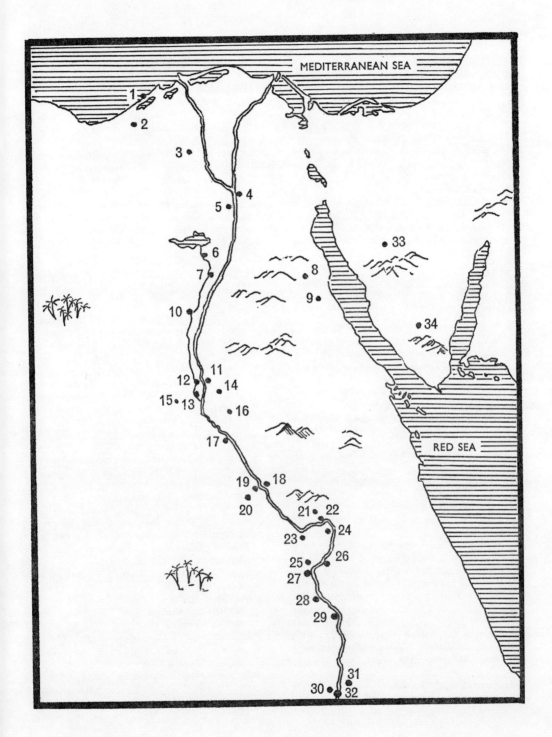

MEDITERRANEAN SEA

RED SEA

223

BIBLIOGRAPHY

There can be no question of providing here an exhaustive bibliography. This can be found:

(i) Up to 1949, in Kammerer, W., *A Coptic Bibliography*, Ann Arbor, University of Michigan Press, 1950.

(ii) From 1940 onwards, in the *Bibliographie copte* which has appeared annually in the review *Orientalia* (Rome) since 1949, compiled by J. Simon.

The studies mentioned here have been selected, either because in the light of long experience – nearly twenty years in the museums and in the field of Coptic art and archeology – they seem to be the most valuable, or because the recent date of some of them required their inclusion, however disputable their value might be.

The arrangement of this bibliography does not correspond with the chapter headings in the text, although it borrows some elements from it (nos. 1, 2 and 3 correspond with chapter III, and no. II with chapter VI), as it has seemed to us better, because of the field covered by the studies cited, to group them firstly as a panorama of Coptic art (no. 4) and then according to the various techniques (nos. 6–10).

1. THE COPTS

du Bourguet, P., 'L'Apport des Coptes au patrimoine universel', *École des langues orientales anciennes de l'Institut Catholique, Mémorial du cinquantenaire 1914–1964*, Paris, Bloud et Gay, 1964, pp. 147–57.

Cramer, M., *Das christlich-koptische Aegypten einst und heute*, Wiesbaden, 1959.

Christentum am Nil. Koptische Kunst. Catalogue of the Exhibition in the Villa Hügel, Essen, 1963.

Leclerq, Dom H., 'Égypte', *Dictionnaire d'Archéologie chrétienne et de liturgie*, pt. XLIII, cols. 2408–2571, Paris, Letouzey, 1921.

2. THE ELEMENTS OF COPTIC ART

Beckwith, J., *Coptic Sculpture*, London, Tiranti, 1963.

du Bourguet, P., *L'Art copte.* Catalogue of the Exhibition in the Petit Palais. Paris, Ministère d'État pour les Affaires Culturelles, 1964.

Drioton, E., *Les Sculptures coptes du nilomètre de Rodah*, Cairo, Publications de la Société d'Archéologie Copte, 1942. (Introduction.)

de Francovich, G., 'Egitto, la Siria e Constantinopoli: problemi di metodo. L'Egitto', *Rivista dell'Istituto Nazionale d'Archeologia e Storia dell'Arte*, new series, vols. 11–12, 1963, pp. 89–229.

Strzygowski, J., *Koptische Kunst* (General Catalogue of Egyptian antiquities of the Cairo Museum), Vienna, 1904.

Torp, H., an account and comparison of several books and recent articles on Coptic art, in *The Art Bulletin*, 47, 1965, pp. 361–75.

Wessel, K., *L'Art copte. L'Art antique de la Basse-Époque en Égypte*, Brussels, Meddens, 1964. Translated from *Koptische Kunst. Die Spätantike in Aegypten*. Recklinghausen, Aurel Bongers, 1963. (English translation: *Coptic Art*, translated by J. Carroll and S. Hatton, London, 1965.)

3. THE COPTS IN HISTORY; COPTIC CHRISTIANITY

Festugière, A. M. J., *Les Moines d'Orient*, I. *Culture ou sainteté. Introduction au monachisme oriental*, Paris, Ed. du Cerf, 1961.

Hanotaux, G., *Histoire de la nation égyptienne*, vol. III. Pierre Jouguet, 'L'Égypte ptolémaïque'; Victor Chapot, 'L'Égypte romaine'; Ch. Diehl, 'L'Égypte chrétienne et byzantine', Paris, Plon, 1933.

Ibid., vol. IV. Gaston Wiet, 'L'Égypte arabe', 1937.

Précis de l'Histoire d'Egypte, vol. II. Henri Munier and Gaston Wiet, 'L'Égypte byzantine et musulmane'.

Rémondon, R., 'L'Égypte chrétienne', *Dictionnaire de Spiritualité*, vol. IV, pts. 26–7, Paris, 1959, pp. 532–48.

Rémondon, R., 'L'Égypte et la suprême résistance au christianisme (V–VIIe siècles)', *Bulletin de l'Institut Français d'Archéologie Orientale*, Cairo, 1952, vol. LI, pp. 62–78.

4. PANORAMA OF COPTIC ART
General studies

du Bourguet, P., *L'Art copte*. Catalogue of the Exhibition in the Petit Palais. Paris, Ministère d'État pour les Affaires Culturelles, 1964.

du Bourguet, P., *L'Art copte*. Paris, Publications filmées d'Art et d'Histoire, 1964.

Christentum am Nil. Koptische Kunst. Catalogue of the Exhibition in the Villa Hügel, Essen, 1963.

Drioton, E., 'L'Egypte et l'art copte', R. Huyghe, *L'Art et l'homme*, Paris, Larousse, 1958, pp. 99–103.

Koefoed-Petersen, O., *Koptisk Kunst*, Copenhagen, 1944.

Krause, M., 'Aegypten', *Reallexikon zur byzantinischen Kunst*, Stuttgart, 1963, pp. 65–90.

Volbach, W. F., 'Copti centri e tradizioni', *Enciclopedia universale dell'arte*, 3, Venice-Rome, 1958, cols. 786–800.

Wessel, K., *L'Art copte. L'Art antique de la Basse-Époque en Égypte*, Brussels, Meddens, 1964.

Specialized studies

du Bourguet, P., 'L'Art copte pendant les cinq premiers siècles de l'hégire', *Christentum am Nil*, Recklinghausen, Aurel Bongers, 1964, pp. 221–32.

du Bourguet, P., 'Die koptische Kunst als mögliche Erbin der pharaonischen Kunst', *Christentum am Nil. Koptische Kunst*, Essen, Verein Villa Hügel e V., 1963, pp. 122–30.

5. PRE-COPTIC PERIOD
General studies

du Bourguet, P., 'L'Égypte pharaonique', *Dictionnaire de spiritualité*, Paris, 1959, pts. 26–7, pp. 501–31.

Drioton, E. and du Bourguet, P., *Les Pharaons à la conquête de l'art*, Paris-Bruges, Desclée de Brouwer, 1966.

Fabre, P., 'La religion romaine', *Histoire des religions*, Paris, Bloud et Gay, 1955, particularly pp. 408–29.

Guillaumont, A., 'Copte (littérature spirituelle)', *Dictionnaire de spiritualité*, vol. II, Paris, Beauchesne, 1953, cols. 2266–78.

des Places, E., 'Les religions de la Grèce antique', *Histoire des Religions*, Paris, Bloud et Gay, 1955, particularly pp. 192–225 and 267–90.

Spceialized studies

Badawy, A., *L'Art copte, les influences égyptiennes*, Cairo, Publications de la Société d'Archéologie Copte, 1949.

Badawy, A., 'L'Art copte, les influences hellénistiques et romaines', *Bulletin de l'Institut d'Égypte*, vol. XXXIV, 1952, pp. 151–205 and vol. XXXV, 1953, pp. 57–120.

du Bourguet, P., 'Die koptische Kunst als mögliche Erbin der pharaonischen Kunst', *Christentum am Nil. Koptische Kunst*, Essen, Verein Villa Hügel e V, 1963, pp. 122–30.

Coche de la Ferté, É., *Les Portraits romano-égyptiens*, Paris, Éditions des Musées Nationaux, 1952.

Delatte, A. and Derchain, Ph., *Les Intailles magiques gréco-égyptiennes*, [principally in the Cabinet des Médailles of the Bibliothèque Nationale, Paris], Paris, 1964.

Doresse, J., *Les livres secrets des gnostiques d'Égypte*, Paris, Plon, 1959. (English translation by Ph. Mairet, *The Secret Books of the Egyptian Gnostics*, London, Hollis & Carter, 1960.)

Drioton, E., 'De Philae à Baouît', *Coptic Studies in Honor of W. E. Crum*, Boston, Byzantine Institute, 1950, pp. 443–8.

Drioton, E., 'Art syrien et art copte', *Bulletin de la Société d'Archéologie Copte*, III, 1937, pp. 29–40.

Puech, H. Ch., 'Les nouveaux écrits gnostiques découverts en Haute-Égypte', *Coptic Studies in Honor of W. E. Crum*, Boston, Byzantine Institute, 1950, pp. 91–144.

6. ARCHITECTURE
General studies

Badawy, A., 'Les Premières Églises d'Égypte jusqu'au siècle de Saint Cyrille', *Kyrilliana*, Seminarium franciscale orientale, Ghiza. Cairo, Éd. du scribe égyptien, 1947, pp. 321–80.

Butler, A. J., *The Ancient Coptic Churches of Egypt*, vol. I, Oxford, Clarendon Press, 1884.

Creswell, K. A. C., *Early Muslim Architecture*, Penguin Books, Harmondsworth, 1958.

Grabar, A., *L'Âge d'or de Justinien*, Coll. l'Univers des Formes, Paris, Gallimard, 1967, pp. 35–40.

Krautheimer, E., *Early Christian and Byzantine Architecture*, The Pelican History of Art, Penguin Books, Harmondsworth, 1965.

Monneret de Villard, U., 'La basilica cristiana in

Egitto', *Atti del IV Congr. Intern. di arch. crist.*, Rome, 1940, I, pp. 291–319.

Müller-Wiener, W., 'Koptische Architektur', *Christentum am Nil. Koptische Kunst*, Essen, 1963, pp. 131–36.

Torp, H., 'Some Aspects of Early Coptic Monastic Architecture,' *Byzantion*, vols. 25–7, 1955–7, pt. 2, Brussels, 1957, pp. 513–38.

Specialized studies

Evers, H. G. and Romero, R., 'Rotes und weisses Kloster bei Sohag; Probleme der Rekonstruktion', *Christentum am Nil*, ed. K. Wessel, Recklinghausen, Aurel Bongers, 1964, pp. 175–99.

Krause, M., 'Babylon', *Reallexicon zur byzantinischen Kunst*, Stuttgart, fasc. 3, 1964, pp. 452–60.

Krause, M., 'Die Menasstadt', *Christentum am Nil. Koptische Kunst*, Essen, 1963, pp. 65–70.

Monneret de Villard, U., *Les couvents près de Sohag*, Milan, Giuseppe, 1925–6.

7. PLASTIC ARTS
General studies

Beckwith, J., *Coptic Sculpture*, London, Tiranti, 1963.

Drioton, E., *Les Sculptures coptes du nilomètre de Rodah*, Cairo, Publications de la Société d'Archéologie Copte, 1942.

Duthuit, G., *La Sculpture copte*, Paris, Van Oest, 1931.

Grabar, A., *L'Âge d'or de Justinien*, Coll. l'Univers des Formes, Paris, Gallimard, 1967, pp. 239–45.

Kitzinger, E., 'Notes on Early Coptic Sculpture', *Archaeologia*, LXXXVII, 1937, pp. 181–215.

Kollwitz, J., 'Alexandrinische Elfenbeine', *Christentum am Nil*, ed. K. Wessel, Recklinghausen, Aurel Bongers, 1964, pp. 206–20.

Strzygowski, J., *Koptische Kunst. Catalogue général du Musée du Caire*, Vienna, 1904.

Volbach, W. F., *Elfenbeinarbeiten der Spätantike und des frühen Mittelalters. Katalog des Römisch-Germanischen Zentralmuseums zu Mainz*, 2nd ed., Mainz, 1952.

Specialized studies

du Bourguet, P., 'Le relief copte. À propos de deux acquisitions récentes', *La Revue des Arts*, 9, Paris, 1959, pp. 9–14.

Labib, P., *Guide du Musée Copte*, vol. III,

Nouvelle aile I, section des pierres, Cairo, State Press, 1955.

Lemerle, P., 'Un bois sculpté de l'Annonciation', *Monuments et Mémoires publiés par l'Académie des Inscriptions et Belles-Lettres*, XLIII, 1949, pp. 89–118.

Sacopoulo, M., 'Le Linteau copte dit d'El-Moâllaka', *Cahiers Archéologiques*, IX, Paris, 1957, pp. 99–115.

Stern, H., 'Quelques oeuvres sculptées en bois, os et ivoire de style omeyyade', *Ars orientalis*, I, Washington, 1954, pp. 119–32.

Torp, H., 'Two Sixth-Century Coptic Stone Reliefs with Old Testament Scenes', *Acta ad archaeologiam et artium historiam pertinentia* (Institutum Romanum Norvegiae), vol. II, 1965, pp. 105–9.

8. PAINTING
General studies

Clédat, J., *Le monastère et la nécropole de Baouît*, Cairo, Mémoires de l'Institut Français d'Archéologie Orientale, XII, XXXIX, 1904–16.

Coche de la Ferté, É., 'Du portrait à l'icône', *L'Oeil*, 77, Paris, 1961, pp. 24–31, 78.

Cramer, M., *Koptische Buchmalerei. Illuminationen in Manuskripten des christlich-koptischen Aegypten vom 4. bis 19. Jhd.*, Recklinghausen, Aurel Bongers, 1964.

Grabar, A., *L'Âge d'or de Justinien*, Coll. l'Univers des Formes, Paris, Gallimard, 1967, pp. 172–81, 185 f.

Quibell, J. E., *Excavations at Saqqara (1905–1910)*, Cairo, 1907–13.

Specialized studies

Piankoff, A., 'Peintures au monastère de Saint-Antoine', *Bulletin de la Société d'Archéologie Copte*, XIV, 1950–7, pp. 151–63.

Schwartz, J., 'Nouvelles études sur les fresques d'El-Bagawat', *Cahiers Archéologiques*, XIII, Paris, 1962, pp. 1–11.

Stern, H., 'Les peintures du mausolée de l'Exode à El-Bagawat', *Cahiers Archéologiques*, XI, 1960, pp. 93–119.

9. TEXTILES
General studies

Beckwith, J., 'Les tissus coptes', *Les Cahiers Ciba*, vol. VII, no. 83, 1959.

du Bourguet, P., *Catalogue des étoffes coptes, Musée du Louvre*, vol. I, Paris, Ministère d'État pour les Affaires Culturelles, 1964.

Grabar, A., *L'Âge d'or de Justinien*, Coll. l'Univers des Formes, Paris, Gallimard, 1967, pp. 323-33.

Kendrick, A. F., *Catalogue of Textiles from Burying Grounds in Egypt*, 3 vols., London, 1920-2.

Mathieu, M. and Lyapunova, K., *Artistic Fabrics of Coptic Egypt*, Moscow-Leningrad, State Publishing House 'Art', 1951 (in Russian).

Wiet, G., 'Tissus et tapisseries du Musée Arabe du Caire', *Syria*, vol. XVI, 1935.

Wulff, O. and Volbach, W. F., *Spätantike und koptische Stoffe aus ägyptischen Grabfunden in den Staatlichen Museen*, Berlin, 1926.

Specialized studies

Berliner, R., 'A Coptic Tapestry of Byzantine Style', *Textile Museum Journal*, I, Washington, 1962, pp. 3-22.

du Bourguet, P., 'La fabrication des tissus coptes a-t-elle largement survécu à la conquête arabe?', *Bulletin de la Société Archéologique d'Alexandrie*, XL, 1953, pp. 1-31.

Brett, G., 'The Coptic Textiles and the Great Palace Mosaic', *Coptic Studies in Honor of W. E. Crum*, Boston, Byzantine Institute, 1950, pp. 433-42.

Egger, G., 'Koptische Wirkerei mit figuralen Darstellungen', *Christentum am Nil*, ed. K. Wessel, Recklinghausen, Aurel Bongers, 1964, pp. 240-56.

Kühnel, E., 'La Tradition copte dans les tissus musulmans', *Bulletin de la Société d'Archéologique Copte*, IV, pp. 79-89.

Kühnel, E., 'Nachwirkungen der koptischen Kunst im islamischen Aegypten', *Christentum am Nil*, ed. K. Wessel, Recklinghausen, Aurel Bongers, 1964, pp. 257-59.

Pfister, R., 'Teinture et alchimie dans l'Orient hellénistique', *Seminarium kondakovianum*, VII, 1935, pp. 1-59.

Picard-Schmitter, M. Th., 'Une tapisserie hellénistique d'Antinoé au Musée du Louvre', *Monuments Piot*, LII, 1962, pp. 27-75.

Shepherd, D., 'An Early Tiraz from Egypt', *Bulletin of the Cleveland Museum of Art*, 1960, pp. 8 et seq.

10. CERAMICS, GLASS AND BRONZE

General studies

Neyret, C., *Les Céramiques coptes du Musée du Louvre* (Mémoire présentée pour le diplôme de l'École du Louvre, 1966).

Strzygowski, J., *Koptische Kunst, Catalogue général du Musée du Caire*, Vienna, 1904.

Specialized studies

Coche de la Ferté, É., 'Un fragment de verre copte et deux groupes de verrerie médiévale', *Cahiers de la céramique, du verre et des arts du feu*, Sèvres, 1961, pp. 264-74.

Piankoff, A., 'Les Deux Encensoirs coptes du Musée du Louvre', *Bulletin de la Société d'Archéologie Copte*, VII, 1941, pp. 1-7.

Piankoff, A., 'Un Plat copte au Musée du Louvre', *Bulletin de la Société d'Archéologie Copte*, VIII, 1942, pp. 25-7.

Ross, M. C., 'Byzantine Bronze Peacock Lamps', *Archeology*, 13, New York, 1960, pp. 134-36.

11. SURVIVAL OF COPTIC ART

Findlay, L., 'The Monolithic Churches of Lalibela in Ethiopia', *Bulletin de la Société d'Archéologie Copte*, IX, 1944, pp. 5-58.

Klasens, A., 'De nederlandse opgravingen in Nubië. Tweede seizoen 1963-1964', *Phoenix*, X, 21, Leyden, 1964, pp. 47-56.

Michalowski, K., *Faras, Fouilles polonaises 1961*, Warsaw, 1962; 'Polish Excavations at Faras 1962-1963', *Kush*, XII, 1964, pp. 195-207.

(The numerals in italics refer to the plates and figures.)